COMPLETE ROSICRUCIAN RITES OF THE FELLOWSHIP OF THE ROSY CROSS

Arthur E. Waite

Ishtar Publishing
www.ishtarpublishing.com

Complete Rosicrucian Initiations of the Fellowship of the Rosy Cross

ISBN (13) 978-0-9735931-7-4 (Hb.)

Book Design: Mamdouh Al-Daye
Cover Designer and Artwork: Athena Amato

Ishtar Publishing
141-6200 McKay Avenue,
Suite 716,
Burnaby, BC
Canada V5H-4M9
www.ishtarpublishing.com

TABLE OF CONTENTS

ISSUED BY FRATER SACRAMENTUM REGIS
MOST HONOURED IMPERATOR
IN ORDINE ROSEA CRUCIS
FOR THE DIRECTION OF CELEBRANTS AND
THE USE OF FRATRES ET SORORES UNDER THE
OBEDIENCE OF AUTHORIZED TEMPLES

The First Order of the Rosy Cross
The Holy Order of the Golden Dawn

World of Action
Part 1

The Ceremony of Reception into
The Grade of Neophyte

$0 = 0$

Privately Printed
1916

The Officers of the Grade

1. The Honorable Frater Philosophus,
   id est, Propositum Conscium Dei
   Master of the Temple

2. The Honorable Frater Practicus,
   id est, Desiderium Conscium Dei
   Warden of the Temple

3. The Honorable Frater Theoreticus,
   id est, Mens Conscia Sponsi
   Guide of the Paths and Grades

4. The Auxiliary Frater Zelator,
   id est, Terra Illuminata
   Proclamator et Lucifer

5. The Frater Thurificans,
   id est, Thuribulum Ferens
   Thurifer

6. The Frater Aquarius,
   id est, Aquam Benedictam Ferens
   Aquarius

7. The Frater Ostiarius,
   id est, Custos Liminis
   Guard

N.B. – The Imperator, or chief of the rite, presides *ex officio* in all grades of the Fellowship, either personally or by his appointed substitute. In those cases where certain offices are taken by Sorores of the Fellowship, the necessary alterations are made in the modes of address.

The Clothing of Celebrants and Officers

1. The Honorable Frater Philosophus wears a green robe over his black habit and a collar of red silk, from which depends a circular lamina, inscribed with the letter Yod. The green color of the Master's robe represents the growth in life that is of God. The symbol of the lion is embroidered thereon, upon the left side, with the inscription: Facies Tertia, Facies Leonis. The Master bears a wand, surmounted by a Calvary Cross, having four circles at the end of the four arms and one circle toward the center of the lowermost arm.

2. The Honorable Frater Practicus wears a yellow robe over his black habit, symbolizing the beginning of transmutation in God. The symbol of the eagle is embroidered thereon, upon the left side, with the inscription: Facies Quarta, Facies Aquilae. His collar is of violet silk, from which depends a circular lamina, inscribed with the letter He, being the first He of the Divine Name. He bears a wand surmounted by a flaming heart.

3. The Honorable Frater Theoreticus wears a blue robe over his black habit, symbolizing the aspiration and desire that initiate the great quest and reflects things unrealized. It bears the symbol of the man embroidered thereon, upon the left side, with the inscription: Facies Secunda, Facies Hominis. His collar is of orange silk, from which depends a circular lamina, inscribed with the letter Vau. He bears a wand, surmounted by an open eye, signifying the eye of the mind.

4. The Auxiliary Frater Zelator wears a cloak of reddish brown, corresponding to the Adamic earth and symbolizing the first movement of the Divine Spirit toward the making of a living soul. The symbol of the ox is embroidered thereon, with the inscription: Facies Una, Facies Cherub. His collar is of blue-green silk, from which depends a circular lamina, inscribed with the letter He, being the He final of the Divine Name. He bears a wand, surmounted by a Calvary Cross, having a crown upon the upper arms. The Frater Zelator is in symbolical correspondence with the Guide of the Paths and Grades.

5. The Frater Thurificans wears a red surplice and a collar of green silk, from which depends a circular lamina, inscribed with an equilateral triangle, having the apex upward, as a symbol of Fire. He is in symbolical correspondence with the Master.

6. The Frater Aquarius wears a blue surplice and a collar of orange silk, from which depends a circular lamina, inscribed with an equilateral triangle, having the apex downward, as a symbol of Water. He is in symbolical correspondence with the Warden.

7. The Frater Ostiarius, who is not strictly an officer, has no special vestments. He carries a wand, surmounted by a dove of peace. There is no sword in a Temple of the Rosy Cross.

8. In addition to the black habit, the Frater Ostiarius and all unofficial members wear a collar of white silk, emblematic of purification in progress, from which depends a crimson Calvary Cross. It is the general jewel of the whole Fellowship on the external side.

9. In grades below the Third Order, the Imperator wears the general Rose-Cross of the Third Order and the clothing of an officiating Adeptus Minor. He carries a wand surmounted by a triple Sephirotic Cross.

The Fellowship of the Rosy Cross

Grade of Neophyte
0 = 0

THE SOLEMN CEREMONY OF OPENING THE
TEMPLE IN THE LIGHT

The arrangement of the temple is shown in the official diagram.

The officers and brethren being assembled within, and the door of the sacred precincts having been secured and guarded by the Frater Ostiarius, who is stationed on the hither side, the Imperator ~ as Inspector of the Temples and Permanent Director of Ceremonies, or him failing his substitute and him failing the Master of the Temple ~ goes before the vacant thrones of the east, gives a battery of one knock and makes the first proclamation thus, uplifting his wand of office:~

IMPERATOR: To order, Fratres et Sorores. The Lord is my light and my help. In the name of Him who rescues us from the darkness and unredeemed places, and by the power in me vested (but in the case of a substitute or Master: By the power to me deputed), I direct the officers and brethren to assume the clothing of their rank and grades. Invest our portals, O Lord, and guard our thresholds. Do Thou clothe us in Thy grace and truth.

If a separate room has been set apart for vesting, this direction is given therein, and the temple is entered subsequently in a processional form, led by the Imperator of the Temple, followed by the Fratres Proclamator, Thurificans and Aquarius, the ordinary members and finally the three celebrants.

In either case it is only after the ceremonial direction that the officers and brethren assume their vestments and insignia, which is accomplished in solemn order and in the reverence of holy silence.

The Imperator goes to the eastern end of the temple, before the thrones, and with uplifted wand recites:

THE PRAYER AT THE EAST

IMPERATOR: O immanent and transcendent source and end of all, Lord of the two worlds, Thou hast set up Thy holy signs in all the quarters of the heavens, a revelation of eternal mind unto the mind of man. Thou dost speak to us by day and by night in Thy greater and lesser luminaries, Thy suns and stars and constellations. Grant, we beseech Thee, that the hidden grace and the radiant Light that abides in the supernal crown may be communicated to the thrones of this temple. May those who Thou hast placed thereon dispense Thy Light and grace, through the mediation of this holy order and by virtue of their high office. May they illuminate the path of Thy mysteries, and may that Light lead us even unto the attainment of the quintessence, the tingeing stone of the wise, the wisdom that has its roots in Thee and the beatitude that is found in Thy presence.

The Imperator goes to his place; the celebrants and lesser officers assume their invariable stations; and the ordinary brethren are ranged north and south, according to the precedence of their grades. All members are seated, and a short pause of inward recollection follows.

Master of the Temple knocks.

MASTER OF THE TEMPLE: All rise!

The Auxiliary Frater Zelator lifts up his lamp and wand.

MASTER OF THE TEMPLE: Fratres et Sorores of the Salvator Mundi Temple (*vel Templum Aliud**), duly assembled under warrants for the mysteries of the Rosy Cross, assist me to open the temple of our Holy Order in the grade of Neophyte. (*or whatever other Temple)

FRATER ZELATOR (*speaking from his place in the west, with uplifted lamp and wand*): The Light of the supernals be upon us in the place of our devotion, and the Lord who is with us from the beginning insure the end.

He lowers his lamp and wand.

MASTER OF THE TEMPLE: Frater Ostiarius, see that the temple is guarded on the further side of the portal, as an outward sign of the mysteries of prudence that are within.

A temple of the Rosy Cross has no outer guarding, like lodges of the lesser mysteries. The Frater Ostiarius therefore makes answer thus:

FRATER OSTIARIUS: Honorable Master, the temple is guarded without by the invisible keepers of the mysteries: the portal is secured within, and I stand on the hither side as a witness of vigilance and a gauge of prudence.

MASTER OF THE TEMPLE *(with raised eyes and uplifted wand):* Fratres et Sorores, let us put away the thoughts of the outer world. The temple is guarded without: let the heart be guarded within.

The Master lowers his wand, and there is the pause of a moment

MASTER OF THE TEMPLE: Auxiliary Frater Zelator, Lucifer of this holy temple, lift up your wand of office and remembering the all-beholding eye, assure yourself that those who are here and now present have seen the Light of the crown.

FRATER ZELATOR: Fratres et Sorores of the Holy Order of the Rosy Cross, I demand the manual profession of the secret light.

It is given by all present with extended hands, the Master and the Lucifer excepted. The Frater Proclamator et Lucifer lowers his wand and communicates the sign to the Master.

FRATER ZELATOR: Honorable Master of the Temple, the orient from on high hath visited us.

The sign is repeated by the Master of the Temple.

MASTER OF THE TEMPLE: Watch with me therefore one hour, ye brethren of the Rosy Cross.

The Master gives a battery of one knock and leaving his throne turns to the east, proceeding to the assoilment of the temple. All present stand up and turn eastward. With the first and second fingers and with the thumb of his right hand, the Master seals his forehead and says: ATEH. He seals his breast and says: MALKUTH. He seals his left shoulder and says: VE GEBURAH. He seals his right shoulder and says: VE GEDULAH. He clasps his hands before him, holding his wand under his left arm, and says: LE OLAMH. AMEN. The operation hereof is more especially for his own cleansing, that he may be worthy to purify without.

The Master traces the cosmic cross of four equal arms ✠, *with uplifted wand in the eastern quarter, and pronounces slowly and distinctly the sacred name: YOD, HE, VAU, HE.*

He moves to the south, carrying his wand uplifted in front of his face. He traces the ✠, *in the south and utters the sacred name: ADONAI.*

He moves in the same manner to the west, performs the same working, and utters the sacred name: EH-YEH.

He moves in the same manner to the north, performs the same working, and utters the sacred word: AGLA.

He returns in the same manner to the east, having thus circumambulated the temple. This is the assoilment of the temple, and is a realization of the reign of God as an indwelling presence in the world of manifested things. The members have faced each quarter in succession, following the Master, who again faces the east, extends his arms as on a cross and says:

MASTER OF THE TEMPLE: Before me, Raphael. Behind me, Auriel. At my right hand, Michael. At my left hand, Gabriel. And above me the Holy Shekinah, the glory of God in His temple.

This is the angelical formula, which brings the holy hills about the Jerusalem of the temple and makes the temple itself as a ring of holy hills about his own Jerusalem within. He finishes, as he began, with the sealing prayer, which signifies the closing of the gates within and without against the images of evil. Every member should join in this sacred working, repeating the words mentally, so that it may have effect upon him.

The Master of the Temple returns to this throne and faces west. The officers and members resume their usual positions.

8

IMPERATOR: Frater Aquarius, in the sign of understanding, and remembering the great sea, I direct you to sanctify with Water this Fellowship of the Rosy Cross.

The Frater Aquarius follows the course of the sun, coming eastward from his place in the temple. He faces the Most Honored Imperator and offers his vessel for benediction. The Imperator blesses with the cosmic cross and says:

IMPERATOR: Sanctify us, O Lord, in Thy mercy, and bless this creature of Water, which I have here set apart to Thy service, as an outward sign of graces that are communicated within.

Dipping the aspergillus in the vessel of hallowed Water, the Aquarius makes a ✠ *therewith before the thrones in the east and sprinkles thrice. He proceeds, sprinkling as he goes, and performs the ceremony in the four quarters, returning to the east, where he faces west before the thrones, lifts up the vessel of Water and says:*

FRATER AQUARIUS: Waters of understanding, Waters of the great sea; I have sanctified with Water.

He returns to his place with the sun.

IMPERATOR: Frater Thurificans, in all symbols of Divine desire, and by the sparks of aspiration flying upward, I direct you to sanctify with Fire this Fellowship of the Rosy Cross.

The Frater Thurificans follows the course of the sun, coming eastward from his place in the west. He faces the Most Honored Imperator and offers his vessel for benediction. The Imperator blesses with the cosmic cross and says:

IMPERATOR: Sanctify us, O Lord, in Thy mercy, and bless this creature of Fire, which I have here set apart to Thy service, as an outward sign of graces that are communicated within.

The Frater Thurificans makes a ✠ *with his thurible and censes thrice in the east. He proceeds, censing as he goes, and performs the same ceremony in the four quarters, facing each point. He returns to the east, where he faces west before the thrones, lifts up his vessel of Fire and says:*

FRATER THURIFICANS: The desire of the house of the Lord hath eaten me up. I have sanctified with Fire.

He returns to his place with the sun.

IMPERATOR: Stand about us in Thy holy place, O Lord, and keep us pure in Thy precincts.

This is said with raised eyes and uplifted wand, and there follows the pause of a moment.

MASTER OF THE TEMPLE: Fratres et Sorores, before this temple is opened, let us recall, with gratitude and reverence, the graces and lights that are represented by the offices of the grade, that they may be realized in the hearts of the celebrants and of all who are here present. Honorable Frater Practicus, Warden of this holy temple, how many are the celebrants-in-chief who communicate the worshipful mysteries of the Rosy Cross in the grade of Neophyte?

WORDEN OF THE TEMPLE: They represent in their triplicity below, the supernal triad that is above. They are the Master of the Temple, its Warden and the Guide of the Paths. They have descended from a world that is above, to administer the benefits and consolations belonging to this holy grade.

MASTER OF THE TEMPLE: What do you testify concerning the lesser officers?

WARDEN OF THE TEMPLE: These also are three, the Ostiarius excepted, who is the novice in the portal of the Rosy Cross and is therefore without the triad. They are the Auxiliary Frater Zelator, who is Proclamator and Lucifer of the Temple; the Frater Thurificans, who carries the sacred Fire; and the Frater Aquarius, keeper of the Holy Water. Their offices are particular to the fourth mystical world, or that comprised by the first order of the Rosy Cross.

The Aquarius, standing in his place, raises the vessel of Water.

FRATER AQUARIUS: My place is in the west of the temple, on the northern side, and I bear the Water of my office. My office is greater than I am, and

I ask to be dissolved therein. In the grace of that union I am the waters of salvation that pour upon the world of the soul. As the heart panteth after the water-brooks, so doth the soul within me desire after Thee, O God. It is in this sense that I sanctify my brethren and co-heirs of the order, and the novice at his reception with Water.

The vessel of Water is lowered. The Thurifer, standing in his place, raises the vessel of Fire, with incense fuming.

FRATER THURIFICANS: My place is in the west of the temple, on the southern side, and I bear the thurible of my office. My office is greater than I am, and I seek to be consumed thereby. In the grace of that union I am the heat of the supernatural Fire that consumes all lusts of the flesh, lusts of the eyes, and pride of life. My soul hath thirsted for the Lord in the pathless and waterless deserts of the dark places. I am the desire of God that has burnt up all earthly roses and has wasted all false gardens of delight, so that the soul can find neither food nor wine therein. It is in this sense that I sanctify my brethren and co-heirs of the order, and the novice at his reception by Fire.

The thurible is lowered. The Auxiliary Frater Zelator, standing in his place, lifts up his lamp and wand.

FRATER ZELATOR: My place is in the middle west, and I bear the lamp of my office. My office is greater than I am, and I ask to be light therein. In the sense of that union I am the secret light that abides in the world of grace, shining there from upon the world of sensible things. I am the body of man in its redemption, looking for a robe of glory. I am he who testifies in the world of action; and I go before the novice at his reception, as God goeth before the elect on the path of their return to Him.

The lamp and wand are lowered. The Guide of the Paths raises his own wand.

GUIDE OF THE PATHS: My seat is in the middle place of the temple, between the pillars of the mysteries, between mercy and judgment, light and darkness. I am the mediator and reconciler between them. My office is greater than I am: I have prayed to be made one therewith. In the faith of that union I am even as the Divine presence between the cherubim on the mercy seat, in the sanctuary of the elect. I am the bond and path of union. I am mind and the light of mind. I have consecrated all the images.

I watch over spiritual espousals and Divine marriages. I am the middle way, by which ascent is possible to the height. I direct, in the grace of purity, all higher aspirations of the soul. In virtue of this my office and of its high symbolism, I am Guide of the Paths, and I lead in the true way.

The wand of the Guide is lowered. The Warden uplifts his wand.

WARDEN OF THE TEMPLE: My place is in the east of the temple, in the northern side. I am love and the desire therein. My office is greater than I am; I have aspired to be one therewith. In the grace of that union I am the Divine love descending, clothed in the light of glory. The Lord has enlightened my darkness. The quest and the end are mine. The truth is with me in the stillness. I follow the way to God. I have seen the height ascending. In virtue of my high office, I am Warden of this Holy Temple, seated on the right hand of the Master who rules therein.

The wand of the Warden is lowered. The Master uplifts his wand.

MASTER OF THE TEMPLE: My place is in the east of the temple, on the southern side. I am the will of man in its redemption, in its union with Divine will. My office is greater than I am; I have wrought that I may be joined therewith. In respect of that union I represent the purpose of God, coming down into the worlds below and raising them to the holy height. I am therefore the Master of the Temple, who rules in all grades. I am he who communicates the mysteries under their sacred seals. I am he who is authorized from beyond to give expression in eternal symbolism to the things that are beyond the veil. I am the point at which faith passes into experience. In virtue of my high office, its titles and prerogatives, behold I serve.

The wand of the Master is lowered.

FRATER ZELATOR *(with uplifted wand):* Blessed be the servant of the Lord in the place of his ministry.

MASTER OF THE TEMPLE: Let us declare the sanctity of God in the reverence of holy prayer, that the light and darkness of humanity may unite to bless the Lord.

The Imperator and celebrants-in-chief descend from their thrones and face east, with the other officers and the rest of the brethren.

MASTER OF THE TEMPLE: Our wills and life are Thine, O will most high. Establish us, Thy children, in the freedom of Thy holy purpose. Our minds and thoughts are Thine, O mind supreme. Transmute our natural minds and let our thoughts be reborn in Thee. The heart and its needs are Thine, O heart and center of all things. Uplift us in the way of our research, that we may attain the knowledge of Thy presence. Enlighten our darkness, increase our light, O Lord of light and darkness.

The Imperator and celebrants return to their places and all face as usual.

MASTER OF THE TEMPLE: Auxiliary Frater Zelator, Proclamator of the temple, in the name of Him who is our strength, our refuge and our term from everlasting. I command you to proclaim that the temple is open in the grace of the world of action.

The Auxiliary Frater Zelator lifts up his lamp and wand, saying loudly and clearly:

FRATER ZELATOR: Fratres et Sorores, blessed is the temple of our order in the Light of the Rosy Cross. I testify that the temple is open in the grade of Neophyte.

The sign of the Neophyte grade is given by all present.

MASTER OF THE TEMPLE: BENEDICTUS DOMINUS (Knock)

WARDEN OF THE TEMPLE: DEUS NOSTER (Knock)

GUIDE OF THE PATHS: QUI DEDIT NOBUS SIGNUM (Knocks)

The Auxiliary Frater Zelator, as Proclamator of the Temple, comes forward to the western side of the altar, carrying his wand only, which he lifts on high.

FRATER ZELATOR: Silence in the mouth of the Almighty One.

He returns direct as he came. The officers and brethren are seated.

Here ends the solemn ceremony of opening the temple in the Light.

THE CEREMONIAL ADMISSION OF A NOVICE
IN THE PORTAL OF THE ROSY CROSS

The postulant is alone in the vestibule on a prie-dieu in full light, with a scroll in his hands containing versicles on the fulfillment of earthly life in life eternal and Divine union. A ewer and basin are provided for the lavabo that precedes his reception.

MASTER OF THE TEMPLE: Fratres et Sorores, I beseech you to lift up your hearts and to pray that the Divine assistance may be with us efficaciously in the work that I am delegated to perform as an authorized Preceptor of the Mysteries. I have been entrusted with a warrant from the Most Honored Imperator of the order for the admission of A... B... to the first circle of initiation in the portal of the Rosy Cross. I depute therefore the Honorable Frater Theoreticus, Guide of the Paths and Grades, to take in charge the preparation of the postulant and to see that the things within are symbolized by the things without.

The Guide of the Paths rises, and having reached the hither side of the threshold, he turns eastward, makes with recollection the sign of a Neophyte and then passes without the portal. His seat is removed from the middle place of the pillars to a convenient point left free for this purpose.

MASTER OF THE TEMPLE: The things that are without are in analogy with the things that are within. The eyes of our postulant at the gate of mysteries are darkened for a period, to symbolize the cloud that rests upon the sanctuary of his soul. The body of our postulant is enveloped to typify the material yoke that he carries in the world of action, seeking the home of the spirit. He cannot walk alone and hence he depends upon our guidance. He will not be deserted in his need. He will be brought safely and surely into the secret place of our light. There is faith and there is hope in his heart, and that which leads him in the narrow way is the hand of love.

During this annunciation the Guide prepares the postulant by administering the rite of lavabo, and thereafter placing the hoodwink over his eyes and a black garment about his body. While this is being done:

GUIDE: From a temple of the spirit, in the name of God and of His Light, I have come into the ways without, that I may bring you into a deeper knowledge of the world that is within. By the brotherhood at the heart of our fellowship, I bid you remember that what is begun here and now will find its fruition only when it ends in God. There is darkness on the eyes of mind, but the mind shall enter into day. The yoke of the world is upon you, but the soul shall enter into freedom.

The preparation being ended, the Guide gives an alarm (knock) ~ on the outer side of the portal. The Ostiarius replies (knock).

OSTIARIUS *(addressing the Frater Zelator)*: Frater Zelator, there is a report on the further side.

FRATER ZELATOR: Honorable Master of the Temple, the mediator between light and darkness, the Guide of the Holy Paths, stands at the door and knocks.

MASTER OF THE TEMPLE: Do you certify, Frater Zelator, that he returns in the name of his mission, for the beginning of a work of redemption?

FRATER ZELATOR: He looks to lead that which is begun in order to a perfect term.

MASTER OF THE TEMPLE: God made the world without as He made that which is within. May the peace of the Lord fill those who are seeking His Light. I give you permission to admit A... B..., who puts aside henceforth in these precincts his earthly titles and dignities, receiving at our hands that name that represents his aspiration on entering here among us. He will be known hereafter as Frater Adveniat Regnum (vel nomen aliud*), and may he that enters the kingdom receive the crown of life. Auxiliary Frater Zelator, with the uplifted wand of your office, by the purifying sign of Fire and in the Holy Water of regeneration, go forward with your assistant officers and receive him who has been called. (* Substitute the power name of the postulant here and throughout.)

This is done accordingly. The lights are turned down. The Ostiarius opens the door and withdraws immediately. The postulant enters the portal, led by the Guide of the Paths. They move slowly forward, preceded by the Auxiliary Frater Zelator, as Lucifer of the Temple, with raised lamp, and followed by the Fratres Thurificants et Aquarius, who have stood as they entered on either side of the threshold. The portal is closed and secured.

GUIDE OF THE PATHS *(as he leads the postulant):* The darkness is also God's minister. The darkness shall lead his servant.

FRATER THURIFICANS: The treasure of the hidden Fire shall shine therein.

FRATER AQUARIUS: It is over the great sea and in the deeps thereof.

LUCIFER OF THE TEMPLE: The night shall be enlightened by the day.

MASTER OF THE TEMPLE: Inheritor of night and time, what seek you in the places of the soul?

GUIDE OF THE PATHS *(as spokesman for the postulant):* Through the darkness of time and night, I have come to the gate of the temple, looking for light within.

MASTER OF THE TEMPLE: Place the postulant on the western side of the altar with his face to the east, symbolizing the desire after that light that God shall grant to the seeker who is well and properly prepared.

This is done by the Guide of the Paths, who so leads the postulant throughout the ceremony that he is not permitted to kneel or rise, or make any movement whatever, of his own accord. The Lucifer of the Temple and his assistants have returned to their places, where they remain standing.

MASTER OF THE TEMPLE: We hold your signed application for admission to this Fellowship, which exists for the increase of spiritual knowledge among those who have awakened in the spirit. We hold also your solemn testimony to a desire conceived in your heart for the realization of eternal life and Divine union. We are taught that the things that are Caesar's must be rendered duly to Caesar but to God the things that are God's, and the secrets of the sanctuary are reserved to the sanctuary alone. Before your reception can proceed, it is necessary for you to take a solemn obligation to maintain the veils of the order, and as in the world without you are bound by the canons of morality and the code of society to keep the laws of both, so you must be covenanted herein to observe the rule of the temples and never to disclose without that which you learn within. But it is just on our part to assure you, as I do now in God's name, that the pledge that we exact does in no wise derogate from the laws of man, but leads to their better fulfillment in the light of Divine law. Are you willing to take this meet and salutary obligation?

The postulant is prompted by the Guide.

POSTULANT: I desire the light of the house, and I take its laws upon me.

The Master of the Temple, in conformity with the symbolism and accompanied by the Warden, descends from his throne and goes to the east of the altar, saying:

MASTER OF THE TEMPLE: It is written that I will visit the hearts of men, for my delight is in the way of justice.

He stands facing the west. The Warden proceeds to the northern side of the altar and the Guide to the southern side. The postulant in the west forms therefore with the celebrants a cosmic cross corresponding to the altar symbol, the rose therein being the common center of both. The Master of the Temple gives a battery of one knock. The brethren of all grades rise and remain standing while the obligation is taken.

MASTER OF THE TEMPLE: Postulant in this home of the spirit, looking for grace to come, in the name of the Lord of grace, who is the fountain of all our light, I bid you kneel down as a sign of worship and obedience. Give me your right hand, which I place upon this holy rose in the center of the cosmic cross. Lay your left hand in mine, as a pledge of the sacred and sincere intention that your heart brings into this Order, that it may be married to the sincerity and holiness that abide in its own heart. Bow your head reverently, as one who has come out of the world looking for those gifts that do not belong to the world. For the first and last time in the presence of this Fellowship, recite your earthly name and say after me.

The postulant follows the Master.

The Solemn Obligation of a Novice
in the Order of the Rosy Cross

I, A... B..., in the presence of the Eternal Father of Light, who recompenses those who seek Him out, and in the presence of the brethren who are gathered here together in the grace of His Divine name, do of my own will and in the consciousness of my proper act and deed, submitted in conformity with the act and will of God, most solemnly pledge the honor of my soul to hold inviolate the glory of the Rosy Cross and the mysteries contained therein. I will not speak of them in the world without when I go forth here from. I will not disclose the name of this holy temple but will keep all secrets of the sanctuary as I would keep those of my king and God, speaking to me in the inmost places of the soul. I will conform to the laws of the Fellowship and to the by-laws of this temple. I will have no part or dealing in respect of the fellowship, its rites, proceedings or its knowledge, with any person, who - for what reason soever - is no longer integrated in the mystical body of the fellowship, nor will I recognize the living membership of any claimant to initiation who is not in possession of the temporal password that is communicated at each equinox by the Imperator of the rite, his substitute or successor, lawfully appointed. I include hereby within the category of this sacred pledge whatever information I may have received concerning the fellowship prior to my admission therein.

I lift up my heart to God, who is my judge, and seeing that I have come hither actuated by the most solemn motives that are conceived by the soul of man, I promise solemnly from this moment that I will persevere with courage and devotion in the path of Divine science, even as I shall abide undaunted through this ceremony that is its image; and whatsoever I may learn or attain in this temple and in the fellowship I will receive as from the hands of God and to His hands will return it in purity. I certify hereby and hereon that I desire above all things the knowledge of the Rosy Cross, and I covenant that at no time and under no temptation will I apply it to the works of evil. I will hold myself dedicated henceforth, so far as in me lies, to the consecration of my outward and inward nature that I may deserve to leave the darkness and dwell in the world of Light. I will abide with my brethren in union, rectitude and purity, remembering that peace is with God.

Bending over this holy symbol of the rose and cross of Light, I swear to observe all parts and points of this pledge without evasion, equivocation, or mental reservation of any kind, praying - as I deal herein, in all high faith and honor - that my secret name may be written in the book of life, even

18

as its symbol will be registered this day in the books of the fellowship. Deal with me, O Lord, in Thy mercy, strengthen my heart and my reins. Into Thy Holy hands, for judgment or reward, I here commit my spirit. Aid me, Thou sun of my soul; enlighten me in the dark places, and bring me in fine to Thee.

A short pause follows.

MASTER OF THE TEMPLE: Rise, novice of the portal grade in the Fellowship of the Rosy Cross.

The novice is assisted accordingly. The Master and Warden of the Temple return to their thrones. The Guide and novice are left standing by the altar. Other members are seated.

MASTER OF THE TEMPLE: Being mindful, O Honorable Guide, that all things are within, all joys, all dangers, all hopes, all fears, with the ways of the height and deep, let the novice be sanctified in the four parts of his personality ~ that having entered into the freedom of our fellowship he may find the life therein.

The Auxiliary Frater Zelator comes forward with his assistants, and they go before the Guide, who has put back the novice toward the western wall of the temple. The Frater Zelator ~ as Lucifer ~ lifts up the lamp of his office before the face of the novice.

FRATER ZELATOR: Be thy body as a robe of light and a vesture of redemption.

The Frater Aquarius comes forward, cross-marks the novice on his forehead and sprinkles three times before him.

FRATER AQUARIUS: In the name of the fountain of living Water, which cleanses the children of earth, I consecrate you with Water.

He falls back. The Frater Thurificans comes forward, raises his thurible before the face of the novice, makes the sign of the cross therewith and censes him three times.

Frater Thurificans: In the name of the Divine desire, which transmutes the life of earth, I consecrate you with Fire.

He falls back to the side of the Frater Aquarius, the Lucifer of the Temple being in front. They move slowly and reverently through the northern side of the temple. The Guide follows, leading the novice.

N.B. In the case of several postulants each must be consecrated separately.

Master of the Temple *(as the procession moves forward):* I asked to be taken from the darkness, and holy hands led me in the covert of holy wings.

The procession pauses in the middle north of the temple. The Warden gives a battery of one knock, and rises in his place.

Warden of the Temple: Change thou the form of thy desire, and thou shalt see the spiritual sun in the place of knowledge.

He resumes his seat. The Frater Aquarius, turning in his place, cross-marks the novice on the forehead and sprinkles three times before him.

Frater Aquarius: In the name of the fountain of living Water, which cleanses the heart of man, I consecrate you with Water.

He turns eastward. The Frater Thurificans, moving about in the same manner, raises his thurible before the face of the novice, makes the sign of the cross therewith and censes him three times.

Frater Thurificans: In the name of the Divine desire, which converts the heart of man, I consecrate you with Fire.

He turns again eastward. The procession moves slowly forward through the northern and eastern sides. While this is being done:

Master of the Temple: I asked to be brought into the Light, and the loving wings were closed about the face of me, lest I should see God and die.

The procession pauses in the middle east of the temple, behind the pillars.

NEOPHYTE INITIATION

The Guide goes in front of the novice and gives a battery of one knock.

GUIDE OF THE PATHS: In stillness and purity of thought prepare the temple of mind as a place of the presence, and that which shall fill thy temple is the spirit of Divine mind.

The Guide resumes his place on the right of the novice. The Frater Aquarius turns to cross-mark the novice on his forehead and sprinkles three times before him.

FRATER AQUARIUS: In the name of the fountain of living Water, which cleanses the thought of man, I consecrate you with Water.

He turns again southward. The Frater Thurificans, moving about in the same manner, raises his thurible before the face of the novice and censes him three times.

FRATER THURIFICANS: In the name of the Divine desire, which transmutes the thought of man, I consecrate you with Fire.

He turns again southward. The procession moves forward through the eastern and southern sides. While this is being done:

MASTER OF THE TEMPLE: I asked to kneel on the steps of the house of God, and they set me in the holy place, even by the tabernacle.

The procession pauses in the middle south of the temple. The Master gives a battery of one knock, and rises in his place.

MASTER OF THE TEMPLE: If thou make unto thyself a new creature of will and an end in holy purpose, thine end shall abide in God and thy will be His.

The Frater Aquarius, turning in his place, cross-marks the novice on the forehead and sprinkles three times before him.

FRATER AQUARIUS: In the name of the fountain of living Water, which cleanses the will of man, I consecrate you with Water.

He turns again southward. The Frater Thurificans, moving about in the same manner, raises his thurible before the face of the novice, makes the sign of the cross therewith and censes him three times.

FRATER THURIFICANS: In the name of the Divine desire, which transmutes the will of man, I consecrate you with Fire.

He turns again westward. The procession moves slowly forward through the southern and western sides, completing the circumambulation of the temple and pausing in the middle west. While this is being done:

MASTER OF THE TEMPLE: O God, how wonderfully is Thy work declared in the heart of man; I will walk in Thy ways for ever.

The procession moves slowly forward to the western side of the altar and there divides. The novice is left kneeling where the obligation was taken previously. The Guide of the Paths moves round the altar to the southern side. The Lucifer of the Temple stands at some distance behind the novice, with Fratres Thurificans et Aquarius on either side. The Master of the Temple rises in his place. The Auxiliary Frater Zelator gives a battery of one knock. The Ostiarius turns up the lights.

FRATER ZELATOR: Light in the place of Light, Light shining in the darkness, Light in the soul of man, for the illumination and deliverance of those who dwell in the house of bondage and in the shadow of death.

The eyes of the novice are unbound. He sees the Master of the Temple, standing at his throne with uplifted arms.

MASTER OF THE TEMPLE: I am the witness of the Light, shining in the darkness of material things, reigning in the soul of man. I am he who declares its mysteries. I am the guardian of the veil, and I speak in the opening of the eyes, proclaiming the path of will and the law of Divine purpose.

The Master of the Temple leaves his throne and passes westward, bearing his wand. The Auxiliary Frater Zelator gives a battery of one knock.

FRATER ZELATOR: Hail unto the Light enkindled, the spiritual Light, the desire of the eyes of the world.

The Master of the Temple pauses between the pillars and says slowly and clearly:

MASTER OF THE TEMPLE: I come in the will of the Light; I come in the Light of purpose; I come in the mercy of the Light. The Light has healing in its wings.

And afterwards at the east of the altar:

MASTER OF THE TEMPLE: Behold, I wait without Thy door and knock. Open thy heart, O novice of this fellowship. Take in thy spiritual hands the desires and aspirations that have brought thee to our holy temple, and kneeling with bended head, place them with humility and reverence on our altar of sacrifice.

The head of the novice is bowed, and he is directed to cross his hands on the altar. The Master of the Temple gives a battery of one knock, and all present rise up.

MASTER OF THE TEMPLE: O Thou who sanctifiest the heart of man, Who leadest our desires into attainment and our aspirations to the steps of Thy house, sanctify, eternal God, this novice of our fellowship. Lead him to the perfection that is in Thee, into the splendor of Thy great white throne. May that which I have here and now restored to him in the outward signs of Thy most blessed sacraments and Thine all sacred symbols be ratified above in Thy presence and realized essentially within him, to the glory of Thy name, world without end, Amen, and to the joy of Thy redeemed hierarchies.

The novice is assisted to rise. The unofficial brethren resume their seats. The Master of the Temple, the Warden, and the Guide join their wands above his head.

GUIDE: Thou who wouldest be saved and hast come out of the ways of darkness, enter into thy holy inheritance.

WARDEN: Thou in whom the world has not anything from henceforth and for ever, come into the Holy Light.

MASTER OF THE TEMPLE: We receive thee into the place of our sacraments, among the signs without of things that are realized within, into the pure and shining mystery, The Salvator Mundi Temple (vel Templum Aliud), in the Fellowship of the Rosy Cross.

GUIDE: BENEDICTUS.

WARDEN: QUI VENIT.

MASTER OF THE TEMPLE: IN NOMINE DOMINI.

The celebrants part their wands and return to their stations.

The seat of the Guide is replaced between the pillars.

The lesser officers also return to their posts.

The novice remains standing at the western side of the altar still facing east.

MASTER OF THE TEMPLE: Auxiliary Frater Zelator, you will now impart to the Neophyte the secret step, sign, token, and words that are allocated to the 0 = 0 grade in the portal of the Rosy Cross. You will communicate also the temporal password proclaimed at the last Equinox.

Leaving his lamp and wand, the Auxiliary Frater Zelator comes forward, turns to the novice with his back to the north, and faces him at a short distance.

FRATER ZELATOR: Frater Adveniat Regnum, (*vel nomen aliud*), by the decree of the Honorable Master of the Temple, receive at my hands the step, sign, token, and words of the portal. The step is given by advancing your left foot, as I now advance my own, the distance being ten inches. This is followed by advancing the right foot in front of the left to the same extent. The step is completed by bringing the left foot level with the right and pausing in an erect posture. It is an allusion not only to the fact that you have crossed the threshold and entered the court of the temple, but to your intention of proceeding further and of following a life of progress in spiritual things. It is in this position that the sign and grip are communicated. The sign is given by extending both arms with the hands raised vertically and the fingers separated. It has reference to the sacred number ten, which is characteristic of the whole Order. The grip is given by crossing and clasping both hands, with interlocked fingers and thumbs joined at the tips. This again has reference to the decade, but also to the triad that rules therein. It signifies further the welding bond of our Fellowship. The secret words are: SILENCE IN THE MOUTH OF THE ALMIGHTY ONE. The answer to this is: UNITAS. The temporal password of the fellowship is changed at each Equinox: at the present time it is *****.

MASTER OF THE TEMPLE: Auxiliary Frater Zelator, let the Neophyte be unclothed and reclothed, to symbolize the transmutation of the lower parts of his personality, so that they may concur in the work of the will, when the will has been turned to the light.

The Auxiliary Frater Zelator removes the coarse garment ~ that symbolizes the unpurified life of earth ~ and clothes the novice in the ordinary habit of the fellowship. He girds him about the waist with a brown cord, interwoven with red.

MASTER OF THE TEMPLE: Let the Neophyte be invested also with the mystical badge of the Fellowship in the world of action.

The Neophyte is invested with the collar of white silk and the red Calvary Cross.

FRATER ZELATOR: By command of the Honorable Master of the Temple, you have received your clothing and insignia. The habit is black, to signify that your purification is still in progress, but the brown cord, interwoven with red, indicates that the earthly element is in course of transmutation by the Divine. The white collar represents the state of purity attained and is that toward which you must work. The crimson Calvary Cross is the general jewel of the whole Order on the external side. It symbolizes Divine life dwelling in the fourfold nature of man.

MASTER OF THE TEMPLE: Let the Neophyte be led to the eastern side of the altar; let him sit with his face to the east.

This is done accordingly, and the Auxiliary Frater Zelator returns to his seat.

MASTER OF THE TEMPLE: Frater Adveniat Regnum, (*vel nomen aliud*), the Fellowship of the Rosy Cross extends to you its loving welcome on your admission as a Neophyte of this temple. May there be joy in the blessed hierarchies at your coming out of earthly into spiritual life, and may that joy in its reflection fall ~ like the rain of love ~ into your heart of hearts. Your preparation as a postulant was in the body, to symbolize that greater preparation that you had made already in your heart before you could be accepted as a Neophyte. The coarse outer garment that was placed upon you represented the common yoke of our mortality, and when it was in fine exchanged this signified the purification that our symbolism is intended to effect in your earthly part. The hoodwink imaged the darkness of the material mind. The cross-marking with lustral water and the mystical sprinkling shewed forth sacramentally the condition on which your name is registered in the book of life. The censing in your several consecrations prefigured the cleansing with Fire from the supernal altar of incense. May your heart and your reins be purified thereby, as if with burning coal. The altar at which you knelt is in the form of a double cube, with its base of necessity concealed, the surfaces exposed to sight, which on the summit is that sacred emblem whereon you were pledged and whereby you are bound in the sight of God henceforth and forever. The altar is black, to portray the state of our natural humanity before the work of God and of His Light is performed therein. But the matter of the work and the root of Light are within us. The cube unfolds as the cross and displays the red rose in the center of its open arms. The white cross placed on the altar is therefore in macrocosmic analogy with the black cube raised to a state of purity and unfolded in the light. The red rose of five petals typifies the immanent divinity, which must be declared in your soul, my brother, if you would unfold in the Light of the Spirit and become the Rosy Cross.

The Master of the Temple gives a battery of one knock. He stands up and extends his arms in the form of a ✠.

All rise.

MASTER OF THE TEMPLE: Thanks be to Thee, O Lord and father almighty, for the secret Light that is conceived and born in the heart. We have accepted Thy cross and Thy Calvary because of the glorious resurrection that is to come. May Thy Light also be born in the heart of this Neophyte. May he grow in grace and truth. May the light of his attainment in its fullness be as the glory of the king of ALL.

The Master resumes his seat, and so also the brethren.

MASTER OF THE TEMPLE: Between the thrones of the east and the altar are the two pillars, which are referred analogically to Seth, Enoch and Solomon, by allusion to the secret tradition and its perpetuation through the guardians of the mysteries. They are symbols of light and darkness, active and passive, mercy and severity, male and female, the pair of opposites in all things, ever seeking equilibrium, which is attained through union at a center. Between them lies the narrow path of ascent in the spirit. It was down this path, my brother, that I passed for your integration in the light. It is the way of your return journey into the land of the Living.

The Master of the Temple on his throne in the east of the temple, at the southern side, personifies the pillar of light, which, in the symbolism of the secret tradition, extends from the kingdom of this world to that of eternal wisdom. It represents the male aspect in all manifested things and the root of the male principle in things that are Divine. For this reason, the Master of the Temple signifies in an especial manner the will of man in its union with Divine will and therefore the Divine purpose that leads humanity at large by the open ways of life, but those who have attained election by secret paths of knowledge and the mysteries of the Rosy Cross, into the substance of things hoped for and the evidence of things not seen. He descends from a temple that is above for the initiation and advancement of the postulant, as an ambassador of wisdom and mercy and the victory of Holy Light. He is the power and will to save the soul alive when it has gone forth seeking the true life. He is also a teaching spirit at the place of the rending of veils.

The Warden of the Temple on his throne in the east of the temple, at the northern side, personifies the pillar of darkness, which, in the symbolism of the secret tradition, extends from the kingdom of this world to that of eternal understanding. It represents the female aspect in all manifested things and the root of the female principle in things that are Divine. The Warden of the Temple signifies the part of our desires, which is in darkness upon Divine mysteries until it is illuminated by that light which is from above; but in union therewith he typifies the Divine love descending, so that the darkness of the mystical pillar is really an excess of light. He also comes down from a temple that is above for the initiation and advancement of the postulant, as an ambassador of understanding in judgment and the glory of God in the highest. From another point of view, the Warden of the Temple is in correspondence with that Divine darkness that is behind all manifested Divine Light, even as the Master of the Temple is in correspondence with the Divine Light breaking forth in the Divine darkness.

Therefore, my brother, the will and the heart of God watch over your progress upward. But that progress is in virtue of middle path between the pillars, and because it is a straight path, leading to the height or the center, it is called in our symbolism the central pillar of benignity. Its living emblem in our temple is the Guide of the Paths, seated between the pillars as the mediator and reconciler between them. The pillars are male and female in the distinction of these principles one from another, while the middle way signifies their union, which takes place in virtue of purity, as the condition of the ascent of the soul. It is in and by this quality that the Guide of the Paths descends from a temple that is above for the initiation and advancement of the postulant, and for the direction of his higher aspirations, as an ambassador from the supreme crown, the everlasting beauty and the foundation built in God. He symbolizes Divine espousals and the return of the mind into union, by the way of purity. Purity is not only the condition, but in sense it is also the term; it is not only the preparer but the escort; it is not only the first link in that chain that leads from earth to heaven, but it is the chain itself. It is the ladder of Jacob, by which the aspirations go up and the great influences come down. We have been taught that religion pure and undefiled before God and the father is this: To visit the fatherless and the widowed in their affliction and to keep oneself unspotted from the world.

The Guide of the Paths passing from between the pillars, and going even outside the door of the temple into the place of the uninitiated, is sent to save that which is in dereliction. His ministry is to those who are widowed of the Divine spouse and to those who are fatherless, being without God in the world. When he goes out, therefore, it is as if a voice said: And God so loved the world.

But the qualities and virtues and graces that are represented by the three celebrants dissolve one into another, and in their unity they all embody that love that is behind the universe, in virtue of which God is so near the heart of man that it is more easy to attain than to miss Him. This is why the path upward is natural and straight in comparison with the downward path.

In respect of the lesser officers, when guiding hands led you through ways of darkness, the light of mystical wisdom went before you, symbolized by the lamp of the Lucifer. Know and remember henceforward that this wisdom, which begins in the fear of the Lord, ends in His palace at the center. The Lucifer is the light of the term that goes before the cohorts of salvation, and in the symbolism of our secret tradition he represents the purified body of man. The Thurificans and Aquarius, who are seated on either side of him, carry the outward signs of those graces that sanctify within. It is in virtue of such lustrations and such consecrations that the postulant comes at length into light, as the quest to its term and desire to its proper attainment.

A short pause follows.

MASTER OF THE TEMPLE: Auxiliary Frater Zelator, I call upon you to proclaim that the Neophyte has been admitted into the mysteries of the 0=0 grade in the Fellowship of the Rosy Cross.

The Auxiliary Frater Zelator rises in his place, together with his assistants as witnesses. He gives a battery of one knock, and lifts up his lamp and wand.

FRATER ZELATOR: In the Name of God who is our Light, and by the ordinance of the Honorable Master of the Temple, I testify that A... B..., who will be known henceforth among us by the sacramental title of Frater (*vel soror*) Adveniat Regnum, (*vel nomen aliud*), has entered the portal of the Rosy Cross and has been admitted into our bond of the Fellowship in the Neophyte grade.

They resume their seats.

WARDEN OF THE TEMPLE: Frater Adveniat Regnum, (*vel nomen aliud*), I charge you to keep in everlasting memory the obligation that you have taken on your admission into our Fellowship. It differs from the pledges that are administered in lesser circles of initiation, for it is concerned with your advancement in the soul. It is therefore a test of merit, and its faithful observance will be to you as a title of salvation. Remember in this sense the mystery that you have received and continue to desire those Divine ends that you have undertaken to seek. But remember also that if those who go before you may place you on the path of attainment, your soul must ascend of itself, till the grace and the power come down to abide in its secret sanctuary. Let the pillars of light and darkness teach you, by their contrast, to distinguish between good and evil; to choose the one and put aside the other, until that time comes when goodness shall fill the heart entirely. Remember, lastly, that the Rosy Cross signifies a hidden knowledge, of which God is the motive and the end.

MASTER OF THE TEMPLE: The titles of your advancement to the next grade of our Fellowship depend in part on yourself and in part on us. Ponder over that which is communicated in the portal of the secret light. In such reflection and in the examination of your own motives you will find a further light, and that light is your warrant.

The Auxiliary Frater Zelator comes forward, bearing his wand only, and faces the postulant.

FRATER ZELATOR: Arise, my brother, and be prepared in your heart, for henceforth you shall be keeper of the threshold.

He leads the Neophyte to the portal, where he is met by the Ostiarius, who commits his wand into his charge and is thus delivered of his duties, but remains near his successor. They are seated. The Frater Zelator returns to his place. The allocution of the Neophyte grade follows, and is delivered by the Imperator, but failing him by his substitute, or by the Master of the Temple.

THE ALLOCUTION OF THE GRADE OF NEOPHYTE

Fratres et Sorores, holding all grades of our fellowship, by the power vested in my office, (*or in the case of a substitute or Master: By the power to me deputed*), I invite you to hear with recollected hearts the allocution belonging to the grade of Neophyte. And you, our brother, who have been received this day among us, to you are addressed more especially these few words, desiring that they may abide in your memory and perform their office within you ~ to your own and to our advantage. We have called down upon you the Light of the spirit, the Light of the Rosy Cross; and we feel that within the secret abode of this Order you may find not only a place of peace and contemplation, apart from the outer world of mans daily solicitude, but a sanctuary where the symbols of Divine knowledge may bring to you some radiance in reflection of the direct light that shines in the temple of the Light ~ that temple which is not entered by earthly feet, or seen with the veiled eyes of this body of our mortality. We trust also that the Order may become to you one of those hearths and homes around which the love of brotherhood is gathered ~ that love which does not fail us in the hour of inward need. In this respect we are pledged to you whom we have admitted, as you are pledged to us. We ask you to remember this, as we also shall remember; and among the last things that we can offer you at this time is the maxim-in-chief of fratrenity, founded on consanguinity of spirit; Brother, the keys of all the greater mysteries are committed to the hands of love.

And now as regards the experience through which you have just passed, we have no occasion to remind you that in the physical order we come forth from darkness into light, or that in the intellectual order most comparisons between light and darkness offer a confused symbolism. The progress of the postulant from the one to the order state in the grade of Neophyte is understood among us in a particular sense. The awakening of consciousness toward God is like light dawning in darkness; and though the second birth of the mystic lies far away in our symbolism of the Rosy Cross, the change of such an awakening is like birth into physical life. It is the beginning of a mystical state, a life of grace in the soul, and hereof is the whole grade a symbol. So also when the desire of the house of the Lord is enkindled within us, our passage from darkness has already begun; we have been called to the living beauty. That which is termed among us the lamp of a hidden knowledge is uplifted and goes before us in the way; it is the experience of those who are our precursors in the ascent of the holy mountain. Through the keen air of high aspiration, uplifted in the region of the mind, may we pass into that world of love wherein are the sons and daughters of desire. When desire and aspiration have attained their term in us, may there be communicated at length that bread and salt of life, which are types of this earth no longer, but a food of souls. May we drink of that wine reserved for those who are athirst in the kingdom of our father. May our rose blossom in the garden of the Lord and our light shine upon the mystic mountain.

During these last words the Auxiliary Frater Zelator places the elements of communication upon the altar, elevating them successively in his two hands before depositing them and bending his head toward the east.

Meanwhile there are many lustrations, and the hallowings also are many, looking for that time when God shall cleanse us from our stains with living water, pouring through the chambers of the mind, and our hearts with that Fire which being enkindled on earth shall hereafter bear us, as a sacred incense, to our term in Him.

During these words the Fratres Thurificants et Aquarius have encompassed the altar, censing and sprinkling around it.

We are dealing, my brethren, and shall continue to deal henceforward, not alone with the question of religion but with its heart and center, behind all the external differences of systems and churches and sects. The grade of Neophyte begins in the approach to the court of the mystical tabernacle and ends in the court itself. It is the beginning of a life of dedication to the ends of all perfection. But regarded in the fullness of their sequence, the grades of the Rosy Cross are stages of our progression in God. As in those that we take through the not less symbolical progression of daily life, it rests with us whether they shall remain symbolism, or whether we shall pass in them, and they shall pass in us, into a living region of experience. But because of that infinite realm which lies behind the woven circle of official religion, I counsel you to remember always the charity of the wise and to respect the outward forms, for there are many paths to the center. The external churches are doors that open for others, if not indeed for you, and there is perhaps one of them that may open also for you into places of peace and the hidden church at the center. Looking unto that region in the Light of the Rosy Cross, let us realize that we all, who are inheritors of a world of change, must enter into another heritage in the world without end.

The minutes of the previous convocation and the other official business, if any, are taken at this point.

THE SOLEMN CEREMONY OF CLOSING THE TEMPLE IN THE GRADE OF NEOPHYTE

MASTER OF THE TEMPLE: Fratres et Sorores, in the banishment of all earthly thoughts and in the recollection of the heart, assist me to close the temple in the grade of Neophyte (Knock).

All Rise.

MASTER OF THE TEMPLE: Let the keeper of the holy place on the hither side of the portal, ascertain that the Temple is guarded.

The new Frater Ostiarius, instructed by him who preceded him, sees that the door is secured.

FRATER OSTIARIUS *(who is prompted)*: Honorable Master of the Temple, on the hither and further side it is surely guarded.

MASTER OF THE TEMPLE: Fratres et Sorores, lift up your hearts. I testify on my part that the world is still without and the price thereof. Auxiliary Frater Zelator, assure yourself that all present have seen the mystic rose in the center of the cosmic cross.

FRATER ZELATOR: Fratres et Sorores, give me the outward sign that is attributed to the first grade of the light within… (*this being done*). Honorable Master of the Temple, they have seen His star in the east and have come to adore Him.

The Frater Zelator communicates the sign to the Master of the Temple, who repeats it in due form.

MASTER OF THE TEMPLE: May the angel of great counsel, the Prince of peace, and the Light that enlightens every man who cometh into this world, give us grace and illumination in our day.

WARDEN OF THE TEMPLE: Let things that are holy be reserved to those that are holy and the sanctuary of initiation to consecrated and initiated men.

The Frater Zelator, as Lucifer of the temple, lifts up his lamp of office.
FRATER ZELATOR: Blessed be the brethren of the Rosy Cross on their return into the outer world, carrying the symbols of the Light.

MASTER OF THE TEMPLE: Let us adore the Holy and eternal God, who is the father and the term of our desires.

The Imperator of the Order with the Master and the Warden of the Temple descend from their thrones and face the east thereat. All turn east, giving and maintaining the sign of the grade until the adoration is over.

MASTER OF THE TEMPLE: O Thou who hast called Thy servants in all generations, who has set apart Thine elect to Thy service, who has filled our hearts with the aspiration toward Thy union, and all Thy channels of grace with the means of its attainment; give us this day and for ever our daily desire for Thee; and grant, we beseech Thee, at the close of this solemn office, which we have performed to Thy glory, that the fullness of Thine efficacious grace may be with us on our going forth into the world, even as on our coming into Thy sanctuary.

The Imperator puts aside his wand and turns west. All face as usual.

IMPERATOR: Fratres et Sorores, holding all grades of the Order, let us in the bodily reception of sacramental food in common remember that Divine substance can be also communicated to the soul.

He goes to the west of the altar and faces east.

IMPERATOR *(communicating in the bread and salt):* Partake with me therefore, I pray to you, of this bread ensavoured with salt, as emblems of earth and its spirit. Remember our part of earth and the salt of regeneration that ensavors it. (*Then raising the cup of wine.*) Drink with me now of this chalice, and may its wine, which symbolizes water, remind us of waters of life. So may our desires and emotions be as wine upon the altar of God. (*Raising the mystical rose.*) Inbreathe with me the fragrance of this rose, a token of air and the breath of the spirit of God. Let the images of our understanding and the thoughts of our mind rise as a sweet incense in the sight of God. (*Then placing his hands over the fire.*) And, lastly, let your hands be touched like my own by the warmth of this natural fire. But remember the fire of the purpose, which consecrates and changes the will, so that it is raised from the body of its corruption into living conformity with the eternal will.

The Imperator raises the lamp to his forehead, carries it round with him to the eastern side of the altar, deposits it in its former place, and serves the Master, raising and handing him each element successively, after which he returns to his throne. This is done in silence by all, as they participate in turn. The order of communication is as follows: The Imperator, the Master of the Temple, the other officers, excepting the Auxiliary Frater Zelator, who stands at the south of the altar with the flagon of wine, the Members according to grade, and then the Frater Ostiarius ~ who is the Neophyte of the day. When the Neophyte is at the east of the altar, the Frater Zelator comes to the west and partakes. Having raised the lamp to his forehead and passed to the east of the altar, he faces east, bends his head and says:

FRATER ZELATOR: In the worship of holy conformity and obedience to the Divine will.

MASTER OF THE TEMPLE: (Knocks) – CONSUMMATUM EST.

The Frater Zelator turns to the west, deposits the lamp and passes to his own place. The sign of the grade is given by all present.

MASTER OF THE TEMPLE: May that which we have received in the body represent in its symbolism to our souls the concord of purifying graces and the eternal communication, O Lord, of that life which comes from Thee for the transmutation of our personality into a true quintessence and for the attainment of our term in Thee.

WARDEN OF THE TEMPLE: Fratres et Sorores, remember the perfect end.

MASTER OF THE TEMPLE: The end of this grade is with us. Auxiliary Frater Zelator, in the name of our consecrated humanity and by virtue of your high office in the world of action, I command you to close the temple.

The Frater Zelator lifts up his wand only.

FRATER ZELATOR: In the name of God, who sanctifies, and by command of the Honorable Master, I close the Salvator Mundi Temple in the grade of Neophyte.

MASTER OF THE TEMPLE: AD GLORIAM (*Knocks*)

WARDEN OF THE TEMPLE: ROSEAE (*Knocks*)

GUIDE OF THE PATHS: CRUCIS (*Knocks*)

The Auxiliary Frater Zelator, as Proclamator of the Temple, comes forward to the western side of the altar, carrying his wand only, which he lifts on high.

FRATER ZELATOR: Silence in the mouth of the almighty One.

He returns direct as he came.

HERE ENDS THE SOLEMN CEREMONY OF CLOSING THE TEMPLE IN THE GRADE OF NEOPHYTE.

The First Order of the Rosy Cross

World of Action

Part II
The Ceremony of Advancement
in the
Grade of Zelator

$1 = 10$

Privately Printed

1916

The Fellowship of the Rosy Cross

—

Grade of Zelator
1 = 10

—

The Solemn Ceremony of Opening the
Temple in the Grade of Zelator

—

The arrangement of the temple is shown in the official diagram.

If the temple should not have been occupied previously in the grade of Neophyte, the ceremonial vesting of officers and members, the invocation or prayer at the east and the assoilment of the temple are performed as exhibited therein. The Master of the Temple takes his place, holding the wand of his office. The officers assume their stations and the ordinary brethren are ranged north and south, according to the precedence of their grades. All members are seated, and a short pause of inward recollection follows. N.B. The titles and duties of officers are identical with those in the grade of Neophyte.

Master of the Temple: (*Knocks*)

All rise.

Master of the Temple: Fratres et sorores in our holy and glorious Fellowship of the Rosy Cross, assist me to open the temple with recollection and great reverence in the grade of Zelator. Frater Ostiarius, I direct you to see that the temple is guarded on the hither and further sides, remembering the treasure that is within.

ZELATOR INITIATION

The Frater Ostiarius opens the portal pro forma, inspects the immediate precincts, again secures the threshold, and turns to the east, with uplifted wand.

FRATER OSTIARIUS: Honorable Master of the Temple, I testify by the pearl of great price that the portal is watched and guarded.

MASTER OF THE TEMPLE: Fratres et sorores, let us see to the guarding of the sacred and beautiful Light that has come in the Rosy Cross to hearts that are prepared within.

This is said with raised eyes and uplifted wand. The pause of a moment follows.

MASTER OF THE TEMPLE: Auxiliary Frater Zelator, I command you to prove the brethren. Assure yourself that all present have been advanced to the grade of Zelator and are zealous students, seeking the holy ends.

The Auxiliary Frater Zelator lifts up his lamp and wand.

FRATER ZELATOR: Fratres et sorores, in the name of the holy watchers, and by the ordinance of the Honorable Master, I demand the sign of this grade.

The same being duly given, the Auxiliary Frater Zelator lays down his lamp and wand. He comes forward and pauses between the pillars.

FRATER ZELATOR: Honorable Master of the Temple, in obedience to your commands, I have received from the fratres et sorores the sign of benediction, which is that of the grade of Zelator.

He communicates the sign to the Master, by whom it is repeated in turn. The Auxiliary Frater Zelator goes back direct as he came.

MASTER OF THE TEMPLE: I testify on my own part, and on behalf of the whole Fellowship, that we who are here present have been dedicated by our own free will, and have pledged and set apart ourselves, seeking the high things belonging to this grade of zeal. Intervene, O Lord, in Thy mercy, and so sustain those who have entered within the gate that they may come at last to Thy presence.

This is said with raised eyes and uplifted wand. The pause of a moment follows.

MASTER OF THE TEMPLE: Let this Fellowship of the Rosy Cross be sprinkled with Holy Water, to symbolize that greater sanctification by which we are purified from stain in our earthly part.

If the brethren have not been purified previously in the grade of Neophyte, the Frater Aquarius comes round with the sun to the throne of the Master, the blessing of the vessel of water takes place in the prescribed form, and the Aquarius returns with the sun to his proper place. Then – and in either case – he advances to the pillars and, standing between them, describes a great cross in the air with his aspergillus and sprinkles freely thrice. He makes obeisance to the east between the pillars and uplifts his vessel.

FRATER AQUARIUS: He that is washed needs not save to wash his feet, but is clean every whit. I have purified the Fellowship with Water.

He returns to his place.

MASTER OF THE TEMPLE: Let this Fellowship of the Rosy Cross be hallowed with sacred Fire, to symbolize that consecration of the earthly part of our nature that God fulfills within us by the Fire of His indwelling presence.

The same form of procedure is followed by Frater Thurificans, and when he pauses between the pillars he describes a great ✠ in the air with his thurible and offers incense thrice, so that the fumes spread freely. Thereafter he makes obeisance to the east between the pillars and uplifts his vessel.

FRATER THURIFICANS: It is written that God shall save both man and beast. I have hallowed the Fellowship with Fire.

He returns to his place. The Auxiliary Frater Zelator comes forward and, standing between the pillars, lifts up his lamp and wand, saying:

FRATER ZELATOR: The body of the Fellowship is cleansed.

MASTER OF THE TEMPLE: In the sanctification of our earthly part, O Lord, grant us to see Thy face.

This is said with raised eyes and uplifted wand. The pause of a moment follows.

MASTER OF THE TEMPLE: Let us recall that part of human personality which receives its plenary consecration in the symbolism of this grade, and the element to which it corresponds, that a sense of our election may be awakened, O Honorable Frater Practicus, in the hearts of those who are here and now present and in the uplifted heart of this Fellowship.

WARDEN OF THE TEMPLE: The work of the wise is performed in the body of man, which is hallowed in this grade and corresponds to the element of Earth. It is written that the earth is the Lord's and His is the fullness thereof.

MASTER OF THE TEMPLE: (Knocks) Now, therefore, fratres et sorores, let us offer up our bodies in adoration, giving glory and thanks and honor to the Lord and King of Earth.

The Master of the Temple descends from his throne and faces the east in front of it, with the other officers and the rest of the brethren, in their respective places.

MASTER OF THE TEMPLE *(holding his wand upraised in the left hand):* ADONAI HA ARETZ, ADONAI MALKAH (*making upon his person the kabalistic sign of the cross*), unto Thee be the kingdom, the power and the glory, MALKUTH, GEBURAH and GEDULAH, the valley of vision, the seat of judgment and the palace of magnificence. Unto Thee be the rose of Sharon, the lily of the valley, the indwelling glory and fountain of all influx, wherewith the garden is watered for ever and ever.

The Auxiliary Frater Zelator comes forward and pauses between the pillars, with uplifted wand and lamp.

FRATER ZELATOR: At the gates, O city of Jerusalem, at thy sanctified gates of light, let the Earth adore ADONAI.

He returns direct as he came. The Master of the Temple faces west, standing in front of his throne, and says, with raised eyes and uplifted wand:

MASTER OF THE TEMPLE: And purified, consecrated, dedicated, let the part of Earth of his servants, the holy body of man, adore ADONAI.

He proceeds by south around the altar to the western part of the temple, and says in his solemn progress:

MASTER OF THE TEMPLE: For the body is a holy sanctuary and the Lord is our light therein. Therefore we look for its adoption, a redemption in perfect transmutation, that it may be as the body of heaven in its clearness.

The Master of the Temple halts in the middle west, facing the tablet of the west, at a convenient distance therefrom. The Warden of the Temple proceeds by south around the altar, where he is joined by the Guide of the Paths, who has taken the bowl of Earth from the altar. They assume their places respectively on the right and left of the Master. The Lucifer of the Temple brings up his lesser officers and stands with raised lamp immediately behind the Master, having Frater Thurificans on his left behind the Guide of the Paths and Frater Aquarius on his right, behind the Warden of the Temple. All present are now facing west.

MASTER OF THE TEMPLE: From the palace at the center, the most secret and holy place, wherein is the king in his beauty, to the palace of material things, wherein reigns the lord of the visible world in the likeness of the Lord of glory, the order and sequence of high graces and mysteries are interchanged without break or interruption, and man ~ by their blessed intermediation ~ communicates with the Eternal in the heights and the depths of his nature. In the mystical name ADAM, the letter Aleph looks toward the Supreme Crown; the letter Mem looks toward the Great Mother in BINAH, who is the Divine Mother of souls; but the letter Daleth looks toward the sephira MALKUTH and the bride in manifestation. May the power of the Lord descend upon me and the brightness of the Lord encompass me, while I recite the sacred invocations.

The Master of the Temple places his wand in the charge of the Warden, and taking from the Guide the bowl of symbolical Earth, he raises it in both hands.

MASTER OF THE TEMPLE: Thou hast clothed us in the earth of the worlds, and thither whence we came at first do we look in our desire and longing. Lead us in the paths thereto, Thou guide of all our ways. Remake us in the image of the ELOHIM, that which is manifest in our nature after the mode of things that are unseen by eyes of flesh, the will below in correspondence with the will that is above. Over fish in the sea, which are the lower emotions of our nature, over fowl of the air, which are wandering thoughts of mind, over cattle and over all the earth, over every material thing, give unto us the rule of kingship, that we may subdue our part of earth. Breathe into our nostrils the breath of life, that many may become a living soul.

With the bowl of symbolical Earth, the Master of the Temple traces the symbol of Earth in the air before him.

MASTER OF THE TEMPLE: Sanctify our congregation, O Lord; clothe us with the garments of salvation; cover us with the robe of righteousness, as a bridegroom is adorned with jewels. In the name of ADONAI MALKAH, the bride and queen of the kingdom, looking toward the gates of light, let the soul of our natural manhood and the earth of our human life adore ADONAI.

With the bowl of symbolical Earth, the Master of the Temple traces the sign of the bull in the air before him.

MASTER OF THE TEMPLE: In the name of AURIEL, the great angel of Earth, in memory of the manifested law, and by the sign of the head of the bull, ye living souls of Earth, adore ADONAI.

The Master of the Temple returns the bowl of Earth to the Guide, and taking from Frater Aquarius the vessel of Holy Water, he makes a cosmic cross in the north and sprinkles thrice, saying:

MASTER OF THE TEMPLE: By the sacred names and letters that are written about the western quarter of the universe, by the inward mystery that they communicate, by the protection from the enemy therein, and by their grace operating within us, ye living souls of Earth, adore ADONAI.

Returning the vessel of Water, he takes the thurible from Frater Thurificans, and making a cosmic cross, he offers incense thrice, saying:

MASTER OF THE TEMPLE: By the footstool of the King of glory, by the kingdom that is His, by the Crown of the kingdom in its splendor, ye living souls of Earth, adore ADONAI.

Returning the thurible, he receives his wand from the Warden and goes back by the northern quarter to his throne in the east. The other celebrants and officers return with the sun to their places. The Guide of the Paths replaces the bowl of Earth on the altar. All members face as usual.

MASTER OF THE TEMPLE *(with raised face and uplifted wand):* Seal us, O Lord, for ever with Thy holy names. May they be written about the hearts of Thy servants. Fratres et sorores, the Spirit and the bride say: Come. And come therefore, my brethren. Bring offerings of aspiration, and come into the house of the Lord. Auxiliary Frater Zelator, in the name of the Holy SHEKINAH, I command you to proclaim that the temple is open in the grade of zeal.

The Frater Proclamator lifts up his lamp and wand, saying loudly and clearly:

FRATER ZELATOR: In the name of ADONAI MALKAH, the house is swept and garnished. The temple is opened duly in the holy grade of Zelator *(Knocks)*.

WARDEN OF THE TEMPLE: *(Knocks)*

MASTER OF THE TEMPLE: *(Knocks)*

The officers and members are seated.

Here ends the solemn ceremony of opening the temple in the grade of Zelator.

THE CEREMONIAL ADVANCEMENT OF A NEOPHYTE
TO THE GRADE OF ZELATOR, 1 = 10

The postulant is alone in the vestibule on a prie-dieu, in full light, with a scroll in his hands, containing versicles proper to the grade.

MASTER OF THE TEMPLE: Fratres et sorores, the dispensation of the high light has been committed to our charge, working toward the will in its conversion ~ through conformity with divine will. And, seeing that I have been entrusted with a warrant from the Most Honored Imperator of the order for its exercise in the person of our beloved Frater Advient Regnum (*vel nomen aliud*), a Neophyte of this holy order, and am empowered to promote him from the portal of the Rosy Cross, now therefore I call upon you to unite with me spiritually in the hallowing of his natural body, for the better manifestation, the greater preparation and liberation of the man within. Do you, O Honorable Frater Theoreticus, Guide of the Paths and Grades, as mediator and reconciler, prince of purity and lord of peace, (*but in the case of a Soror acting as Guide of the Paths, substitute*: spirit of peace and purity), go forth and prepare the postulant, in the grace and the light, the benediction and mystical beauty, of your all-saving office.

The Guide of the Paths rises in his place and makes obeisance with the sign of the grade.

GUIDE OF THE PATHS: I will take unto me the strength of the eagle; I will unfold the wings of the dove; and all who desire in their hearts the graces and lights that abide in the holy place I will bring unto the mercy-seat and the rest of an eternal Sabbath.

The Guide leaves the temple by south and west.

MASTER OF THE TEMPLE: Fratres et sorores, the Neophyte is prepared in the body because he has been prepared already in his mind. He bears the outward warrants of advancement, being warranted from within the Order, seeing that we are acquainted with his zeal. The light is not hidden that he received in the portal of the Rosy Cross. I invite you to prepare for him a place in your own hearts, that the love of brotherhood may encompass one who is on the quest of divine love and the sacred word therein. Concur with me also in his advancement, that with recollection and reference we may bring him beyond the gate and place him at the entrance of that most hidden path that leads from the court of the temple through the holy place, from the place that is holy to that which is Holy of Holies, and thence into the mystery of God.

In the meantime the Guide of the Paths has greeted the postulant on the further side of the portal saying:

GUIDE OF THE PATHS: Blessed is he who comes in the name of the Lord. May his light shine in this temple as a glory of the Rosy Cross.

The Guide prepares the Neophyte, who wears the collar of his grade and is given a fylfot cross to carry in his right hand. In the act of giving the cross:

GUIDE OF THE PATHS: Purify this earthly part, O Lord; purge away the old leaven, sanctify the acts of man. And remember on your part, my brother of the Rosy Cross, that it is light of grace in the soul that enlightens the body as its temple. I say unto you, therefore, O Frater Advient Regnum (*vel nomen aliud*); Hallowed be thy soul.

While this is being done in the precincts:

MASTER OF THE TEMPLE: Auxiliary Frater Zelator, when the Neophyte, under gracious guidance, gives the symbolical battery of the grade, signifying the great law of unity, as a title to the freedom of the elect, you will admit him in traditional form. Fratres Thurificans et Aquarius, follow with your mystical vessels and perform your allotted part by the consecration of the Neophyte for the last time in the solemn ceremonies of this temple.

The Auxiliary Frater Zelator and his lesser officers rise in their places and proceed to a convenient point in proximity to the door.

The Guide of the Paths has instructed the Neophyte, who gives the battery of the grade (Knocks).
The Frater Ostiarius turns down the lights, and at a signal from Frater Zelator he opens the door, so that it is just ajar.

GUIDE OF THE PATHS *(speaking for the postulant, while they are still on the further side):* Let me enter by the gate of the temple, for without are darkness and sorrow, and the eye opens in vain.

The Frater Ostiarius throws back the door, so that they stand now on the sacred threshold.

FRATER ZELATOR: May that which has opened at your knocking be even as the house of God and to you as the gate of heaven.

The postulant crosses the threshold, let by the Guide.

GUIDE OF THE PATHS *(again speaking for the postulant):* Open to me the gates of righteousness; I will go into them; I will praise the Lord.

The Frater Ostiarius closes and secures the door behind them.

FRATER ZELATOR: Come in peace. The Lord loves the gates of Zion more than all the dwellings of Jacob.

The Guide of the paths advances to the middle west with the postulant. They halt at a short distance behind the pillars. The Auxiliary Frater Zelator and his lesser officers fall in and follow behind them. All pause and turn east on hearing the voice of the Master.

MASTER OF THE TEMPLE: The beginning of wisdom is the most true desire of discipline, and the care of discipline is love; but love is the keeping of her laws; and the keeping of her laws is the firm foundation of incorruption; while incorruption brings near to God. Therefore the desire of wisdom brings to the everlasting kingdom.

GUIDE OF THE PATHS: I have passed through the gates of understanding; I have come to the gate of wisdom; I have crossed the threshold thereof. O give unto me the path of peace, the path that leads to the temple and the place where wisdom dwells. I will build my tabernacle thereby and abide in the light of that presence.

MASTER OF THE TEMPLE: Except the Lord build the house, they labor in vain that build it. Except the Lord keep the city, the watchman wakes but in vain. May He keep your city for ever, O Neophyte of the Rosy Cross. May He build your house in beauty. By what aid have you come to our portal? Who has brought you across the threshold? Who leads you on this holy ground?

GUIDE OF THE PATHS: A call has come from the Imperator of this Temple, who by a gracious act of intervention has decreed the advancement of this our beloved brother. But the call is dual and the call is also one; it is from the depths of the heart of our postulant and from that which rules in the Fellowship ~ a sacred motive working in goodwill toward man. The Neophyte enters therefore by an act of permission and an act on his own part. The aids to entrance are in the sense of this twofold motive. It is written that the earth is the Lord's and the fullness thereof; the Neophyte is guided by ADONAI, the Lord of Earth. He is prepared in his mind by faith in a path to the heights; he is recognized by the warrant that you hold; the secrets of the portal grade are treasured in his heart; and he carries the sacred swastika as a badge of admission.

The Guide of the Paths takes the symbol and exalts it toward the east.

WARDEN OF THE TEMPLE: The fylfot cross, or swastika, is a great astronomical symbol that speaks to those who can interpret concerning the divine in the universe. It is formed of 17 squares extracted in a peculiar manner from a square of 25 squares. Observe that the sun is in the center and that it is surrounded by the four symbolical elements and the twelve zodiacal signs. You also are a center in the universe, brother novice of the Rosy Cross; let your light shine before it. You are a center of your own system; let the light of your consciousness be poured over your elements, over the parts of your personality, over your seals and characters and signs. The portents of the outward universe testify to the universe within.

The badge of admission is laid aside.

MASTER OF THE TEMPLE: Honorable Frater Theoreticus, you will place the Neophyte between the pillars, with his face toward the east.

This is done in the authorized form, the Guide leading the postulant.

MASTER OF THE TEMPLE: Auxiliary Frater Zelator, I direct you to receive from the Neophyte the step, sign, token, secret words, and temporal password communicated at the last Equinox in the portal of our order.

The Auxiliary Frater Zelator puts aside his lamp and wand. He comes round with the sun to the postulant. Having received the official secrets, he faces east, giving the salute of the grade, and says:

FRATER ZELATOR: Honorable Master of the Temple, I have received the secrets of the first portal grade.

MASTER OF THE TEMPLE: They are outward forms of our mysteries. Let us remember that the body of our sacred ritual is not without its spirit.

The Guide resumes his seat in the middle space between the altar and the thrones of the east. The Auxiliary Frater Zelator takes charge of the postulant.

MASTER OF THE TEMPLE: He who certifies that ADONAI is his guide when he enters our holy temple shall ever command our aid. The ministers of the Rosy Cross wait upon the followers of God. Stand therefore, frater, and ~ erect between the mystical pillars ~ bear witness to your high intention. Do you covenant to maintain the same honorable and perfect silence on the mysteries of this grade that you have been pledged already to preserve in respect of those belonging to the portal of our Fellowship? Will you never reveal them to the world? Will you never confer them on a Neophyte, except in an authorized temple, under warrant from the Imperator of our Order, when you are acting in the capacity of Master? And do you testify with true lips ~ in the presence of the brethren who are here and now assembled ~ that the dispositions that brought you to the portal have passed into a sense of dedication, and that you will continue to the best of your ability to be worthy of your high calling?

THE NEOPHYTE *(being prompted by Frater Zelator and repeating the words after him):* I pledge my soul to silence; I will communicate only as I have received in the ceremonies of the temple; and the sense of my dedication burns like a holy fire in my heart.

The Auxiliary Frater Zelator comes round with the sun to the western side of the altar, removes the bowl of Earth and returning faces north, on the eastern side of the pillars, close to the postulant.

MASTER OF THE TEMPLE: I now bid you kneel down; place both hands in the vessel presented before you, which contains emblematical Earth and salt. As one who calls upon his proper body in testimony, repeat in a clear voice: When his earthly part has been purified, the spirit of man shall ascend, as the sparks fly upward. I give my body to the work of divine life; I will follow the call of the spirit. I swear by the Earth of Zion, which became a living soul, and by the body with its activities and all the train of their consequences. Let me be uplifted on the mountain; let me tread the wine-press of the kingdom.

This is repeated by the postulant – following the Master. The Auxiliary Frater Zelator takes charge of the bowl.

MASTER OF THE TEMPLE: And even as the immemorial soul, may your heart continue to demand the higher things. Frater Ostiarius, in virtue of the testimony that has been born on his knees by the postulant, let there be a light upon his way.

The Frater Ostiarius turns up the lights of the temple. The postulant remains upon his knees. The Master of the Temple rises with uplifted arms.

MASTER OF THE TEMPLE: With water from the wells of understanding, do Thou cleanse us, O Lord, from sin; with fire from the altar of incense, do Thou consecrate us again to Thy service; that we may offer up a clean sacrifice in Thy holy place.

And then, having resumed his seat:

MASTER OF THE TEMPLE: Fratres Thurificans et Aquarius, approach in the grace and sanctification of your respective offices; purify the earthly part of our beloved postulant.

The Frater Aquarius comes round the pillars with the sun, holds up his vessel of water in obeisance to the thrones of the east, turns westward, cross-marks the postulant on the forehead and sprinkles three times before him, saying:

FRATER AQUARIUS: Waters of purification, waters of the great sea, for the cleansing of Earth and man, I purify with Water.

He turns eastward, again elevates the vessel and resumes his former place, moving with the sun. The Frater Thurificans comes round the pillars in the same manner, holds up his thurible in obeisance to the thrones of the east, turns westward, makes a ✠ with the thurible before the postulant and censes him thrice, saying:

FRATER THURIFICANS: Fire from the altar that is above; Fire for the consecration of Earth and man; I consecrate with Fire.

He turns eastward, again elevates the thurible and ~ moving with the sun ~ resumes his former place.

MASTER OF THE TEMPLE: Rise, Neophyte of the Rosy Cross, an accepted Postulant for advancement to the Grade of Zelator.

The Postulant rises.

The Auxiliary Frater Zelator places the bowl of Earth in the two hands of the postulant, and moving with the sun proceeds to a convenient point behind him, where he directs the postulant in a low voice to lift up the bowl to the full height of his arms and say after him clearly:

THE NEOPHYTE *(following the Frater Zelator):* Into thy hands, O soul of mine, for the work of the Rosy Cross, I commend my body of life.

The Auxiliary Frater Zelator should perform this part of the ceremony so that attention may be directed to the postulant rather than to his own prompting. The bowl is replaced on the Altar.

MASTER OF THE TEMPLE: The blessing of the Order overshadows you, its welcome awaits you, its God-speed goes before you, as you pass from the court of the temple toward the sanctuary that is within. You have knelt between the pillars, to lay down the uneasy yoke and intolerable burden of the old unconsecrated life. You have risen between the pillars, to the new and dedicated life. Between the pillars you have been purified and made ready in the sense of the life of dedication; its vistas stretch before you. I bid you lift up the eyes of your spirit, for this is holy ground, and that which lies before you is the path of your attainment and return. Hail unto you, our postulant and brother, for your blessed dispositions toward the Light.

The Guide of the Paths rises in his place, with uplifted wand, facing westward to the altar.

GUIDE OF THE PATHS: Guide us, O Lord, and guard in all our ways. Watch us, going forth and returning; watch us, our King, for ever. Lead us to our term, O Hidden Master of the Rosy Cross, that we may come alive into Thy presence.

The Guide resumes his seat.

WARDEN OF THE TEMPLE: And the Lord God planted a garden eastward in Eden; and there He put the man whom He had formed. And out of the ground made the Lord God to grow every Tree that is pleasant to the sight and good for food; the Tree of Life also in the midst of the garden, and the Tree of Knowledge of good and evil. It is the Tree of divided Knowledge; but it shall be made one with the supernals in that higher knowledge that is unity; and it shall become the Tree of Life.

GUIDE OF THE PATHS: In the correspondence of things that are above with those that are manifested below, there is a supernal and there is a lower Eden. The one is the place of our desire and the place whence the influx comes; the other is that of our purgation.

WARDEN OF THE TEMPLE: The one is in a world of understanding that is called in our traditional system the SEPHIRA BINAH; the other is in the kingdom of this world, which is called the SEPHIRA MALKUTH.

MASTER OF THE TEMPLE: From MALKUTH, which is the tenth sephira, the manifested world, there extends a path of Life, and it is the way of your return to the heights, O frater Advient Regnum (*vel nomen aliud*).

GUIDE OF THE PATHS: The legend of Eden is an allegory of our first estate, when divine substance was communicated to the soul of man in a paradise that is above. But since that immemorial pre-natal time he has been the denizen of an inferior garden. Yet the vestiges of his old transcendent state have not been removed utterly, and scattered fragments of the divine food allure him still amidst the quests of material life. To him who can receive they are administered in the sacraments of nature and grace for ever and ever. They are aids and consolations on the way of his return homeward; they are sanctities in his path of liberation. You who have been nourished on fruits of the Tree of Knowledge, remember the Tree of Life. Whence you have come remember, an also whither you are going. Lift up your eyes, looking to the land of life, beyond the mountains of salvation.

ZELATOR INITIATION

The Auxiliary Frater Zelator prompts the postulant in an undertone, from behind him.

THE NEOPHYTE *(following Frater Zelator):* I stand between the mystical pillars; I seek the way to the heights and the path of life, in the name of ADONAI.

The Guide of the Paths rises in his place, with uplifted wand.

GUIDE OF THE PATHS: I have watched long for your coming, O son of truth.

He proceeds slowly westward, and says in his progress:

GUIDE OF THE PATHS: I rise in the place of benignity. I come in the name of the light. I come from the mercy seat. I am the preparer of the way that leads to the celestial Light. Peace and reconciliation are in my hands. I have the power and will to perfect all who shall enter by the path of prudence. I have seen the Tree of Life and the twelve manners of fruit. Make way for me, ye lords of truth. I carry the grace of mediation, and before I have finished my course I look to make all things one.

He is standing in front of the postulant, who is directed by the Auxiliary Frater Zelator to kneel with bent head.

MASTER OF THE TEMPLE: May God be with you for ever, true Guide of the Paths and Grades. Fulfill your ministry of mercy, in the performance of which you represent in this world of action the glorious love ~kindness descending from the Supreme Crown through the unmanifest and manifest worlds.

The Guide of the Paths gives the ritual benediction of the grade over the bowed head of the postulant. It is given with both arms extended horizontally, the fingers separated and inclined downward, symbolizing the good will of the order flowing over the personality of the recipient.

GUIDE OF THE PATHS: Frater Advient Regnum (*vel nomen aliud*), may God be with you in your quest, and seeing whence you have come down, may His own wisdom teach you the most practical of all lessons, which is how to go back.

The Guide of the Paths lifts up the postulant by his two arms and draws him through the pillars.

GUIDE OF THE PATHS: You who are zealous of the Light, I will lead you, I will bring you, even unto the house of Light.

Having brought him across the threshold, the Guide of the Paths returns with the sun to his place. The postulant remains standing, a little in front of the pillars, facing east. The Auxiliary Frater Zelator and his assistant officers go back to their own seats.

MASTER OF THE TEMPLE: Frater Advient Regnum (*vel nomen aliud*), you were admitted in the grade of Neophyte through the portal of a holy house, typically represented by that place of God that was built of old in Israel. You came already within the precincts, even into the court of the tabernacle, where stood the altar of burnt offerings, on which animals were immolated in sacrifice. On such an altar you have dedicated your body of life to the high ends of the spirit, that in your soul you may see the Light.

GUIDE OF THE PATHS: When the Light of the spirit is declared, my brother, in your consciousness may the life be communicated to you therein.

WARDEN OF THE TEMPLE: Between the altar of burnt offerings and the entrance to the holy place stood the laver of brass, wherein the priests washed before they entered the tabernacle of the congregation.

GUIDE OF THE PATHS: Remember, O brother of the Rosy Cross, that through the fires and waters of this earthly life we are prepared for the things that are of heaven.

MASTER OF THE TEMPLE: Having been cleansed in the laver of brass, having made his offering at the altar of burnt sacrifice, the priest then entered the holy place.

The Guide of the Paths rises, with uplifted wand.

GUIDE OF THE PATHS: From earthly into spiritual life, from places of lesser purification, come into the place that is holy. Enter into the presence of God.

MASTER OF THE TEMPLE: The path of your symbolical progress in this grade has brought you from the court of the temple into the holy place. Beyond it is a Holy of Holies, and yet beyond is another mystery of religion, leading by successive stages to a central place of experience, unto which all faiths testify, which all set forth in types.

The Guide of the Paths has resumed his seat.

WARDEN OF THE TEMPLE: The golden table of shewbread stood on the northern side of the holy place, and the twelve loaves placed thereon were symbolical of the bread of life, of which those who partake in the spirit are joined together into one mystical body and community of the elect. They signify to us that the material nourishment of man may become the food of souls by the power behind the sacraments, the grace and life and light that it is the purpose of all the signs of nature to communicate under their proper veils. For this reason the twelve loaves typify the universe of manifested things, behind which the divine immanence abides like a secret Light. And because the word of God ~ which is sought and found in our Fellowship after an arcane manner ~ finds expression in creation, but is veiled also therein, the twelve loaves are referable to the twelve simple letters of the Hebrew alphabet. They signify further ~ but this is in the sense of the microcosm ~ the twelve tribes of Israel, understood mystically as those who have been called and chosen, out of all tribes and tongues and peoples and nations, for divine work in the world. They are in correspondence also with the figurative crown of the twelve stars on the head of ADONAI MALKAH, the most Holy SHEKINAH, the bride and queen in manifestation, ruling in the spiritual MALKUTH, which is sanctum regnum, the kingdom of the elect, in sacramental analogy with the kingdom of this world, which is also a city of God. The loaves of the table of shewbread may be likened again to twelve petals composing the rose of creation; and on the microcosmic side of the symbol, seen under this aspect, they typify finally the rose of our humanity, in the center of which is consciousness enlightened by God, as the world itself is enlightened by virtue of the immanence within.

GUIDE OF THE PATHS: The seven branched candlestick stood on the southern side of the holy place, wrought about with golden lilies, lighting the altar of incense and the table of shewbread. It corresponds in our secret tradition with the seven emblematical palaces of the world of action, or the material world, and with the seven double letters of the Hebrew alphabet, signifying the divine efficacy therein, by which the palaces of action become the holy place. This place is the glorious palace of holiness and the secret temple at the center. The seven branched candlestick is also in analogy with the seven churches of Asia; and even as the petals of a rose, like the branches of the light bearer in the temple, are bound together, springing from one root and one stem, so are the seven churches one holy church of the elect. And as the angels of the churches are stars for the enlightenment thereof, so is there a mystical lesson in the days of the week. For those days are like seven churches, and it is yours, O chosen brother, so to consecrate and rule your life within them that they shall be one church and one most holy temple, with God dwelling therein. Thus shall you deserve to be crowned at the end of all with that chaplet of seven stars, which are the gifts of the spirit.

The Master of the Temple descends from his throne and proceeds to the eastern side of the altar. The Frater Thurificans comes up from the west and hands his thurible to the master, who ~ turning to the east ~ makes a ✠ in the air therewith and offers incense thrice.

MASTER OF THE TEMPLE *(at the first censing):* Glory be to God, who is declared in the heart of man to those who are pure in heart. (*At the second censing*) Glory be to God, who is manifested in the light of created things. (*At the third censing*) Glory be to God in the transcendence, in the place of concealed mystery. We adore Thee in the presence of the veil. O take us in Thine own good time, Thy gracious and saving time, beyond all veils, behind Thy palms and pomegranates, into the Holy of Holies.

He gives back the thurible to Frater Thurificans, who returns to his place. The Master of the Temple now faces westward to the postulant.

MASTER OF THE TEMPLE: Before the veil of the Holy of Holies stood the golden altar of incense; but this altar stands in the middle place of our temple. It is in the form of a double cube, presenting the surface of things to the eye of sense, but concealing the root and the source, as He is concealed in the universe Who is author and cause of all. The altar of incense was golden to signify that perfect state which is possible for our human nature to attain in union with its source, and wherein our human will becomes an acceptable offering, integrated in the will of God. But this altar is black, because we await the conversion of our personal elements from the state of impurity into the state of living gold, because of the divine darkness, and because the witness of nature to grace is a witness in the night of time. Upon the golden altar were incense, oil and fire, corresponding to Aleph, Mem, and Shin, the three mother letters of the Hebrew alphabet. The divisions of this Alphabet, of which you have heard briefly in connection with the table of shewbread, the seven branched candlestick, and the altar of incense, are but a part of the deep symbolism that lies behind the letters of the word of man ~ itself a shadow and reflection of that eternal word to the quest whereof we are dedicated ~ that word which is concealed everywhere, but is declared in the secret heart. From the throne of your imperishable spirit, O Frater Advient Regnum (*vel nomen aliud*), may the triad and the unity therein look forth upon the kingdom that is yours; may the seven spirits and the seven graces encircle it; and may the twelve fruits of the Tree of Life ripen in your external part.

The Master of the Temple returns to his throne and the Auxiliary Frater Zelator comes forward, leaving his lamp and wand. Taking the postulant by his two hands, he turns him with his back to the north and faces him at a short distance.

MASTER OF THE TEMPLE: Auxiliary Frater Zelator, you will now impart to the postulant the secret sign, sacred words, password, and mystical number that are allocated to the 1 = 10 grade in the Fellowship of the Rosy Cross.

FRATER ZELATOR: Frater Advient Regnum (*vel nomen aliud*), by the decree of the Honorable Master of the Temple, receive at my hands the official secrets that are reserved to the grade of Zelator. You will advance to me in the first place with the step of a Neophyte. It is in this position that the secret sign is communicated. The sign is given with both arms extended horizontally, the fingers separated and inclined downward, as if in the act of benediction. It signifies the goodwill of the order flowing over him who receives it, and it was by this memorable sign that the Guide of the Paths bestowed his blessing upon you, on the part of the whole Order, as you knelt between the pillars. The sacred words are ADONAI MALKAH, and ~ as understood among us ~ they have reference to the bride or queen of Earth, to which symbolical Element this grade is attributed. The password is NAH, which signifies ornament. It is formed from the two Hebrew letters Nun and He, the numerical value of which is 55; and this is the mystical number. The grip of the Neophyte grade obtains throughout the first order, and also the step.

The grip having been exchanged between them, the Auxiliary Frater Zelator leads the postulant to a seat between the altar and the pillars.

MASTER OF THE TEMPLE: The three great banners in the east are signs of the paths that connect the grades of Malkuth with the grades of sephiroth that are above. These banners are inscribed respectively in their centers with the Hebrew letters Resh, Shin, and Tau. The paths refer to the mode of symbolical ascent through the grades and sephiroth comprised in the second order of the Rosy Cross. They are symbols, my brother, and the realities to which they correspond are states of high experience belonging to the life of the soul on its search for God. I bid you remember that there is an eternal covenant between the divine in man and the Divine in the universe, by which there is ~ world without end ~ a way of return to God.

WARDEN OF THE TEMPLE: The four-square tablet that stands in the middle west of the temple contains divine and angelical names referable to the western quarter of the heaven and ~ by correspondence ~ to the element of Earth. They teach us that the universe and man who dwells therein are encompassed by the powers and the providences, the graces and benedictions of the Divine. They serve, moreover, to remind us that God has given His angels charge over all those who work for the hidden wisdom and follow the quest of Him.

MASTER OF THE TEMPLE: I now confer on you the mystical title of Pereclinus de Faustis, which signifies that on this earth you are as one who walks in a wilderness, and it bids you therefore create a garden of the soul therein. Your work is the regeneration of earth in your own personality, that you may renew it in that which is about you. I give you therefore the symbol of ARETZ, being the Hebrew name of Earth. May you so work, my brother, that through nature you shall enter into grace. May you be worthy of your high calling. May you come with joy and go forth in gladness. May God still guide you, if haply our leading fail in the path that goes to the heights.

There is here the pause of a moment.

MASTER OF THE TEMPLE: Auxiliary Frater Zelator, lift up your wand of office, lift up the light that you carry, and declare in this holy temple that our Frater Advient Regnum (*vel nomen aliud*) has been advanced to the grade of Zelator and has received, by a regular communication, the titles conferred therein.

ZELATOR INITIATION

The Auxiliary Frater Zelator comes with the sun to a point in front of the postulant.

FRATER ZELATOR: The Name of ADONAI is before us; the name of MALKAH is before us; the lord of Earth, the bride and queen of the kingdom. Honorable Master of the Temple, in those Names and obeying your high ordinance, I proclaim that Frater Advient Regnum (*vel nomen aliud*) has been advanced in traditional form to the grade of Zelator, 1 = 10 in our Fellowship, and has received the mystical title of Pereclinus de Faustis, with the symbol of ARETZ.

He returns to his place with the Sun.

WARDEN OF THE TEMPLE: Malkuth is a place of the darkness, a place of the shadowed light, a place of illumination in holy and secret sanctuaries. The powers and the glories, the graces also and mercies, through paths and worlds of the sephiroth above, are sent down therein. It is the first sephira in the way of our return whence we came, and it is therefore called 1 in our system. But seeing that on the outward path by which man traveled into manifestation, it is the tenth and last sephira, so also its number is 10; and it is in such sense that the grace to which you have been advanced is described as 1 = 10. A corresponding symbolism of numbers obtains through all grades of the order on the ascent to the heights. In this dual quest of the spirit of man, the world of Malkuth is denominated a path by the secret tradition of Israel, and it is termed also the resplendent intelligence, a root and fountain of light. But this is in the restored state, when the kingdom of manifest things has become the kingdom of God. I counsel you to remember, my brother, that for you in the work of our Fellowship the kingdom of heaven is at hand.

MASTER OF THE TEMPLE: Frater Advient Regnum (*vel nomen aliud*), your title to further advancement in the grades of this Order will continue to depend upon the maintenance of that Holy Fire that your zeal has kindled within you. Guard therefore that Fire, as we on our side will guard your memory in our hearts; and be sure that when you come again to our temple, carrying the proper warrants, asking in humility and reverence for tidings of the Holy of Holies, we shall hear your voice, and when you knock we shall surely answer. Meanwhile, you are appointed keeper of the threshold in this grade of sacred zeal.

The Auxiliary Frater Zelator comes forward, removes the chair of the postulant and leads him to the door of the temple, where he is met by the acting Ostiarius, who delivers to him his wand of office.

The allocution of the grade follows, and is delivered by the Imperator, but him failing by his substitute, or by the Master of the Temple.

THE ALLOCUTION OF THE GRADE OF ZELATOR

Fratres et sorores, by the faithful witnesses whose counsels have been transmitted from of old, we know that the Tree of Knowledge becomes the Tree of Life and is made one with the supernals in that higher knowledge which is unity. In some high region of the mind, above the distinctions that obtain between good and evil, and merged in an absolute goodness that fills the soul entirely, there is an union that the soul attains, so that knowledge is on all sides and is universal and holy. Looking to that end of our desire, I invite you to hear in the repose and the stillness that follow each stage of our activity, marking progress in the work, the allocution belonging to the grade of Zelator. And you, our postulant, who have this day crossed that threshold to which you were brought only in the previous degree, I solicit and claim your attention to a few salutary inferences that should be taken away from the experience through which you have just passed, being that of the advancement which follows reception into the house of our Fellowship. Here, as in other departments of intellectual and spiritual life, advancement is in knowledge and experience acquired slowly. It is the continued communication of that light which is conferred symbolically on the postulant in the grade of Neophyte and which it is prayed that he may realize within him. He is brought to the door of the temple, and if it be only in symbolism that he has earned the title for a further share in its mysteries, he is still instructed to knock, and what follows is that the door opens. He enters amidst the harmonious rumors that move about the activity of the spiritual house and of the mystical city. His face is set toward the east, as one who should see Zion on the sacred hill when the orient from on high has flooded it, when the night and its shadows are over. Let us pray that for him and those who are like him all scales and bandages may fall from the inward eyes and that there shall be no more darkness within.

From his base on this earth he looks toward the city that is beyond and the house of his desire; he sees the great distance stretching before him ~ an immeasurable distance that he is prepared to enter. He will understand also, if he have brought within the circle of our Fellowship something of the light of thought, that distances themselves are nothing, nor do places signify, because that which we reach in the height is already here. There are no greater opportunities than those of today; there are no hindrances so insuperable that will and desire cannot ~ in their transmutation and with their tingeing power ~ convert into perfect paths. When the voice of the master speaks to the postulant of the great old allegories, of the Tree and the garden, he knows that their inward meanings are here and now among us, that Earth's kingdom is also a garden, the paradise that is below, while the Tree is not separable from these. Fratres et sorores, here is the way of the Tree of Life, now is the call thereto; and if some swords are broken at the entrance gate, if for some the sword of the Kerubim keep that way too keenly, there is also a sword of the spirit, before which even the Kerubim raise their guard, so that those who are born for the sanctuary may enter and go in.

Amidst such intimations, and such awakenings within, is the postulant brought from the court of the temple to the holy place, and is told of the mysteries that are beyond, of religion behind religion, and of that which is the center of all, worlds without end of symbolism and one world of experience ~ the key and explanation of all. But in the deep places of his mind he will know that the world about him is truly the court of the temple, that here is the holy place and a Holy of Holies within it for those who are qualified to enter. So also ~ and whether we are conscious or not of His divine presence ~ the reconciler is always with us, speaking from the mercy Seat and preparing the way to the Celestial Light. In God's most spiritual temple ~ at once manifest and concealed ~ you are the burnt offerings, my brethren; you are also the altar. It is by the sacrifice of your proper selves, and so only, that you can enter truly and essentially that holy place which you have now entered symbolically. There is the bread of life, which is shown in our symbolism to correspond with the whole of creation, because God nourishes His children, substantially and super substantially, on all the planes; and the high angels, which guard the inmost precincts of the mysteries, do communicate ~ to those who can receive ~ the food of souls, in every region of the universe. In that temple also are held ~ as if in archives ~ the hidden doctrines of divine mystery, leading by steep paths to the crown of all experience in the term of sanctity. After this manner does the mystical temple, of which this is the type and symbol, contain all things. The last message that it communicates to the postulant in this grade is that the path of life in which it has pleased God to call him in the nearest way of his election. The mystery of the tenth path, about which you have just heard, shows that Malkuth is understood after more than one manner, that the pearl of great price is in your own house, in the temple of your own personality, while that which is begun on earth from every point of departure may be completed also on earth in the heaven within you.

For there is a certain mode of mind that is other than logical understanding ~ more resplendent and more highly enthroned. A light descends therefrom through an ordered channel; it is called the Light of the Spirit; and this channel is the path by which the Zelator goes up.

If the minutes of any previous meeting or other official business are to be taken in the grade of Zelator, the temple must be reduced at this point to the grade of Neophyte. By the power of his wand, the Master must close in the higher grade, open by fiat in the lower, and after the business has been completed must similarly close therein and re-open in the grade of Zelator.

The Solemn Ceremony of Closing
The Sacred Temple in the Grade of Zelator

MASTER OF THE TEMPLE: (*Knocks*)

All rise.

MASTER OF THE TEMPLE: Fratres et sorores Zelators, I pray you to assist me with one mind in the closing of the heart against the world.

WARDEN OF THE TEMPLE: Honored Master of the Temple, I testify on behalf of the brethren, I testify on my own part, that the heart is guarded.

MASTER OF THE TEMPLE: Let that which is watched within, even in the sacred precincts, be protected also beyond, in the world to which we return. Frater Ostiarius, remembering the correspondence between things within and without, I direct you to see that the temple is duly secured.

The Frater Ostiarius, having seen that the door is fast:

FRATER OSTIARIUS: Honorable Master of the Temple, the precincts are guarded without by the invisible keepers of the mysteries; the door is secured within; and I stand on the hither side as a witness of vigilance and a gage of prudence.

MASTER OF THE TEMPLE: The earth is full of His goodness; the pillars of the earth are the Lord's; the earth is full of His riches. Let us adore the lord and king of Earth.

The Master and Warden descend from their thrones and face east, with uplifted wands. All present face east.

MASTER OF THE TEMPLE: ADONAI HA-ARETZ, ADONAI MAL-KAH, we have desired thee in all generations. Spirit of the Lord, say: Come. Bride of the Lord, say: Come. We have watched in the night because of Thee; we have worked in the day because of Thee; we die in the endurance of our longing. Make us alive in Thee. O Earth. Earth, Earth, part of the Earth in us, hear the word of the Lord. Amen.

The Master of the Temple turns westward with extended arms.

MASTER OF THE TEMPLE: The guide of the elect, the abiding and in-dwelling presence, remain with this temple for ever, and in the hearts of the brethren. Hail unto the Holy SHEKINAH on the mercy seat, between the folded wings of the Kerubim.

The Master of the Temple lays aside his wand and turns to the Warden, who turns also to him and lays aside his own wand. They approach one another. The Master gives the benediction of the grade to the Warden, who receives it with bowed head.

MASTER OF THE TEMPLE: Remember the end, my brother.

WARDEN OF THE TEMPLE: The end is unity.

The Master of the Temple returns to his throne and there remains standing. Members face as usual. The Guide of the Paths lays aside his wand and turns to the Warden of the Temple in the middle east. They approach one another. The Warden gives the benediction of the grade to the Guide, who receives it with bowed head. They exchange the previous formulary. The Warden returns to his throne and there remains standing. The Guide of the Paths turns westward and proceeds with the sun to a point in front of the pillars. The Auxiliary Frater Zelator comes forward and pauses between the pillars. The Guide gives the benediction of the grade to the Frater Zelator, who receives it with bowed head. The formulary is exchanged between them. The Guide returns to his seat with the sun and there remains standing.

  The Auxiliary Frater Zelator returns direct as he came, and standing in his own place he turns to the Frater Thurificans, who turns also to him. The Auxiliary Frater Zelator gives the benediction of the grade to the Frater Thurificans, who receives it with bowed head. The formulary is repeated. The Frater Thurificans carries the benediction to the Frater Aquarius, who receives it with bowed head. The formulary is repeated.

  The Frater Aquarius proceeds with the Sun to the first unofficial brother in the south-east and gives the benediction of the grade. The formulary is repeated. It is communicated from member to member on the southern side in the same manner. Meanwhile the Frater Aquarius proceeds with the sun to the first unofficial brother in the north-east and gives the benediction. It is communicated from member to member on the northern side. The last recipient gives it to the Frater Ostiarius, who is the postulant of the day.

  The Frater Ostiarius, under direction from the Frater Aquarius, proceeds with the sun to a point between the altar and the pillars, facing east.

The Most Honored Imperator of the Order comes round to that point with the sun and receives the benediction of the Grade from Frater Ostiarius with bowed head. The formulary is exchanged, as in all cases previously. The Frater Ostiarius is led back to his place and there remains standing.

The Most Honored Imperator turns eastward with extended arms.

IMPERATOR OF THE FELLOWSHIP: And God shall be all in all.

Having said this in a clear voice, and with great reverence, the Imperator returns to his place. All face as usual.

MASTER OF THE TEMPLE: Our hearts are licensed to go forth into the world without, carrying the memorials of the covenants made within. Depart in the peace of the eternal. Depart to your proper places, your paths in life and their activities. Frater Zelator, by virtue of your high office in the world of action, I command you to close the temple.

The Frater Zelator lifts up his wand only.

FRATER ZELATOR: The graces and benedictions of ADONAI be upon us, as children of the restored world. Be we ready for the call of His service, under the banner of the Rosy Cross. In the name of the Holy SHEKINAH, I declare this temple closed in the grade of zeal.

MASTER OF THE TEMPLE: (*Knocks*)

WARDEN OF THE TEMPLE: (*Knocks*)

GUIDE OF THE PATHS: (*Knocks*)

HERE ENDS THE RITUAL OF THE GRADE OF ZELATOR,
AND
HERE ENDS THE FIRST ORDER OF THE ROSY CROSS.

The Second Order of the Rosy Cross

World of Formation

Part I

The Ceremony of Advancement

in the

The Grade of Theoreticus

2 = 9

Privately Printed

1916

The Fellowship of the Rosy Cross

—

Grade of Theoreticus 2 = 9

—

THE SOLEMN CEREMONY OF OPENING THE TEMPLE IN THE GRADE OF THEORETICUS

—

The arrangement of the temple is shown in the official diagram of the first point.

The celebrants or officers of this grade are the Master of the Temple, the Warden, and the Guide of the Paths, in addition to the Ostiarius, who should be the last candidate to have received advancement therein.

If the temple should not have been opened previously in one of the lower grades, the ceremonial vesting of officers and members, the invocation or prayer at the east, and the assoilment of the temple are performed as exhibited therein.

The Master of the Temple assumes his throne, holding the wand of his office. The other celebrants repair to their stations, and the ordinary brethren are arranged north and south, according to the precedence of their grades. All members are seated and a short space of inward recollection follows.

MASTER OF THE TEMPLE: (*Knocks*)

All rise.

MASTER OF THE TEMPLE: Fratres et sorores, by the bond of our Fellowship, which is the union of consecrated minds, and in the name of the Lord of hosts who leads the cohorts of salvation, assist me to open this temple of the Rosy Cross in the grade of Theoreticus, as a light of salvation to minds that are called herein. Frater Ostiarius, I direct you to see that the temple is guarded on the hither and further sides, that we may keep without the gate those who distract from the term.

The Frater Ostiarius opens the portal pro forma, inspects the immediate precincts, again secures the threshold, and turns to the east with uplifted wand.

FRATER OSTIARIUS: Honorable Master of the Temple, the guard is maintained duly on the outer side by those who have kept the threshold from the beginning of our sacred mysteries. I keep the guard within, and I will ever remember the end.

MASTER OF THE TEMPLE: Honorable Frater Theoreticus, you will receive from those who are present the external warrants in virtue of which they have entered our holy temple in this grade.

The Guide of the Paths, standing in his place, lifts up his Wand of Office.

GUIDE OF THE PATHS: Fratres et sorores, united in the Mystical Fellowship of the Rosy Cross, I demand the sign of a Theoreticus.

He turns in succession to the four quarters and receives it from all present, the master of the Temple excepted. The Guide turns to the master, giving it on his own part.

GUIDE OF THE PATHS: Honorable Master of the Temple, the glory of the holy heights and the splendor of the great white crown uplift the minds of the Fellowship.

The sign is repeated by the Master.

MASTER OF THE TEMPLE: I have also beheld that Light, and because of it I am glad for ever. Herein is the consecration of the mind part of the Fellowship. The brethren who can give this sign have entered the Theoreticus grade. Unto them be the graces thereof and the mystery of YESOD revealed in the sanctuary of thought.

This is said with raised eyes and uplifted wand. There follows the pause of a moment.

MASTER OF THE TEMPLE: Let us recall the abiding graces that prevail in the mysteries of this grade, that their living presence may be declared in our own consciousness and renewed in the mind of the Fellowship.

GUIDE OF THE PATHS: The grade of fratres Theoretici is the grade of the sephira YESOD, and the presence of SHEKINAH is therein, as mistress of the middle pillar, and the form of our desire for God.

WARDEN OF THE TEMPLE: It is in correspondence by symbolical attribution with the macrocosmic element of air, and with the natural understanding in man. The children of disobedience shall become the sons and daughters of the law, and the law shall enlighten the mind by the rays of the sun of justice.

GUIDE OF THE PATHS: In the mystical astronomy of the soul, the moon is like natural reason, a realm of reflected light, peopled by wandering thoughts and plastic images. But we seek, O Honorable Master, the direct illumination at another and eternal source. I am the reconciler between them, standing in the middle path, looking towards the glorious sun of TIPHERETH, as a purified moon of mind, and testifying to the bond of union.

WARDEN OF THE TEMPLE: The way of attainment is the way of progression in the Tree, even unto the Holy of Holies, into the great mystery of which our entrance is by the 32nd path, the path of Tau. This is the ladder of Jacob, and a sure testimony that man is made for the heights.

MASTER OF THE TEMPLE: (*Knocks*)

The Master of the Temple descends from his throne, and faces the east thereat. The Warden also descends. All members face east. The Master uplifts his wand.

MASTER OF THE TEMPLE: Ye who are in search of the Life of life, lift up your hearts in worship. Lift them in aspiration and in longing unto Him who lives for ever. Praise unto Thee, EL CHAI and SHADDAI, Lord of the heavenly spheres, Lord and king of mind. Our thoughts are stayed on

Thee, the head and the heart are Thine. O lead us on the holy mountain, in the paths that approach to Thee. Raise into the consecrated places those who are born from Thy sanctuary. Beyond the natural reason, out of the errant thoughts and the flux of images, draw us ~ we beseech ~ and raise us. Take us into the still rest of the active center. May we be fixed on Thee, and after all reflections, and all the borrowed luster, give us Thy light for ever. Amen.

The Master of the Temple turns westward, with arms uplifted.

MASTER OF THE TEMPLE: Fratres et sorores, let us offer up our minds in dedication, giving glory and thanks and honor to the Lord and king of Air.

The Master of the Temple turns to the middle east. The Warden and Guide of the paths take up their places behind him, so that the three form a triangle of which the Master is the apex. All present are still facing east. The Master of the Temple traces the symbol of Air in front of him, using the head of his wand.

MASTER OF THE TEMPLE: Let there be lights in the firmament of heaven to enlighten the earth of our humanity. Thou have given us, O Master, the borrowed light of mind, to rule in the night of our mortality. Give unto us Thy sun of justice, and it shall be day therein. Show unto us Thy knowledge in the night; shine upon us more and more until it be perfect day.

He takes up the mystical rose that is placed on the altar before the tablet of the east, and describes with it the sign of the man.

MASTER OF THE TEMPLE: In the names EL CHAI and SHADDAI, the living God almighty, Lord of the heavenly spaces, adore your Creator. Minds of the brotherhood, adore Him. Word of the mind, confess Him. Receive the word of the Holy One. Breath of the spirit of life, enter and abide within us, that we may live in Thee. In the sign of the holy living creature, the mystic head of man, adore, adore, adore.

He makes the sign of the cross with the mystic rose.

Master of the Temple: From the places of reflections and of images, from the realm of flux, from the world of created light, seek in aspiration and in purity the fixed and constant refuge. In the name of RAPHAEL, the great angel of Air, invoked for the consecration of this all wandering element; by that which it signifies within us, in whom are all the keys, by that which we have cleansed and dedicated, ye living minds of men, adore your Creator.

He replaces the mystical rose, and again uplifts his wand.

Master of the Temple: By the power of the sacred names, names from everlasting to everlasting, names of the eastern quarter, set about the height and the deep for the protection of the mind of man, spirit of the inmost mind, height and deep of thought, adore your Creator. By the word of the living God, adore, adore, adore.

The celebrants return with the sun to their places. All members face as usual.

Master of the Temple: Fratres et sorores, we have come out from the magia of illusory things, in thought seeking the realization that is within. May the symbols and sacraments of all that testifies without lead us from the world of images into union with the mind of God. Honorable Frater Theoreticus, Guide of the Paths and Grades, from your place in the world of formation I direct you to announce that the temple is open in the 2 = 9 Grade.

The Guide of the Paths turns westward, with uplifted wand.

Guide of the Paths: Praise unto Thee, EL CHAI and SHADDAI, Lord of life and thought. In Thy most holy name I declare that this temple of the Rosy Cross is open in the grade Theoreticus for the dispatch of God's work in this world.

Guide of the Paths: (*Knocks Twice*)

Warden of the Temple: (*Knocks Twice*)

Master of the Temple: (*Knocks Twice*)

The celebrants and members are seated.

Here ends the solemn ceremony of opening the temple in the grade of Theoreticus.

FIRST POINT

The ceremonial admission of a Zelator in the path of Tau.

The postulant is alone in the vestibule on a prie-dieu, in full light, with a scroll in his hands containing versicles proper to the grade.

MASTER OF THE TEMPLE: Fratres et sorores, may the union of dedicated minds be overshadowed by the mind of God, and directed to the service of our brethren in the offices of this holy rite. By the power to me committed for the authorized communication of mysteries, I declare that the lineal path of Tau, the 32nd Path, leading from the deeps to the height, is open to those who are prepared for the sacrament of this grade of our Fellowship, and other manner of ascent has not been revealed to us in the world of symbolism. It is also our high duty to give of that which we receive, and I hold a warrant from the Most Honored Imperator of the order for the advancement of our Zealous Frater Adveniat Regnum (*vel nomen aliud*), who has dwelt as a Zelator amongst us. Honorable Frater Theoreticus, Guide of the Paths and Grades, the postulant stands at the door. Teach him to knock thereat; prepare him that he may enter worthily, and bring him across the threshold.

The Guide of the Paths rises in his place, takes the bowl of Earth from the altar, passes by south and west to the door of the temple, where he turns eastward and makes obeisance with the sign of the grade. His chair is removed.

GUIDE OF THE PATHS: Between the sacred pillars of the temple, pillars of severity and mercy, pillars of the four worlds, I will keep for ever and ever a free path to the east, and it shall be called the path of benignity.

The Frater Ostiarius opens the door, and the Guide leaves the temple, which is immediately secured behind him.

MASTER OF THE TEMPLE: Fratres et sorores, our Frater Adveniat Regnum (*vel nomen aliud*), having been brought in the grade of Zelator from the court of the tabernacle into the holy place, was left to contemplate therein the embroidered veil, the curtain of palms and pomegranates, before the entrance to the Holy of Holies. He has guarded the fire within; he has maintained the zeal of quest; he desires to pass behind the veil into the mystery of symbolism that is beyond. He does not know that which awaits him, but he has heard of the land of life; he is moving on the path of attainment and return to the central place of experience. By the force of perseverance, by the grace of patience, he has earned a title to advancement. He stands now on the threshold of the path of Tau, leading from the world of action, which is that of manifested things, to the world of formation in God. Do you therefore, my brethren, unite your intention with mine, that he who comes among us in the darkness of natural mind may attain the inward light, and that he who carries the mystical cross may rise at last to the crown.

Meanwhile, the Guide of the paths has greeted the postulant on the further side of the portal, saying:

GUIDE OF THE PATHS: Glory be to God in the highest, and grace to the mind uplifted towards divine attainment in the Light of the Rosy Cross.

The Guide prepares the Zelator by placing in his hands the bowl of sacramental Earth and the cubical cross about his neck.

GUIDE OF THE PATHS: Purify the mind, O Lord; consecrate the world of images; sanctify the thoughts of man. And remember, on your part, my brother of the Rosy Cross, that it is the pre-occupation with God and His union that hallows the mind of the postulant. The body is the holy place and the mind is the Holy of Holies, when God dwells therein. I say unto you, therefore, O Frater Adveniat Regnum (*vel nomen aliud*), hallowed be thy mind.

While this is being done in the precincts the Frater Ostiarius rises, and following the sun, proceeds to the east of the temple, and sees that altar symbols of the Elements are set as follows: The rose on the eastern side; the lamp on that of the south; and the cup of Water on the north. The place of the bowl of Earth is on the western side.

The Guide of the Paths gives the battery of the grade: (knocks twice).

The Frater Ostiarius turns down the lights and opens the door. As the Guide of the Paths enters with the postulant:

GUIDE OF THE PATHS: Come from the natural to the supernatural light, from the material that is without to the spiritual that is within.

The door is closed behind them. The Guide of the Paths pauses with the Zelator at or near the entrance.

MASTER OF THE TEMPLE: There is a path that no fowl knows and that the vulture's eye has not seen. Teach me Thy way, O Lord, and lead me in a plain path. I will go in the light of Thy commandments, and Thou wilt show me the path of life. I have loved Thy service from the beginning. Thou shalt draw me; Thou shalt bring me to Thy high city and Thy hill.

The Guide of the Paths advances again, very slowly, leading the postulant, who bears the bowl of sacramental Earth.

GUIDE OF THE PATHS *(as they step forward):* Show me Thy way, O Lord; teach me Thy paths. Hold up my goings therein, that my footsteps slip not. I have come from afar in the darkness; send me Thy saving light.

As the Guide of the Paths comes to a pause and stays also the Zelator:

MASTER OF THE TEMPLE: Honorable Frater Theoreticus, Guide of the Paths and Grades, you will lead the Zelator to the west, and place him between the mystical pillars, as at the portal of that path by which he will be led in his progress from the kingdom of holiness in Malkuth to the sanctuary that is in the Holy of Holies, unto the mysteries and graces whereof we have prayed that our hands might bring him in the meet and acceptable time.

The Guide of the Paths leads the Zelator and he is placed in the middle way between the pillars.

MASTER OF THE TEMPLE: Frater Adveniat Regnum (*vel nomen aliud*) you will communicate to the Guide of the Paths the proof of your regular advancement to the grade of Zelator.

The Guide of the Paths takes the bowl of sacramental Earth from the postulant and sets it aside for the moment. He passes round the pillars with the sun and faces the postulant.

GUIDE OF THE PATHS: Give me the sign of benediction with which you were blessed on the part of the whole Fellowship in the grade of Zelator. Give me the step and the grip that you received in the grade of neophyte. Give me the word of a Zelator. Give me the mystical password, and the number drawn therefrom. Give me the title and symbol that you received in the last grade.

These things are done accordingly by the postulant, but he is prompted if need should be. The Guide of the Paths gives back to him the bowl of sacramental Earth, and turns eastward with uplifted wand.

GUIDE OF THE PATHS: Honorable Master of the Temple, I have received from our Frater Pereclinus de Faustis the proofs of his regular advancement to the grade of Zelator.

He returns behind the pillars, following the course of the sun.

MASTER OF THE TEMPLE: They are also a condition of your advancement to the next grade of our mystery. In virtue of the sign of benediction you were brought from the portal of the Rosy Cross, even from the court of this tabernacle into the holy place and the kingdom of manifested light. May the step that you have taken be the first sign of that progress which will bring you to the holy mountain. May the grip foreshadow the union of the divine in the universe with that which is divine in your nature. May the bride and queen of the kingdom lead you by secret paths to the kingdom that is within. May the word ornament given to you in the grade of Zelator mean for you the adornment of your dedicated life and lead you to the goal of the blessed. In virtue of all these saving signs and emblems, I demand whether you are willing to keep the laws of the sanctuary and the silence imposed thereby, even as you took and have maintained the pledges of the kingdom and the rule of the holy place in the previous grades.

THE ZELATOR *(prompted by the Guide of the Paths):* I will dwell in the house of the Lord for henceforth and for ever. I will keep the secrets of the house.

As directed by the Guide of the Paths, the Zelator raises the bowl of sacramental Earth to the full height of his arms, and says after him:

THE ZELATOR: May my earthly part in the manifest world of action be henceforward a clean vehicle wherein the body of redemption can be prepared by the powers of the formation world.

The Guide of the Paths takes the bowl from the Zelator and going behind him raises it over the head of the Zelator.

GUIDE OF THE PATHS: Fratres et sorores, in the Fellowship of the Rosy Cross, I testify that this consecrated earth of humanity is earth of the city of Zion, and that the temple is built thereon.

The Master of the Temple gives a battery of one knock and rises in his place, with uplifted arms.

MASTER OF THE TEMPLE: Transmutamini, transmutamini, de lapidibus mortuis in lapides verso philosophicos.

He resumes his throne. The Guide of the Paths moves with the sun and deposits the bowl of sacramental Earth on the western side of the altar. He returns, bearing the sacramental rose, which he places in the hands of the postulant, and then resumes his station behind the pillars.

MASTER OF THE TEMPLE: Frater Pereclinus de Faustis, come in peace, and in the spirit of brotherhood. Offer up your mind in sacrifice, praying that the Divine Light may be enkindled within you. I hid you therefore kneel down.

THE GUIDE ASSISTS THE POSTULANT: Lift up the rose that you carry, and say in clear voice: By the wisdom and understanding that are above the knowledge of Malkuth; by the aspiration of the mind's eye that is fixed thereon; by the light and bearers of light in the great dome of Heaven, give unto me the Light that I seek.

This is repeated by the postulant, following the Master.

MASTER OF THE TEMPLE: Rise, Zelator of the Rosy Cross, and accepted postulant for advancement to the grade of Theoreticus.

The postulant rises. The Guide of the Paths directs him in a low voice to raise the mystical rose to the full height of his arms and to say after him clearly:

THE ZELATOR: Into Thy hands, O Lord, for the work of the Rosy Cross, I commend my life of mind.

The Guide of the Paths should perform this part of the ceremony so that attention is directed to the postulant rather than his own prompting.

MASTER OF THE TEMPLE: It is written that there shall be no more night. May all material darkness dissolve; may there be no cloud upon the sanctuary of your mind. The darkness of the temple that is around you is the veiling of the divine glory.

The Guide of the paths moves with the sun round the pillars, and faces the postulant, whom he draws between the pillars.

GUIDE OF THE PATHS: Bring us forth into the light, O Lord. Shine upon the way of prudence, the path that leads to Thee.

He takes his place on the right of the postulant. They are now facing the east.

MASTER OF THE TEMPLE: From the manifest world of Malkuth, from the grades of neophyte and Zelator attributed in our system, three paths lead to the degrees that are beyond. They are the 31st, 32nd and 30th paths, and their banners are inscribed with the corresponding letters of the Hebrew alphabet, as displayed before you in the east. The Guide of the Paths shall lead you, seeking the goal of quest, that you may pass in your journey of the mind from natural to supernatural light, from the material that is without to the spiritual that is within.

The Guide of the Paths moves forward slowly in the north of the temple, leading the postulant.

GUIDE OF THE PATHS (*speaking on behalf of the Postulant*): Guide us, O Lord, and guard us in all our ways. Behold, I am purified in the body and confess the dedication therein. All that is within me desires to dwell in the presence of the lords of truth. Let us enter the path of severity, because Zion shall be redeemed with judgment.

When they have reached the middle north, they are brought to a pause by the Warden of the Temple rising from his throne with outstretched wand, holding the vessel of Water in his left hand.

WARDEN OF THE TEMPLE: There is peace upon the heights in the presence of the holy desires, and the still fountains shine. There is peace upon the deeps of the waters, and the waters reflect the heights. Who are ye that move in the twilight, with faces born of the twilight, and foreign to this holy ground?

GUIDE OF THE PATHS: We come from between the mystical pillars, seekers for a way to the heights and the path of life, in the name of the living God almighty.

WARDEN OF THE TEMPLE: I am desire and emotion, manifesting in the soul of man. The desires of my soul are purified; the desires of the soul are indrawn; this is the way of peace. I am on the seat of judgment, trying and sifting the elect, but not beyond their strength. You have called upon the name of the Lord; return in that name of majesty. Not here is your path to the heights.

He makes the sign of the eagle with his cup. The Guide leads back the Zelator by the same way, that is, against the sun, and sets him between the pillars.

GUIDE OF THE PATHS: Watch us going forth and returning; watch us, O Lord, for ever. Let us enter the path of mercy.

The Guide of the Paths moves forward slowly, leading the postulant through the south of the temple, and therefore against the sun.

GUIDE OF THE PATHS: The light shall disperse the darkness, and in the Holy of Holies the mind shall be uplifted.

When they have reached the middle south, they are brought to a pause by the Master of the Temple rising from his throne with outstretched wand, holding the sacramental Fire in his left hand.

MASTER OF THE TEMPLE: There is no part of me that is not in conformity. I have fulfilled the precepts. I stand at the apex of all the ways that are below, to indicate those that are above. Who are ye that move in the darkness, with faces born of the darkness, and foreign to this holy ground?

GUIDE OF THE PATHS: We come from between the mystical pillars, seekers for a way to the heights and the path of life, in the name of the living God almighty.

MASTER OF THE TEMPLE: I am the will in the covenant of its obedience, united to the Divine will. My rule is on the side of mercy. I am the providence of God in its compassion, over-watching the elect of Israel. It is not in the law and the order to overleap everything and attain perfection at once. Return in the name of the Lord; not here is your path to the heights.

He makes the sign of the lion with his lamp. The Guide leads back the postulant by the same way, and sets him again between the pillars.

GUIDE OF THE PATHS: Lead us to our term, O Lord, that we may come alive into Thy presence.

MASTER OF THE TEMPLE: The way of ascent in this grade is by the path of Tau only, the 32nd path, in the middle place of progression.

WARDEN OF THE TEMPLE: Straight and narrow is the path that leads to the height. May it be unto you a reflection of the mystery of union and the rest of the great Sabbath.

GUIDE OF THE PATHS: Let us enter the path of benignity. I am the mind in consecration, and the mind is the light of the world, as God is the light of the mind.

The Guide of the Paths again moves forward slowly, leading the postulant, but this time through the middle way of the temple to the due east.

GUIDE OF THE PATHS: My seat is on the intellectual throne. I have coordinated the wandering thoughts and the flux of mental images. I rule and govern therein.

MASTER OF THE TEMPLE: When the body is made whole and clean, when it is dedicated and set apart to the service, let us enter into the region of the mind, that this may be also consecrated, that the thoughts that dwell therein may be pure and fixed and holy.

WARDEN OF THE TEMPLE: O Lord of Light, the darkness flees from before Thee. Thou art our lamp, O Lord. The Lord will enlighten my darkness.

GUIDE OF THE PATHS: We traverse the paths of darkness. We draw to the hour of light.

They have reached the western side of the altar, which stands in the due east, between the thrones, having the banner of the path Tau above and behind it. The Guide of the Paths falls back behind the postulant. The three celebrants raise their wands and join them above the head of the postulant.

MASTER OF THE TEMPLE: Amidst the darkness of material things, O Lord of Light, lift up our thoughts unto Thee.

WARDEN OF THE TEMPLE: Bring us forth into the Light, O Lord. Shine upon the way of prudence, the path that leads to Thee.

GUIDE OF THE PATHS: Open thy mind, O brother of the Rosy Cross, and receive the light of the world.

The Frater Ostiarius turns up the lights of the temple.

MASTER OF THE TEMPLE: The darkness is past; the light shines; the cloud has been removed from the sanctuary.

The celebrants part their wands. The Guide of the Paths takes the mystical rose from the postulant, whom he faces, and raising it in his right hand, makes with it the sign of Aquarius.

GUIDE OF THE PATHS: I am the spirit of the path of Tau, which is the furthest extension of the paths that lead outward from within, and the first of those that go back to our source and end. The light shall dawn in the mind.

He lays the rose on the eastern side of the altar. The Master of the Temple lifts up his hands over the head of the postulant.

MASTER OF THE TEMPLE: Enter into the mind and purify; come into the thoughts and consecrate; Holy, Holy Light. Illuminate the thoughts of the mind, that in Thy Light we may see light.

The chair of the Guide has been replaced and the Guide returns thereto. The celebrants resume their seats. The postulant remains standing before the altar.

WARDEN OF THE TEMPLE: The cubical cross on your breast is composed of 22 squares inscribed with the letters of the Hebrew alphabet, to intimate that Divine Word of which the expressed word is an echo and reflection from afar. Behind the logical understanding and the natural mind of man there is realization after another mode. The word transcendence is represented by silence rather than by the uttered voice. It is breathed into all things and is the divine immanence in all. It is in Earth, Air, Fire and Water, corresponding to the parts of our personality, or the four utterances of the sacred word in man. It is the testimony of all that is visible to all that is unseen by the eye of flesh. May the word be realized within you.

The master of the Temple indicates the diagram on the altar.

MASTER OF THE TEMPLE: The lesson in chief of that path of Tau, through which you have passed in your progress from the grade of Malkuth, is shown in the great symbol of the path. Within an oval of 72 circles there is depicted a female figure having the lunar crescent on her head. The four living creatures of Ezekiel's vision, placed outside the oval, are in correspondence with the four letters of the sacred name JEHOVAH, while the circles forming the oval are in correspondence with other divine names communicated in our secret tradition. They signify together the divine powers that stand about the whole creation, the indwelling of that word which is intimated everywhere in nature, but passes into expression nowhere. This is on the macrocosmic side, on which also the female figure represents the perfection of the universe as an expression of divine law and order. The two wands signify active and passive, the positive and negative currents, the fixed and volatile, the inbreathing and outbreathing that alternate continually in nature. Of these the female figure is at once the equilibrium and the synthesis. In another form of symbolism, she is in the act of dancing, to indicate the ecstasy and joy with which the harmonious creation came into manifested being. She is thus archetypal nature and for this reason is shown to the Zelator on his issue from that world of action that is nature in travail. You now see her in all the original perfection with which she was adorned at the beginning as an image in the divine mind. But she is manifested with a veil about her, because nature is a woman, and her mystery is not declared in this grade. The lunar crescent intimates that all her lights are borrowed or reflected, and that their source is in God. The star of the heptagram above her refers to the number of creation. There is also the macropsychic side of the symbol, but its deep unfolding of the life of souls in God belongs to a later stage of your progress. I can say only that she is the law and state of paradise, the divine presence within and without ourselves, represented by the SHEKINAH. There is, however, the personal, or microcosmic side of the symbol, and as such it typifies that state which is delineated by the work of the world of formation in the Fellowship of the Rosy Cross; the remaking of man, male and female, in the perfect terms of the archetype. For us and for our concerns, the female figure is therefore the restorer of worlds, and of you, my brother, in the likeness of the Elohim. For this reason she is shown to you on the threshold of the world of forma-tion, whereat you now stand. She is the guardian of the gate.

The Guide of the Paths comes forward and takes charge of the postulant.

MASTER OF THE TEMPLE: Frater Adveniat Regnum (*vel nomen aliud*), remember the abiding glory between the Cherubim on the mercy seat. Remember the indwelling presence within you. You have traversed the path of Tau. I salute you as son of the path. Follow your Guide, who will lead you outside the temple, and the ceremony of your reception in the grade of Theoreticus will take place on your return.

GUIDE OF THE PATHS: The great symbol of the path is surrounded by a sacramental lamp, rose, vessel of Water, and bowl containing Earth. They typify the four mystical Elements, the four parts of our human personality. They are in correspondence also with the four living creatures and the letters of the divine name. They stand for modes of the utterance of that name in man. These symbols were in use at various points of your passage through the path of Tau. They rest now on the altar, as the parts of your personality will repose, my brother, when they have attained the perfect consecration.

The Guide of the Paths leads the postulant by south and west to the door, without passing through the pillars. The postulant leaves the temple.

This completes the admission of Zelator in the path of Tau.

Second Point

The Ceremonial Admission of a Zelator to the Grade of Theoreticus, 2 = 9

The arrangement of the temple is shown in the official diagram of the second point. The temple is in light.

Master of the Temple: (*Knocks*) To order, Fratres et Sorores. The Lord lift up the light of His countenance upon us; the Lord give us peace in our work.

There is here the pause of a moment.

Master of the Temple: Honorable Frater Theoreticus, like the paths of the Lord, there is mercy in all your ways. I bid you go forth, therefore, carrying the gifts of mercy. Bring back into our holy temple the zealous Frater Adveniat Regnum (*vel nomen aliud*). See that he enters duly, giving the battery of the grade, and that he carries his title of admission.

As the Guide of the Paths rises from his seat, and moves with the sun eastward.

GUIDE OF THE PATHS: God shall send forth His mercy and His truth. I will lead those who are given me. I will bring them by a sure way from the wilderness and the waste place to the court of the tabernacle, from the court into the holy place, even into the Holy of Holies.

He has now reached the door, and, giving the sign of the grade, he leaves the temple. He prepares the Zelator by decorating him with the badge or collar of an Auxiliary Frater Zelator, but not with the other insignia belonging to that office.

N.B. This badge has been worn previously by the Guide of the Paths beneath his own collar, as a jewel about his waist. While so doing:

GUIDE OF THE PATHS: Purified in the earthly body and now consecrated in the mind, O brother of the Rosy Cross, I bid you remember that the spirit of man ascends by a path of love, and that he who traverses the path of Tau enters into the life of benignity.

While this takes place in the precincts:

MASTER OF THE TEMPLE: Our brother came recently among us to the threshold of the path of Tau, carrying a cross of 22 squares, another meaning of which is the operation of sephirotic graces in the heaven of the zodiac. It is macrocosmic under this aspect, but it applies here more especially to the astronomy of the soul. For within us are the height and the deep, the abyss of light and the abyss of darkness. Brethren, let us pray that the Divine that is concealed in the Zelator may be also made manifest within him.

The battery of the Zelator being heard without (knocks twice):

MASTER OF THE TEMPLE: To those who have knocked it shall be opened. Frater Ostiarius, guarding the hither side of the portal, give free way in the west.

The Ostiarius having opened the door, the Guide leads in the Zelator.

GUIDE OF THE PATHS: Open unto us a door of utterance, that we may enter into the house of the Lord, with lips of praise, keeping a clear mind and a heart of thanksgiving.

The Guide of the Paths pauses with the Zelator in the north-west of the temple. The door is secured behind them.

MASTER OF THE TEMPLE: In the name of the living God almighty, be welcomed on your return to the temple. This is the Divine name that is magnified in the life of all. It is that which is ever living, with and within all. May it be magnified in your own spirit my brother, for every spirit that can utter it in the true form shall know the eternal joy in God our savior.

The Guide of the Paths leads the Zelator and places him between the pillars.

MASTER OF THE TEMPLE: The court of the tabernacle, to which you were brought in the grade of neophyte, is the places of the proselytes of the gate, the places of novices, of those who desire to be cleansed, that they may dwell in the holy house. The more external offices of purification are symbolized in this grade. In that of Zelator you entered the house itself and were taught that the body in its purification becomes the holy place. You stand now at the threshold of the Holy of Holies, the place of the ark and the Kerubim that covered the ark, the place of SHEKINAH, manifesting on the mercy seat.

WARDEN OF THE TEMPLE: By what sign have you entered this secret place of the temple, O son of thought?

THE ZELATOR *(as prompted by the Guide):* It is borne on the heart of the Auxiliary Frater Zelator in the grades of the world of action; it is borne on my own heart. It is the sign of SHEKINAH descended and dwelling in the hearts of men.

The Master of the Temple rises in his place with uplifted arms.

MASTER OF THE TEMPLE: O Lord of truth, Who has given us knowledge of the manifested world, grant us to know the hidden world of cause in the mind that is linked therein.

The Master resumes his seat.

GUIDE OF THE PATHS: I have passed through the gates of heaven, O Lord of truth. I have carried up the holy mountain the higher aspirations of the mind.

MASTER OF THE TEMPLE: By the purified mind of the postulant, by his thoughts in the dedication thereof, bring him across the threshold.

The Guide of the Paths comes round with the sun, and draws the Zelator through the pillars.

GUIDE OF THE PATHS: The mind from its base in Malkuth shall rise by aspiration to the throne of God in Kether. The wings of the intellectual faculty shall abide in wisdom and understanding.

MASTER OF THE TEMPLE: You stand now amidst the mystery of the Holy of Holies, or the place of divine presence, manifesting as the glory of SHEKINAH on the mercy seat. It is represented in our temple by the rose resting in the center of the cross on the altar. It has therefore an intimate correspondence with the great symbol belonging to the path of Tau, as it has also with the table of shewbread and the seven branched candlestick in the grade of Zelator. The SHEKINAH is always with us in the mysteries of the Rosy Cross, and the rose is her chief symbol. She is more especially presented to your consideration in this grade because of the Holy of Holies, and the fact that you have entered within those all-sacred precincts should lead you to realize that you are passing through priestly offices in the rites of our Fellowship, from the time of your first purification as a neophyte in the court of the tabernacle, like the ancient priests of Israel in the laver of brass, to the present stage of your advancement, when in virtue of the mind's consecration you have entered that place which the high priest of old could enter but once a year. Herein and hereby, therefore, I give you counsel of the grade, and this is ~ holiness to the Lord.

The Guide leads the postulant to the western side of the altar, and resumes his seat.

The Master of the Temple leaves his throne and passes by south to the western side of the altar, where he stands on the right of the postulant. He indicates with his wand the diagram above the altar.

MASTER OF THE TEMPLE: Look upon this symbol, which represents at once, according to our traditional teaching, the immemorial journey of your spirit, by which it was brought into the manifest world, and also the path of your return. Before you is the Tree of the Sephiroth, having its roots apparently in Malkuth, the world of action, the incorporation of man's spirit in flesh. As such, it is the Tree of Knowledge of good and evil. It is only by righteous judgment between the two qualities that man can ascend whence he came. But there is a certain place or point of the ascent at which the Tree of Knowledge becomes the Tree of Life, which stood in the midst of the garden, and is that mystery of divine life by which Malkuth is united with Binah (these Sephiroth are indicated by the Master with his wand). The path to the Tree of Life is by the way of knowledge, and the union with the supernals in Daath, or divine knowledge, is by the middle path of benignity. In the ritual of the path of Tau, you came out from the Sephira Malkuth by a straight road (which the Master indicates on the diagram). It is called the 32nd path in the secret tradition, and also the executive intelligence, being a reference to the immanent power behind the manifested world. This is the furthest extension of paths leading outward from within, and the first that takes us back to our source. It is in union with its hidden power that the path is traversed by postulants, the veil of the Holy of Holies is raised on the further side, and those who are chosen for the mystery approach and go in. From the path of Tau, wherein you were consecrated mystically, you have been brought, therefore, into the Sephira Yesod, into the region of the purified mind, and this is the Holy of Holies (*The Master indicates Yesod on the diagram*), the heart of the world, the place of the voice, the place of the daughter of the voice, who is SHEKINAH. There are 22 paths by which the Sephiroth are connected one with another, and they are inscribed on this symbol with the letters of the Hebrew alphabet. But the Sephiroth are themselves counted as paths, the number of which is, therefore, 32. That of Yesod corresponds to the 9th Path, and it is called the purified intelligence, an understanding in the heart. May that name of grace sink into your own heart. May you be purified in all your ways, as one who is clothed with fine linen, clean and white, which is the righteousness of saints.

The Master of the Temple returns with the sun to his throne, and standing thereat says, with extended arms and uplifted eyes:

MASTER OF THE TEMPLE: Almighty Lord, and Lord Who livest for ever, we have consecrated our brother by the sacramental offices of this holy temple. We have given unto him a clean mind and a pure body. Do Thou keep him in perfect peace. May his mind be stayed on Thee, remembering Thy covenants.

The Master resumes his seat. The Guide of the Paths comes forward, places the postulant with his back to the north, and assumes a position facing him.

GUIDE OF THE PATHS: Frater Adveniat Regnum (*vel nomen aliud*), the sign of this grade is given by placing both hands thus upon the forehead, with all the fingers interlaced and the palms turned outwards. It refers to the ten Sephiroth of the Tree of Life grafted in the mind of the postulant. The sacred words are SHADDAI and EL CHAI, the living God almighty. The password is MAH, a secret name of the world of formation, formed of the two Hebrew letters Mem and He, the numerical value of which is 45, and this is the mystical number. I invest you with the girdle of a Theoreticus, the color of which is blue, being that assigned to the moon in the symbolism of the Rosy Cross. The moon is referred to this grade because it is an emblem of SHEKINAH, the moon of heaven and earth. In the spiritual mystery of the elements, the grade of Theoreticus is in correspondence with Air, symbolizing the mind in nature, the world of thought in man. It is these that we seek to re-establish according to the law of the Holy of Holies, which is the law of wisdom and understanding, the fountain of life and generation. Yesod is a mystery of generation. The four-square tablet that stands in the middle-east of the temple, containing divine and angelic names referable to the eastern quarter of the heaven, is in correspondence with the element of Air, and is set up as a symbol in our temple for the sanctification of the mind in man.

The tablet is indicated by the Guide, who again turns the postulant to the east, and then goes back to his place.

WARDEN OF THE TEMPLE: The banners before you are symbolical banners of the paths leading from the grade of Theoreticus to the Sephiroth of the further grades. That in the south-east signifies the path of entrance to the grade of Philosophus, and that on the north-east the path to the grade of Practicus. The banner in the due east is that of the path that leads to higher mysteries beyond the world of formation. It is a straight and vertical path, leading to the term of our desire. Keep in your heart, my brother, the memory of the straight way.

MASTER OF THE TEMPLE: The mystical title of Poraios de Rejectis is conferred upon you in this grade. It means that you are saved from rejection. Fear not, therefore, the infernal mansions, the false and treacherous seas or the wastes about the garden of the wise. I now give you this title, and I give you the symbol of RUACH, as a memorial of the Divine breath that imparts the Life of life. Honorable Guide of the Paths, I bid you announce that he who was once a Zelator, in the Fellowship of the Rosy Cross has been advanced to the grade of Theoreticus.

The Guide of the paths comes forward and taking the postulant by the right hand leads him about the altar, where they turn to the west, so that he is in the general sight of the brethren. The Guide uplifts his wand.

GUIDE OF THE PATHS: In the name of the living God almighty, and by the ordinance of the Honorable Master of the Temple, I proclaim and testify that Frater Adveniat Regnum (*vel nomen aliud*) has been admitted by a lawful communication to the grade of Theoreticus, that he is a son of the 32nd path, and that he has received the mystical title of Poraios de Rejectis, with the symbol of Ruach. May he enter into his inheritance in the world of the Life of life.

The Guide turns eastward with the postulant.

MASTER OF THE TEMPLE: Having attained in the symbolism of this grade to the state of purified intelligence, I commend to you the realization of its sanctity in all the thoughts and operations of your mind. Herein is the study in chief that will qualify you for further advancement in the grades of our order. It is in such manner that the true and inward Adam is made in the likeness of the Elohim. So is the sign of the man manifested, and so shall He also be declared Who is the son of man, the hierophant of the mysteries of ADONAI. The archangel Raphael, who is referred to the element of Air, goes before this man, proclaiming to the living and the dead that He is come Who was expected, and we do not look for another. Enter, O Frater Theoreticus, into the sacred places of the mind.

The Guide of the Paths leads the postulant with the sun to his proper place in the temple, which is that of Ostiarius, and he receives from his predecessor the wand of that office. The Guide resumes his seat.

The allocution of the grade follows, and is delivered by the Imperator, but him failing by his substitute, or by the Master of the Temple.

THE ALLOCUTION OF THE GRADE OF THEORETICUS

In the name of that splendid and uncreated light that passes through the worlds that are within, in the name of God who is within, almighty and everliving, I invite you, Fratres et Sorores, Cohaeredes et Sodales, and you in particular who have been received this day among us, I invite you, on behalf of this Fellowship, to hear the inward message and allocution of the 2 = 9 grade. Hereof is a part in symbolism of the long story concerning that holy house which is not entered by earthly feet, for it is in that region of our spiritual being that does not confess to limitations of time and space. We have set before you, O Frater Theoreticus, a shadow in ritual of your further interior progress, that having carried the signs and warrants of your manifestation here on earth, you may being to realize your life as a process of formation in God. Be therefore the aspiration of your mind, henceforth and forever. Open ye gates, and open ye everlasting portals, and let the King of glory enter, even into our penetralia.

The making of the second Adam in the image and likeness of the Elohim continues in this grade. It is one of the successive consecrations performed in the Fellowship of the Rosy Cross, so that all parts of the personality may be transmuted and become a quintessence, even that great quintessence, the condition of which is the summum bonum. It is in particular the hallowing, the dedication of the postulant's natural mind, and we pray, as a result of his experience, that his inward faculties of thought may be brought into the harmonies of dedicated life, into the fixed intent of unity. May you therefore, O Frater Theoreticus, so occupy the period that will intervene between your advancement on this day and the next stage of your progress that the things that you have learned in ceremony may pass into the grade of life. So shall the moon of your natural mind be a mirror in its fullness of the sun of beauty, its reflection and its glass of vision. The sun is like thought in its intentness, when thought is fixed upon our last end and upon things Divine. The moon is like thought in its inconstancy, a reflected light and a wandering fire. The sun is like that life of higher consciousness which dwells behind the logical understanding. The moon is like natural reason, which again is a reflected light. Practice the fixation of this grade, that you may see through your glass, brightly.

Remember the deep intimations of that cubical cross which you bore in the course of your progress through the path of Tau. Remember the symbolism of those letters out of which are formed in their expression the words of all wisdom, human and Divine. But remember more than all that secret word which is expressed only in the heart ~ of which all letters are the shadow ~ because it is declared in silence rather than in speech. Yet is it instilled everywhere and abides in all, the executive intelligence of the 32nd path, the immanence of Divine power in the essence of created things, the grace behind the manifest. From things of the body of man into things within and beyond; into realms of hidden force, into their mysteries and graces, you have entered symbolically in the Sephira Yesod. So from the light that is within nature do we pass to the light that is beyond; but the light without testifies to the light within, as nature beats witness to grace.

The grade of Theoreticus is the grade of the Holy of Holies, and in its true understanding this is a hidden world. You have made acquaintance therein with the mystery of the Tree of Life, which is the immemorial story of the soul, and a prophecy of its future destiny. The Tree of Life is also the Tree of Knowledge at the beginning of the return journey, because man must ascend in virtue of those principles by which his descent was brought about. In this sense, the evil itself must assist him towards the height. He goes back whence he came in proportion as he escapes from its toils; it is, therefore, his great opportunity. No one knows the evil in its true nature until he has embraced the good, and he is then as the cross that it carries. You are assumed in this grade to have made that choice beyond which lies the way of the true knowledge and the point of union between the Tree of Knowledge and the Tree of Life.

Stand, therefore, frater, seeking the one thing needful, so that your higher part may rest upon Daath, as upon the threshold of a supernal world, the wings of aspiration and desire, upon Chesed and Geburah. From these stages of attainment we shall rule the inconstant thoughts within us, interpreting the witness of the mind, the testimony of the senses, and all the forces about us that minister to these, distinguishing the things of illusion, their marvels and enchantments, from the grace of the great reality, and the truth that comes down with power. Stand with your gates open to receive that truth and grace in their plenary descent.

Let us pray that at some far time of our searchings that which is immortal in us, and did once proceed from Him, may be delivered from the age long spaces and be withdrawn in God to the repose and activity of the center ~ even from the created light into that which is eternal. And seeing that the name of the Lord is set in all things and is the seal of all things, let us so order the many forces of our nature that the name may be declared in us, and that we, in our own degree and from the height of intellectual thought, may be even as a light of the world, as an orient from on high visiting it.

If the minutes of any previous meeting or other official business are to be taken in the grade of Theoreticus, the temple must be reduced at this point to the grade of Neophyte. By the power of his wand, the Master should close in the higher grade, open in the lower by fiat, and after the business has been discharged should close similarly therein and re-open in the grade of Theoreticus.

THE SOLEMN OFFICE OF CLOSING THE SACRED TEMPLE IN THE GRADE OF THEORETICUS

MASTER OF THE TEMPLE: (*Knocks*)

All rise.

MASTER OF THE TEMPLE: To order, Fratres et Sorores Theoretici, incorporated for the work of illumination, the fundamental work, and the work of sanctity, in the Fellowship of the Rosy Cross. Let us realize in our minds and hearts that we have striven to attain the term, within the measures to us allotted in this grade of mind.

There is here the pause of a moment.

MASTER OF THE TEMPLE: The mysteries of the temple are guarded in the heart of the temple, and the holy grades lie behind one another, circle within circle, leading to the central point. Frater Ostiarius, in the name of the palace at the center, I command you to see that the temple is guarded without.

The Frater Ostiarius opens the portal pro forma, inspects the immediate precincts, again secures the threshold, and turns to the east with uplifted wand.

Frater Ostiarius: Honorable Master of the Temple, the Lord keeps the mystic city, and the watchman wakes not in vain.

Master of the Temple: Do we therefore, both now and henceforward, maintain the inward vigil, cherishing the Divine messages that come to us in this holy place, expecting on the mountains that encompass it, O Fratres et Sorores, beautiful feet upon the mountains, bringing all high tidings near.

This is said with raised eyes and uplifted wand. There follows the pause of a moment.

Master of the Temple: Honorable Frater Theoreticus, assure yourself that all present have heard with their own ears that which was told by our fathers, the men of vision, and that which you and I have testified continually to one another concerning the hallowed grade of Theoreticus.

The Guide of the Paths, standing in his place, lifts up his wand of office.

Guide of the Paths: Fratres et Sorores, consecrated in body and mind, give me the outward sign of those who are saved from rejection.

He turns in succession to the four quarters and receives the sign of the grade from all present, the Master of the Temple excepted. The Guide turns to the Master, giving it on his own part.

Guide of the Paths: Honorable Master of the Temple, the Divine protection stands about the mind of the Fellowship, keeping it for salutary and holy service, and saving it from the void of unreason.

The sign is repeated by the Master.

Master of the Temple: Let us offer up our minds in worship to the Lord of understanding (*knocks*).

The Master of the Temple descends from his throne, and faces the east thereat. The Warden also descends. All members face east. The Master uplifts his wand.

THEORETICUS INITIATION

MASTER OF THE TEMPLE: Life of life and Light of light, living God almighty, like burning coals upon the altar of the heart is heaped our love for Thee. Grant us the desirable end ~ to fall into Thy holy hands, wherein we commend our spirits. Amen.

The Master and Warden turn again to the west. The Guide uplifts his wand, still facing the east, with the unofficial members generally.

GUIDE OF THE PATHS: Let us raise our wandering thoughts, and fix them upon the Lord of all (*knocks*). Seal us, O Master, with the simplicity that seals nature. Give unto us recollection; give us aspiration and desire; give unto us the knowledge of that secret way, through which we shall pass behind the things of material reason into the living sun of Thy truth. All roads are straight, and every way is fair that leads to our end in Thee.

Then, with raised eyes and uplifted arms:
MASTER OF THE TEMPLE: Depart in the peace of the eternal; depart in the eternal name, O brethren of the Rosy Cross. Ye who have been called to the work are licensed to depart therefrom. May the spirit of the Lord, who rules the realm of the mind, and the grace of the spirit be upon you. Rest, but remember His service, and be ready at the call thereto.

The Master and Warden of the temple resume their thrones, but remain standing thereat.

WARDEN OF THE TEMPLE: Peace in the palaces of mind, peace in the halls of thought; rest unto all who wander; satisfaction to those who yearn; attainment to those who seek. O be there peace in your places, brethren; peace in the world that does not belong to the world; and may you return in purity when called to our holy convention.

MASTER OF THE TEMPLE: Honorable Guide of the Paths, the purified mind beholds the theory of the work in transmutation of the self and its environment. The end of this rite is upon us, and having attained our term therein, I direct you to close the temple in the grade of Theoreticus.

GUIDE OF THE PATHS: Fratres et Sorores, as guardian of the mysteries of Yesod, with the generations of mind therein, and in the name of the living God almighty, I close this holy temple in the grade of Theoreticus.

GUIDE OF THE PATHS: (*Knocks Twice*)

WARDEN OF THE TEMPLE: (*Knocks Twice*)

MASTER OF THE TEMPLE: (*Knocks Twice*)

HERE ENDS THE RITUAL OF THE GRADE OF THEORETICUS.

The Second Order of the Rosy Cross

World of Formation

Part II

The Ceremony of Advancement

in the

Grade of Practicus

3 = 8

Privately Printed

1916

The Fellowship of the Rosy Cross

—

Grade of Practicus
3 = 8

—

THE SOLEMN CEREMONY OF OPENING THE
TEMPLE IN THE GRADE OF PRACTICUS

—

The arrangement of the temple is shown in the official diagram of the first point.

The celebrants or officers of this grade are the Master of the Temple, the Worden and the Guide of the Paths, in addition to the Ostiarius, being the last candidate who has attained advancement therein.

If the Temple should not have been opened previously in one of the lower grades, the ceremonial vesting of officers and members, the invocation or prayer at the east, and the assoilment of the temple are performed as exhibited therein. The Master of the Temple assumes his throne, holding the wand of his office. The other celebrants repair to their stations, and the ordinary brethren are ranged north and south, according to the precedence of their grades. All members are seated, and a short pause of inward recollection follows.

MASTER OF THE TEMPLE: (*Knocks*)

All rise.

98

PRACTICUS INITIATION

MASTER OF THE TEMPLE: Fratres et Sorores, united in the Mystical Fellowship of the Rosy Cross, I bid you remember the end, being mindful also of the paths that lead thereto. And because of our zeal concerning them, assist me ~ I pray you ~ to open this holy temple in the grade of Practicus, for the further progress of the work and the contemplation of its joyful mysteries. Frater Ostiarius, in recollection and great reverence, I direct you to see that the desire of the world is outside these holy gates.

The Frater Ostiarius opens the portal pro forma, inspects the immediate precincts, again secures the threshold and turns to the east with uplifted wand.

FRATER OSTIARIUS: It is written, O Lord of the east, that flesh and blood cannot inherit the kingdom of God. I testify that they have no place herein; they cry at the gates in vain. The temple of light is guarded.

MASTER OF THE TEMPLE: Let them not enter, my brethren. There is a sacred Fire in the heart, and so is the temple guarded. It is reserved for the Lord of hosts, who is the desire of all generations. Honorable Frater Practicus, prove in the perfection of their work the brethren here assembled. See that they are practiced in God's presence, in the work of dedication and in the peace of the heart in its stillness.

The Warden of the Temple, standing in his place, lifts up his wand of office.

WARDEN OF THE TEMPLE: Have you sought Him in the heart, my brethren? Give me the outward sign of the inward grace. I demand the sign of a Practicus.

He receives it from all present, the Master of the Temple excepted. The Warden turns to the Master, giving it on his own part.

WARDEN OF THE TEMPLE: Honorable Master of the Temple, the desire of the holy height has sealed the hearts of the Fellowship.

The Master of the Temple has turned to the Warden, repeating the mystical sign; and then facing west:

MASTER OF THE TEMPLE: I testify at the east of the temple that God is known of the heart. Hide us in the secret of Thy presence, in the house of Thy dedication. Fratres et Sorores, the Lord send you help in His sanctuary, and be the beauty of His countenance herein.

This is said with raised eyes and uplifted wand. The pause of a moment follows.

MASTER OF THE TEMPLE: May the grace of our symbols be with us. May the sense of their plenary attributions be awakened in power within us. May their presence be declared in our consciousness and renewed in the soul of the Order.

WARDEN OF THE TEMPLE: The grade of Practicus is in correspondence by symbolical attribution with the macrocosmic element of Water, typifying the emotions and desires in the microcosmic world of man. We cast out the evil that is within them, remembering, O Lord my God, Thy desirable ways and the land to which we return.

GUIDE OF THE PATHS: The planet Mercury is a symbol in the celestial heavens of that which is desired by the wise. I testify to the mystery herein. There is a star of peace and truth that rises over the stillness of emotion and shines upon its crystal sea. There is a desire that is below, and a desire also that is above, in a holy heaven.

MASTER OF THE TEMPLE: In man is found the corner stone of all life. It is by man that we may experience Mercury as both a symbol of the physical nature and of the emotional nature. It is within this grade of Practicus that the postulant shall manifest changes within his spiritual realm.

WARDEN OF THE TEMPLE: Honored Guide of the Paths, do you testify that by the physical nature of Mercury that man can change and develop his placement upon the throne of stars?

GUIDE OF THE PATHS: It is not by the physical nature, Honored Warden of the Temple, that the postulant will brace his development upon the throne. His development comes from within the womb of the stars.

The Warden of the Temple, facing north with uplifted wand.

WARDEN OF THE TEMPLE: It is the balancement of both the interior and exterior that man may experience that of which is above, and below. By Adam, man may experience both.

MASTER OF THE TEMPLE: Within this light, we can balance good and evil.

He proceeds to the north, bearing his wand, and encompasses the altar, following the sun. He takes the vessel of Water from the altar and holds it in his left hand. The Warden of the Temple descends from his throne and goes northward. In the middle region of the temple he is joined by the Guide of the Paths. Both follow the Master, who says in the course of his progress:

MASTER OF THE TEMPLE: We are the vessels of Thy desire. The desire after Thee and Thy justice is the Tree of Life. Make us lovers of good things in Thy presence. Still the hunger that Thou has kindled; satisfy the thirst for Thee.

The Master of the Temple halts in the middle north, facing the tablet of the north. The Warden takes up his place at a certain distance on the right, in the same line. The Guide of the Paths occupies a point behind them, so that the three form a triangle, with its apex downward. All present are now facing north.

Having placed his wand in charge of the Warden, the Master traces the symbol of Water with his aspergillus in the air before him.

MASTER OF THE TEMPLE: Let there be a firmament in the midst of the waters, and let it divide the waters from the waters, the lights of the world above from the light of understanding in man. Let the desire after things unseen raise him from the desires of earth; that he may have dominion over the lower attractions and over material emotions, as over the fish of the sea; that he may rule over the waters within him, as over seas of the greater world. In the Name of Elohim, which is the sacred name in manifestation, in the name of ELOHIM TZABAOTH, the Lord of hosts, Lord of the great waters, Lord and King of life. By the graces and powers that are above, powers and graces that are below, let the heart of our natural manhood, and the desires of our human life, adore the Lord and God.

He describes the sign of the eagle with the aspergillus.

MASTER OF THE TEMPLE: Waters that are below the firmament, Waters that are above; the waters that are below desire after the Waters that are above. Thoughts and emotions that are beneath and the still thought of the Holy One, who is inaccessible to the heart of man, except in the mystery of union. May the peace of that union be upon us; be we dissolved therein. In the name of Gabriel, the great archangel of Water, bearer of Water from heaven, by which evil is expelled from the habitation of the heart of man, and in the mystical sign of the eagle, ye living hearts of men, adore your Lord and God.

Then making the sign of the cosmic cross with the aspergillus.

MASTER OF THE TEMPLE: Bind about the part of our emotions, O Lord, the seals of Thy divine names. Send down Thy messengers to receive and carry our prayers upwards. O powers of the heart within us, soul of desire within. By the power of the sacred names, names that are emblazoned forever in the northern quarter of the heaven, set about the height and the deep for the protection of our human life, ye living hearts of men, adore your Lord and God.

He lifts up the aspergillus on high.

MASTER OF THE TEMPLE: By the Waters of understanding, by the sea of glass, clear as crystal, by the river and fountain of life, ye living hearts of men, adore your Lord and God.

He receives his wand from the Warden, and the celebrants return to their places, following the sun. The Master, in passing, deposits the vessel of Water on the altar. All members face as usual.

MASTER OF THE TEMPLE: The powers and the graces that are shown forth in the world without are shadows of those that are within. The sprit of God moved upon the face of the Waters, and the spirit of the most high God shall move upon the Waters of the soul. He shall say unto them: Peace, be still ~ and there shall follow a great calm. We shall know His voice in the stillness, passing over our great Waters, stilling the heart in Him. Honored Frater Practicus, Warden of this House of God, I direct you to announce that the secret sanctuary is open in the 3 = 8 Grade.

The Warden lifts up his wand.

WARDEN OF THE TEMPLE: ELOHIM TZABAOTH, Lord of the great armies, Lord of the hosts within, in Thy most holy name, Thy great and glorious name, I open this temple of the Rosy Cross in the grade of Practicus, which is a grade of our desire for Thee.

WARDEN OF THE TEMPLE: (*Knocks Three Times*)

MASTER OF THE TEMPLE: (*Knocks Three Times Rapidly*)

GUIDE OF THE PATHS: (*Knocks Three Times at Intervals*)

The celebrants and members are seated.

Here ends the solemn ceremony of opening the temple in the grade of Practicus.

FIRST POINT
THE CEREMONIAL ADMISSION OF A
FRATER THEORETICUS IN THE PATH OF RESH

The postulant is alone in the vestibule on a prie-dieu in full light, with a scroll in his hands containing versicles proper to the grade.

MASTER OF THE TEMPLE: Fratres et Sorores, the Lord give us a perfect heart, a heart of understanding, a new heart and a new spirit, whereon He may look with compassion when we prepare our ways to His service. By the power to me committed as a guardian of the veil and an expositor of mysteries to the souls of those who are chosen under the obedience of the Rosy Cross, I declare that I hold a dispensation for the advancement of Frater Adveniat Regnum (*vel nomen aliud*) in the way of the secret Light. By virtue of the same power, and for the same high purpose, I open the path of Resh, leading from the Sephiroth that are below to the glory that is revealed in HOD. Consecrated in body and mind by the sacraments of the preceding grades, the postulant shall receive at our hands a new quality of virtue in another world of whiteness. May that which we impart in symbolism be received in the vital essence as a reality to the man within. Honorable

Frater Theoreticus, Guide of the Paths and Grades, let the high office of your mercy be continued in respect of our beloved brother, that the blessing that we have set about him in the way of his mystical progress may not fail of their fruit in his nature. Seek him in the place of vigil; tell him that you have explored the vistas and have found another path to the height.

The Guide rises in his place.

GUIDE OF THE PATHS: Visit me in Thy grace, O Lord, because of the mission that Thou has given me, in the paths that lead to Thee. I will bring Thee a true account of my stewardship when I have finished my work. I will cast myself freely into the abyss if I may draw Thy children out of it. I have sworn that I will save all souls that come into my hands. I will marry the east and the west, the north, and the south. I will bring the four Elements from the four quarters into the place of the quintessence at the center. I will mediate in all the Sephiroth and prepare in all the paths that lead to the Divine.

Taking with him the sacramental rose from its place on the altar, the Guide of the Paths passes by south and west to the door of the temple and there gives the sign of the grade. The door is secured behind him.

MASTER OF THE TEMPLE: Fratres et Sorores, our frater Adveniat Regnum (*vel nomen aliud*) has traversed the path of Tau and has entered with uplifted mind into the Holy of Holies. He has received therein the high intimations of the sanctuary concerning the covenant between God and man, the scheme of our reintegration in God. He has heard also the rumors of a secret doctrine that lies between the mysteries of the expounded law. Where do we consecrate, my brothers, the heart of the postulant, the emotions and desires of nature, that he who came among us to receive good service at our hands may be innocent henceforth in his own and may go up the mountain of god? It is here in the Sephira Hod; it is here in the Light of glory, which was said to be good by the Elohim and is reserved to the sons of desire. In the passage of the 32nd path the restored state of humanity was shown to our postulant in a symbol, and in the passage of the path of Resh he shall learn that we go back whence we came by the purging of the fire within us.

In the meantime the Guide of the Paths has greeted the postulant on the further side of the portal, saying:

GUIDE OF THE PATHS: I come in the purification of desire. Glory be to God in the highest and peace in the heart uplifted to divine attainment by the Light of the Rosy Cross.

The Guide of the Paths prepares the postulant by placing in his hands the sacramental rose and about his neck the cross of 13 squares.

GUIDE OF THE PATHS: Purify the heart, O Lord; transmute the natural emotions; sanctify the desires of man. And remember on your part, my brother of the Rosy Cross, that it is the hunger after God and His union that ordains the heart of the postulant. I say unto you therefore, Frater Adveniat Regnum (*vel nomen aliud*), seek after light and consecration, and hallowed be thy heart.

The Guide of the paths gives a battery of the grade (Knocks three times).

When this has been done in the precincts, the Frater Ostiarius turns down the lights and opens the door. In the act of opening:

WARDEN OF THE TEMPLE: Open in the grace and the power of God. Open in the name of God, in the name of the Lord of hosts, and remember the great rest.

The Guide of the Paths brings in the postulant saying:

GUIDE OF THE PATHS: He has put a new song into my mouth. I will praise the name of God, in a song before the throne of Him. He has prepared His throne in the heavens, and the same is upheld by mercy.

The door is secured behind them. The Guide of the Paths pauses with the postulant at or near the entrance.

MASTER OF THE TEMPLE: Thou has led me in the path of the elect; Thou has brought me by a straight road to a sure place. I have given Thee my heart for ever. I have ascended; I have seen the heights. So do we arise out of the evil, leaving it in our purgations behind us and for ever going up to Thee.

The Guide of the Paths leads the postulant and places him between the pillars. As they are moving slowly forward:

GUIDE OF THE PATHS: I have finished my quest; I have found the perfect way. Be assured of my guidance in the darkness, for I know that there is light beyond.

As they stand between the pillars, the Guide being a few inches behind the postulant:

MASTER OF THE TEMPLE: Hail unto the guide of the perplexed, on the threshold of the height of Zion, glorious in the leading of the soul. And do you, O Honorable Warden, receive from our brother in the spirit those external titles and warrants that were communicated to him in the previous grade of our mystery.

The Warden descends from his throne and proceeds with the sun to the west, where he pauses, facing the postulant between the pillars. The Guide of the Paths has taken the sacramental rose from the hands of the postulant.

WARDEN OF THE TEMPLE: Frater Adveniat Regnum (*vel nomen aliud*), as a Frater Theoreticus, where do you plant the Tree of Life in giving the sign of the grade?

FRATER THEORETICUS *(who is prompted by the Guide):* In the purified world of mind.

The Guide directs him to give the sign of the 2 = 9 grade.

WARDEN OF THE TEMPLE: Unto whom was your homage in the mind when you stood in the Holy of Holies, in the place of purified intelligence?

FRATER THEORETICUS *(who is prompted by the Guide):* I called upon the name of eternal life, upon Him Who is the Life of life, the living God almighty.

WARDEN OF THE TEMPLE: What is the mystical number and the word from which it is formed?

FRATER THEORETICUS *(who is prompted):* It is the word of the world of formation, wherein is the power of the Elohim to remake man in their image, as a reflection below of the grace and glory above. The word is MAH, the number is 45, and this is reduced to its mystical root by the pentad, the issue of which is 9, being the number of the grade itself, and 2 is its equivalent in our system, signifying the two consecrations through which I have passed in the body and mind.

The rose is returned to the postulant. The Warden passed with the sun to his throne and there faces the Master.

WARDEN OF THE TEMPLE: Honorable Master of the Temple, I have received from our frater Theoreticus the proofs of his regular advancement to the 2 = 9 grade.

The Warden resumes his seat, and the Master addresses the postulant.

MASTER OF THE TEMPLE: May their graces abide in your heart and be increased within you. May you grow in the likeness of the Elohim. May your world be reformed in God.

WARDEN OF THE TEMPLE: Frater Adveniat Regnum (*vel nomen aliud*), testify concerning yourself. Beyond the Holy of Holies there is another sanctuary, which you are about to enter by the path that leads thereto. Will you keep the secrets of that sanctuary and the mystery of the ways within? Will you enter with clean thoughts and an ordered mind, offering the heart in sacrifice and praying that the Divine Light may be increased within you?

THE FRATER THEORETICUS (*prompted by the Guide of the Paths*): I testify concerning myself. I will keep the pledges of the path and the house of God.

As directed by the Guide of the Paths, the Frater Theoreticus raises the sacramental rose in his right hand and says after him:

FRATER THEORETICUS: May the powers of the mind bear witness, the thoughts of the mind bear witness, and the images that are types of truth in the world of human understanding.

The Guide of the Paths takes the sacramental rose and holding it in his right hand raises it over the head of the postulant.

GUIDE OF THE PATHS: Fratres et Sorores in the Fellowship of the Rosy Cross, I testify that the purified mind of humanity is mind of the city of God, and that the consensus of all its holy ones is the sense of the Holy Spirit.

The Master of the Temple gives a battery of one knock and rises in his place, with uplifted arms.

MASTER OF THE TEMPLE: Remember the glorious end, O Frater Adveniat Regnum (*vel nomen aliud*). Remember the way of its attainment. The end itself shall draw you, lest you enter the desert or fall unawares into the abyss. You are the natural mind, conceiving by dedication the presence of the Divine within it.

He resumes his throne. The Guide of the Paths moves with the sun, deposits the sacramental rose on the eastern side of the altar and returns with the vessel of Water, which he places in the hands of the postulant and then resumes his station behind the pillars.

MASTER OF THE TEMPLE: Frater Adveniat Regnum (*vel nomen aliud*), I now bid you kneel down (*the Guide assists the postulant*); place both hands in the vessel of sacramental Water (*the Guide holds the vessel for this purpose*); and say in a clear voice: I will consecrate the Waters of desire. I seek the fount of living Waters. Purge me with Water and with Fire. Bring me forth, O Lord, unto the light, for my life and my salvation art Thou.

This is repeated by the postulant, following the Master. The vessel is removed by the Guide, who hands a white napkin to the postulant for the drying of his hands.

MASTER OF THE TEMPLE: Rise, Frater Theoreticus, an accepted postulant for advancement to the grade of Practicus.

The postulant rises. The Guide of the Paths replaces in his hands the vessel of sacramental Water, directing him in a low voice to raise it to the full height of his arms and says after him clearly:

THE FRATER THEORETICUS (*following the Guide*)**:** Into thy hands, O soul of mine, for the work of the Rosy Cross, I commend my heart of life.

He lowers the vessel. The Guide of the Paths should perform this part of the ceremony so that attention is directed to the postulant rather than to his own prompting.

MASTER OF THE TEMPLE: May the glory of understanding in the great sea of BINAH be reflected in the Waters of your soul.

The Guide of the Paths moves round with the sun and faces the postulant, whom he draws between the pillars.

GUIDE OF THE PATHS: Lead us in Thy Light, O Master; lead us in the dark ways. The darkness and the light are both alike to Thee.

He takes his place on the right hand of the postulant. They are now facing the east.

MASTER OF THE TEMPLE: From the Sephira Yesod and the grade of Theoreticus attributed in our system, three paths lead to theSsephiroth that are beyond. They are the 28th, 26th, and 29th paths, and their banners ‑ inscribed with letters of the Hebrew alphabet thereunto attributed ‑ are displayed before you in the east. The Guide of the Paths shall lead you, seeking a goal of quest, looking towards the path of your return, as the soul in its darkness looks to Thy city, O Lord, the city of an eternal sun.

The Guide of the Paths moves forward slowly, leading the postulant through the middle way of the temple towards the due east.

GUIDE OF THE PATHS: Let us enter by the path of benignity, O brother of the Rosy Cross. It is the way, as you have been told, to the heights.

MASTER OF THE TEMPLE: A glory of ineffable radiance comes down from a region of life, from the land of the living.

WARDEN OF THE TEMPLE: The turbid waters of the soul are troubled in its quest for the Divine. The rapid and flowing waters of the soul, clear as crystal, set towards the great sea. The stilled waters of the soul receive the Spirit of God moving upon the face of its waters.

As the Guide of the Paths and the postulant are brought to a pause at the western side of the altar, the Master and Warden descend suddenly from their thrones and come to the east of the altar, barring further progress.

WARDEN OF THE TEMPLE: The middle path opens upon higher mysteries that are beyond the Second Order of the Rosy Cross.

MASTER OF THE TEMPLE: Keep in your heart the memory of the straight way. Look to that time, and desire it, when you shall enter by the path of Ayin; but the time is not yet.

The Master and Warden return, as they come, to their thrones. The Guide also leads back the postulant by their way of advance ~ that is, against the sun ~ and sets him again between the pillars.

GUIDE OF THE PATHS: There rose a fire in the south and a great wind that fanned it. Thou has burnt up all my houses, and henceforth I have no refuge but in Thee.

The Guide of the Paths moves forward slowly, leading the postulant through the south of the temple and therefore against the sun. When they have reached the middle south, they are brought to a pause by the Master of the Temple rising from his throne, with outstretched wand.

MASTER OF THE TEMPLE: The counsel of God is a pure fountain of life. He has given us the law of life and the knowledge of His Light therein. Return on the path that you have traveled, in the name of that sacred law. Not here is your ascent to the heights.

The Master of the Temple is again seated on his throne. The Guide leads back the postulant by the same way and sets him again between the pillars.

GUIDE OF THE PATHS: I say unto you that I will finish my quest. I will satisfy the longing of the soul in the deep ocean of God.

WARDEN OF THE TEMPLE: The way of ascent in this grade is by the path of Qoph only. Let the postulant pass though the pillars and thus issue from Yesod on the way of his progress upward.

GUIDE OF THE PATHS: I say unto you that the quest draws to its term, and that the glorious light rises.

The Guide of the Paths again moves forward slowly in the north of the temple, leading the postulant with the sun.

WARDEN OF THE TEMPLE: His law is a fountain of Water. His doctrine is a river of life. He has refreshed us from wells of salvation.

MASTER OF THE TEMPLE: A pool of living waters in Lebanon, and the pool is deep.

GUIDE OF THE PATHS: He has filled the Waters of the soul with sweetness. He has sealed the sea with peace.

They have reached the throne of the Warden, and he has risen with uplifted arms. The banner of the path of Qoph stands at his right hand.

WARDEN OF THE TEMPLE: Heal Thou our waters, O Lord. Pour upon our waters of desire. Encompass our waters with Thy presence. The voice of the deep within us calls upon Thine eternal deep.

GUIDE OF THE PATHS: Open thy heart, O brother of the Rosy Cross, and receive the Water of Life.

MASTER OF THE TEMPLE: Kindle Thy justice in our hearts, as the light of a lamp is kindled, as the torch of a faithful guide in the way of darkness.

The Master has risen at his throne, and the Frater Ostiarius now turns up the lights of the temple. The Master resumes his throne.

The Warden lifts up his hands over the head of the postulant.

WARDEN OF THE TEMPLE: Fountain of fountains, and of all fountains; chalice of saving rain; grace on the soul descending, as rain on the dry grass; life giving rain of doctrine; mystical fruit of the doctrine; dew of divine speech, falling in stillness on the heart, filling the soul with knowledge; enter into the heart and purify; come into the soul and consecrate.

The Warden resumes his throne. The Guide of the Paths leads the postulant with the sun to the western side of the altar and directs him to deposit thereon the vessel of sacramental Water. The postulant is left standing, and the Guide returns to his seat. While still standing thereat:

GUIDE OF THE PATHS: The rivers of Eden flow from a central source in Daath, which is the higher knowledge. Lead us, O Lord, in Thee to the union of Chokmah and Binah.

The Guide resumes his seat.

MASTER OF THE TEMPLE: As God is the desire of the world, so did Divine desire for the manifestation of eternal beatitude bring the universe and its creatures into being. It is in this sense that the secret law of love, the eternal love, lies within the manifest world, as the immanence of the Father of all. The manifestation of love is the Light begotten of the Father, by which the worlds were made, according to the gifts of understanding. The union of Light and love signifies the bond of the spirit, the comforter who is with all things and leads them into the truth of love. The testimony is without in the world, my brother, and the testimony is also in the soul. But emotion and desire must die in the mystical sense, yet so only that they may be born again. I ask you to regard the old life of desire as dead henceforth within you, for you have entered into a new world of emotion, a new era in your psychic path; and this is the life of the sanctuary.

There is here the pause of a moment.

MASTER OF THE TEMPLE: The cross that you bear on your breast, as one of your titles of admission to the path of Qoph, communicates an analogical message to that in the grade of Zelator. On the surface it depicts the sun encompassed by the zodiacal signs, which are collected, according to their triplicities, on the arms of the cross. The correspondences of those triplicities are found in the part of your personality ~ the will, the rational mind, desire or the part of emotion, and the physical organism by which they manifest in the world of action. In the center of all is the self-knowing spirit, and the sun of that spirit is love.

The Warden of the Temple descends from his throne and proceeds to the eastern side of the altar.

WARDEN OF THE TEMPLE: The path by which you have traveled is that from which you will enter the holy Sephira Hod in the second point of the grade. It is called the corporeal intelligence, and it is referred by the secret tradition to the principles of natural life, growth and development in the world of manifested things. But on the path of the soul and her progress it has reference to the life that is above nature, the world that is beyond and within. The mystery of this path is therefore one of development and growth in grace, and the intelligence of this mystery is called corporeal by allusion to the vesture of the soul.

The Warden of the Temple turns eastward, with wand uplifted.

WARDEN OF THE TEMPLE: Give unto our souls, O Lord, the robe of glory, that we may approach and contemplate in Thee. Give unto us the mantle of the Master. In the darkness of material things, clothe us with purified desire; lift up our hearts to Thee; and in the world to come, which is the portion of our inheritance, unclothe us from all our vestures, that as naked we came forth into separation so naked we may return into union.

He turns again to the altar.

WARDEN OF THE TEMPLE: There is also the 31st path of Shin (*indicating the banner in the north*), by which the influences of Hod are communicated to the Sephira Malkuth, but it is not traveled in our system, and you were sent back therefrom when you entered it in the grade of Theoreticus. It is called the collecting intelligence, and it summarizes the law of grace, which is concealed in the pillar of severity, the loving kindness that prevails in all things, and the art of wisdom by which we overrule all things in virtue of that law. Receive its message into your heart; so shall it be traveled in the spirit.

Both paths are in communication with the pillar of severity, and that Qoph, through which you have passed in your progress from the grade of Yesod, is shown in the great symbol of the path. On the surface it is an emblem of justice, adorned with all her attributions. The mind of our natural humanity conceives this virtue and brings it to birth in life; but there is also a justice that is above, working in the souls of the chosen ones. It is said in the secret tradition that he who is on the seat of judgment has Hades upon his left hand, paradise on his right, the sword of the angel of death suspended over his head, and the Tree of Life behind him. Herein is the justice of the elect, reflected from her who is president of the supernal tribunal, the most Holy SHEKINAH. The outward attributions of justice are as her vesture, and herein, as in one of her aspects, she leads the soul through the pillar of severity from the life of separation into the mystic life of union.

The lesson in chief of that path of Shin on which you have looked in your journey, is shown in the symbol of the path. It is called the tower and exoterically it is that of Babel, as signifying utter overthrow, ruin and confusion. It is therefore in analogy with all symbolical events that carry the same suggestion, and most obviously with the traditional fall of man. But in the secret tradition, Babel is the wisdom of man, or the word of man in separation from the word of God, and the confusion visited on its builders is that which befalls the human mind in its divorce from things that are Divine. You have been in this state of separation, my brother of the Rosy Cross. You have erected in your own personality a tower of Babel, a palace of art, hoping to reach up into heaven from the roof thereof, which is the apex of the natural mind. When you enter into the mystical life, this tower has to fall, and that by which it is destroyed is the glorious and all holy violence of the Divine will, called down by your Divine spirit to break up the kingdom of this world within you, to cast out the kings of old who have reigned therein. Then shall your tower be rebuilt after another manner, and the mystery of its building shall be that of Babel no longer, but it shall be a tower of ivory, a house of gold, and He who shall reign therein will be truly king of Israel.

The Warden of the temple returns direct to his throne and takes his seat thereon.

MASTER OF THE TEMPLE: The desires of the soul in its darkness are like the troubled face of the deep when the earth was without form and void, when darkness dwelt thereon. The desires of the soul in their stillness, when the purified heart reflects the divine image, are like the shining face of the waters when the Spirit moved thereon. Frater Adveniat Regnum (*vel nomen aliud*), the benediction of purifying love be with you henceforth and for ever. You have traversed the path leading to the glory of Hod and have received consecration therein. I salute you as son of that path. I bid you retire for a season, to contemplate with recollection of the heart on the experience through which you have passed, and to prepare for the greater mysteries that will be communicated in the grade of Practicus.

The Guide of the Paths comes forward and leads the postulant by south and west to the door, without passing through the pillars. The postulant leaves the temple. The door is secured behind him.

This completes the ceremonial admission of a Frater Theoreticus into the path of Qoph.

SECOND POINT
THE CEREMONIAL ADVANCEMENT OF A
FRATER THEORETICUS TO THE
GRADE OF PRACTICUS, 3 = 8

The arrangement of the temple is shown in the official diagram of the Second Point. The temple is in light.

MASTER OF THE TEMPLE: To order, Fratres et Sorores (*knocks once*). The Lord shall heal our soul, the heart and the breaches thereof, the bruises of our desire for Him. The Lord shall heal our captivity; in Hod is the place of healing. O lead our captivity captive, my Lord and my God. We shall put away the raiment of bondage and shall enter at some far time into the liberation of Thy union.

There is here the pause of a moment.

MASTER OF THE TEMPLE: Honorable Guide of the Paths, do thou pass with free offerings and gifts beyond the gate of this temple, for there is one in the ways without who has prayed in a land of captivity, and the same shall do service in freedom to the honor of our holy house.

As the Guide of the Paths rises from his seat and moves with the sun westward:

GUIDE OF THE PATHS: In the name of the heavenly spouse on the day of ineffable union; in the name of Hod, which is glory; he shall follow the spouse on that day. He shall enjoy celestial peace to the end of time.

The Guide has reached the door and, giving the sign of the grade, he leaves the temple. The door is secured behind him.

The Guide of the Paths prepares the frater Theoreticus by decorating him with a badge or collar corresponding to that which is worn by himself, or alternatively with his own collar.

N.B. The Guide also wears the He final of the Divine Name, as a jewel about his waist.

GUIDE OF THE PATHS: Purified in body and mind, and then made clean of heart, O brother of the Rosy Cross, remember now and henceforward the Waters of Divine grace, and pray for their descent into the soul.

While this takes place in the precincts:

MASTER OF THE TEMPLE: The glory of understanding in the great sea of Binah descends upon the Waters of the soul. He who has purified his desire shall find in a great upreaching that the desire will sustain him, and he who has beheld in his heart the messenger of the greater mysteries shall afterwards hear also that which is the voice of understanding. What powers of Divine nature, O Fratres et Sorores, move upon the face of the deep waters within us? The path of the Lord of hosts is over the great Waters.

As directed by the Guide of the Paths, the battery of the frater Theoreticus is given without (knocks three times).

The Ostiarius opens the Door, and the Guide leads in the Theoreticus.

GUIDE OF THE PATHS: We have walked in the shadow of Light. We have offered up a new light declared in the heart.

The Guide of the Paths pauses with the frater Theoreticus in the north west of the temple. The door is secured behind them.

MASTER OF THE TEMPLE: Honorable Frater Theoreticus, Guide of the Paths and Grades, I have opened a secret door that gives entrance from the path of Resh to the holy Sephira Hod. In the name of the Lord of hosts, who is the King of glory, may our eyes look upon the King. Let us go to worship and to seek Him, O Frater Adveniat Regnum (*vel nomen aliud*).

You have opened the temple that is within you. You have passed through the court of the tabernacle at the beginning of your life of consecration. In the purification of your active part, symbolized by the natural body, you have dwelt in the holy place. The dedication of your mind has revealed it to you as a Holy of Holies, in the suggestive mystery of our symbolism. Behind the Holy of Holies, the great official religions and the temples built with hands, there lies a secret church and a higher state of soul. Behind the logical understanding there lies another realm of consciousness, which is also a world of memory. These two are one, and both are represented in our system by the mystical garden of Eden, wherein, as the secret doctrine teaches in its living parable, the soul was nourished by fruits of the Tree of Life, not by the material Tree of Knowledge, the admixture of good and evil. You are now in that garden of Eden, the place of the two Trees, wherein is also the altar on which Adam sacrificed the clean oblation of desire and will to the Lord of glory and received, by the mediation of the Tree of Life, the mysteries of eternal wisdom. Honorable Guide of the Paths, you will place our beloved brother between the pillars of the temple.

It is so done accordingly, and as they stand, facing the east:

GUIDE OF THE PATHS: This is the gate of the Lord; let the pure in heart enter thereby.

WARDEN OF THE TEMPLE: By what sign have you come to this secret place of all temples, O son of desire?

FRATER THEORETICUS *(as prompted by the Guide):* It is borne on the heart of the Guide, who leads me in the paths and grades; it is borne on my own heart. It is the symbol of the Sephira Yesod, the place of purified mind, the sacred letter Vau, which is the Tree of Life.

WARDEN OF THE TEMPLE: Remember, O Frater Adveniat Regnum (*vel nomen aliud*), that consecrated aspiration that brings the sons of desire into the presence of the Lord of glory.

The Master of the Temple descends form his throne and pauses before it, facing west.

MASTER OF THE TEMPLE: By the purified heart of the postulant; by his desire in the conversion thereof; by the stilled sea of passion, and in the name of that peace which stills it, bring him across the threshold.

The Guide of the Paths comes round with the sun and draws the postulant through the pillars.

GUIDE OF THE PATHS: There is for ever and ever a secret gate that gives upon the garden of Eden.

As the Master of the Temple approaches the western side of the altar:

MASTER OF THE TEMPLE: And still in the hush of the night, for those who study the doctrine, the Lord Who is blessed comes down and speaks with them in the garden of Eden.

The Guide of the Paths leads the Frater Theoreticus to the western side of the altar, where the master is now standing, and then returns to his place.

MASTER OF THE TEMPLE: Frater Adveniat Regnum (*vel nomen aliud*), the most practical of all paths is that by which we go back whence we came ~ from the exile of the soul in separation into the paradise of the soul in union. The temple in this grade is a memorial of that sanctuary that is called the lower Eden, the place of the just clothed in ethereal envelopes, signifying all perfect purity. Herein is reflected the supreme mystery of faith and the living presence of SHEKINAH. As such, it is that garden that is watered by the glorious and unfailing river flowing down from the Eden that is above. There is the supernal paradise, the place of which is in Binah, and there is the Divine presence of Matrona and Taboona, the SHEKINAH in transcendence. This altar in the middle place of our temple represents the altar of sacrifice that was erected, speaking symbolically, for the unspotted offerings of desire and will in the world before the traditional fall of man. That world is understood as the lower Eden, and it is sometimes identified with Malkuth; but it is not the kingdom of this world in a material sense. It is rather a spiritual place or state preceding, in our symbolism, that which is physical, and intermediate for man between the earth on which he now dwells and the heaven to which he belongs.

The altar by which you stand is in the form of a double cube, and the cube unfolds as a cross. On such a cross is the figure of a man extended in the great diagram before you, which represents the Tree of Life in the transcendence. Above Kether the power and the glory of unmanifest Deity descends from the region Ain Soph. Prior to the generation of beings and of things it is called the closed eye of the unknown darkness; but for the evolution of the cosmic worlds and the manifestation of the Divine therein, it is said that the eye opened, and the radiance of the ineffable Spirit poured through the aeons and the spaces. Kether represents the first movement of the Divine in self-unfoldment through begotten worlds and for manifestation to hierarchies of intelligence generated therein and thereby. Kether is called the place of God and His SHEKINAH in the state of absolute union; but the procession of the great law brought them forth in a state of distinction, which is not to be understood as separation. They became in this manner the Abba, or father, in Chokmah and the great mother, Aima, who is the transcendent SHEKINAH in Binah, corresponding respectively to the letters of Yod and He of the Divine name. These are male and female, and they produced ~ as the fruit of their union ~ a Divine son, who is shown in the diagram extended on the sephirotic cross. His head rests upon Daath, which is supernal knowledge; the arms stretch to Chesed and Geburah, while Tiphereth is over the region of the heart; and that which in the purity of the secret tradition is termed an organ of holiness is veiled by the Sephira Yesod. The feet of the figure rest on Malkuth; to indicate that the kingdom of this world is in subjection to the kingdom of heaven. Among the letters of the Divine name, this Divine son is in correspondence with Vau. He is the first begotten of the mighty ones, by He came into generation with Her who is His Divine bride and sister, the He final of the sacred name and the second aspect of SHEKINAH. She was at first contained within Him, as Eve in the nature of Adam, but was afterwards brought forth like Eve, and they abode together in the unity of mystical marriage.

There came, however, a change upon the face of things, and this union was broken. The He final was divided from the Vau and descended or fell to Malkuth, where the lower SHEKINAH is located in the great diagram. It is part of the legend concerning the fall of man, whom she followed into the exile of separation, being driven out with him. But her expulsion was for the salvation of the world, and a day will come when all nations shall enter under the wings of SHEKINAH; the Vau will raise up the He; the divided name will be restored in all perfection; and man ~ having entered into his birthright ~ will dwell with God in unity. It is she meanwhile who leads him on the path of his return to God.

Such is the legend of the grade of Practicus, derived from the secret tradition, and it is to be understood in the following manner, for in the life of the mystic we are concerned with Divine principles and not with personalities as such. The ADAM MICROPROSOPUS, or son, is the Divine nature that is immanent in the manifest universe, and in the soul of the universal humanity. For the great theosophists of Israel, He is the messiah or deliverer to come, the eternal word of the Father, by whom the worlds were made. The SHEKINAH, the twin sister, who came forth from Him, is the soul in the universal sense, as He ~ in Christian theosophy ~ is the Christ spirit, with whom each soul of man is called to dwell in unity. From another point of view she is the love part of humanity, directed to Divine things. And as all creation is a question of marriages, to intimate everywhere that the marriage of the soul with God is the last end of being, so is SHEKI-NAH the state of espousals understood upon all planes, because of analogy, but above all things in the spiritual and Deific sense. The soul's Divine origin is symbolized by the coming forth of SHEKINAH from the great Adam of the universe, and the soul's return is symbolized by the raising of the He final. Eden is the return accomplished, the state of mystical marriage. The supernal Eden is that state which is called mystically absorption in God, not that we are satisfied with the expression, but because the heart needs a language to body forth its longing.

In our Fellowship of the Rosy Cross, the Master of the Temple reflects the power and the grace coming down from the Father in Chokmah, while the Warden mirrors the influences descending from the great Mother in Binah. The Guide of the Paths represents the herald and vice-gerent of the Divine son, the bride in union with the spouse. You, lastly, my brother, are the man of election on the way of his return to the heights. Hereof is the mystery of love revealed to the purified heart in the grade of Practicus. For all that is intimated in this most holy parable, remember that a way of attainment is reserved for you here and now.

The Master goes back to his throne. The Warden of the Temple comes forward. He turns the postulant with his back to the north, and assumes a position facing him.

WARDEN OF THE TEMPLE: Frater Adveniat Regnum (*vel nomen aliud*), the sign of this grade is given by laying both hands thus upon the heart, with the fingers interlaced and the palms turned inward. It refers to the ten sephiroth of the Tree of Life rooted in the heart of the postulant. The sacred words are ELOHIM TZABAOTH, and in the ordinary sense of scripture they signify Lord of hosts; but in the secret tradition they contain an allusion to SHEKINAH under her title as Lady of Battles in the world of action. The password of the grade is ELOHA, another Divine name, formed of the Hebrew letters Aleph, Lamed and He, the numerical value of which is 36, and this is the mystical number. I invest you with the girdle of a Frater Practicus, the color of which is yellow, being that assigned to Hod in the symbolism of the Rosy Cross. Mercury is referred to this grade, in the sense of philosophical Mercury, or desire in a state of fixation on the end in God. It is that which is sought by the wise. In the spiritual mystery of the Elements, the grade of Practicus is in correspondence with Water, symbolizing the psychic nature, the emotions and desires of man. It is these that we seek to establish under the law of paradise.

The four-squared tablet that is placed in the middle north of the temple, containing Divine and angelical names referable to the northern quarter of the heavens, is in correspondence with the element of Water, and is set up as a symbol in our temple for the sanctification of the heart of man… The banners before you are symbolical banners of the paths leading from the grade Practicus to the sephiroth of the Grades beyond. That in the due east is the way of the greater mysteries. That in the south east communicates between Hod and Tiphereth, wherein is another grade in the sacred and glorious world that is called the Third Order. The banner in the due south is that of the path that you will travel to enter Netzach, at the next stage of your progress. The Sephira Hod is called in the secret tradition an absolute and perfect path, reserved to the sons of the King. It is a channel that draws from above and communicates to that which is below. It is on the side of severity and judgment; yet it is a path of roses, and the red rose of SHEKINAH sheds down its fragrance thereon from the realm of Geburah. It contains also within it a hidden peace and mercy. Remember, on your part that when purity is restored to the soul, when there is peace upon its crystal sea, then is the reign of mercy.

The Warden returns to his throne.

MASTER OF THE TEMPLE: You are qualified to receive in this grade and ~ by the power to me entrusted ~ I now confer upon you the mystical title of Monokeros de Astris, which means the Unicorn from the Stars, signifying the imputed purity of soul and the restored virgin state that you have received in the ceremonial consecration of your desire part. I give you also the symbol of MAIM, which is the Hebrew name of Water. Let them both be memorials of your cleansing within, and may that which is fulfilled in ritual be realized in your life and essence. The Lord of Hosts be with you. The Lord of the power without be declared in the power of grace through the depths and heights of your being. Honorable Warden of the Temple, I bid you announce that he who was Frater Theoreticus in the Fellowship of the Rosy Cross has been advanced to the grade of Practicus.

The Guide of the paths comes forward and taking the postulant by the right hand leads him about the altar, where they turn to the west, so that he is in the general sight of the brethren. The Warden of the Temple rises in his place with uplifted wand.

WARDEN OF THE TEMPLE: In the name of the Lord of Hosts, and by the ordinance of the Honorable Master of the Temple, I proclaim and testify that frater Adveniat Regnum (*vel nomen aliud*) has been admitted to the grade of Practicus in virtue of a lawful communication, that he is a son of the 30th Path, and that he has received the mystical title of Monokeros de Astris, with the symbol of MAIM.

The Guide of the Paths turns eastward with the postulant.

MASTER OF THE TEMPLE: The students of the mystical doctrine are grafted on the Tree of Life, and if those who have been so integrated should neglect the study of the doctrine they would be cut off from that glorious Tree. It is nourished by the sacrifice of prayer and by aspirations from the heart of the elect, going up the path of attainment. This is the middle pillar and the holy pillar of benignity. For these reasons, but in another form of symbolism, the Tree is itself the elect. The blessings that are poured continually upon the outer world descend from it and from them. They are the blessed company in the sanctuary of the hidden church. When the elect shall enter into perfect liberation, the whole world will be nourished by the Tree of Life, sustained and enlightened by SHEKINAH. That faith which passes into experience is the means of attainment in respect of the Tree of Life. Remember this saving faith. Remember also that prayer is the organ of Divine intercourse; but there is the prayer of silence. Contemplate the mysteries into which you have been received this day. Go before the ceremonial advancements that still await you in the Fellowship by a return in the purified heart along the road that leads to God. Through worlds of symbolism our steps can guide your course, but to the palace at the center you must approach alone, my brother, and you will enter also alone.

The Guide of the paths leads the postulant with the sun to his proper place in the temple, which is that of Ostiarius, and he receives from his predecessor the wand of this office. The Guide resumes his seat.

PRACTICUS INITIATION

The allocution of the grade follows, and is delivered by the Imperator, but him failing by his substitute, or by the Master of the Temple.

THE ALLOCUTION OF THE GRADE OF PRACTICUS

Fratres et Sorores, by the power in me vested for the communication of sacraments of knowledge through channels of symbolism, I say unto you: SURSUM CORDA. Lift up your hearts. And I pray that my lips may be cleansed to pronounce the allocution belonging to the grade of Practicus. To you, my brother, who have received it this day at our hands, I speak ~ as before ~ especially, and I would remind you of certain things that have been implied in the course of your progress. The mystery of the Neophyte grade was to you as a mystery of purifying love and the beginning of supernatural life, leading through the experience of religion to the heart thereof, even the secret shrine. The grade of Zelator typified a stage of advancement in spiritual life, an opening of the portal of wisdom, the dream of the mystic city. Something of the legend of the soul was exhibited in the high ceremony to the seeker after the path of life. He saw also the holy place and learned, as he stood symbolically therein, that the Reconciler is always with us, to those who on the altar of the heart can offer up themselves in sacrifice. In the grade of Theoreticus he learned more concerning the holy house, the making of the second Adam, and he entered into the Holy of Holies, as one who after long wandering in the outward ways discovers that within his own consciousness there is a gate that opens into a secret and sacred world. But the grade of Practicus signifies a further progress, a fuller and more fruitful image. The spirit of God moves upon our waters of desire, that the heart may be made in His likeness, the soul filled with sweetness, and its deeps sealed with peace. It is throughout the imagery of aspiration exalted above the formless world, the ebb and flow of reflections, to be fixed henceforth on the center, that point of being and of life in union with which a mystic cannot err.

The ritual of the path of Qoph is concerned with the purification of desire for the attainment of its fruition in God. Having entered the Sephira Hod, in the ceremony of the grade itself, the postulant is led beyond the Holy of Holies, to behold in a vision the hidden world of paradise, which is the world of a sanctuary withdrawn, of a secret church in the heart. Therein is the Light of the supernals, the reflected splendor of the superior Eden, sphered in the Waters of understanding, the great sea of Binah. The separation of the soul and the word is typified by the descent of SHEKINAH, and the law of reunion is typified by the providence that brought about the descent. The state of paradise is that of the immanent Divinity in man realized, and the oneness of this immanence with that which is Divine in the universe embraced by consciousness. Beyond it there are deeper states, and these are symbolized in the higher grades of the Rosy Cross.

Frater Adveniat Regnum (*vel nomen aliud*), now Practicus of our Order, I bid you remember that man in his material state, apart from the life of the spirit, is an earth that is formless and void. But when the spirit, established in consciousness, rules the whole man, a King ~ as you have been told ~ is reigning over the Israel within. The Waters of understanding sweep away the old order and mystery; the glory of God illuminates the heaven of purified heart and mind; and the material parts of our personality participate in the service of the Lord. For the soul that so enters into liberation, the rays of Divine influence extended and impinge everywhere. This is symbolized by the Greek cross, with the Sun in its center and all the grades of its manifestation gathered about it in the zodiac.

May God be with you, my brother. May He grant that what here and now you have come to discern in symbolism, by your own efforts and our instruction, shall so sink into your heart that you will be penetrated by its active meaning, and will attain it at first hand in the way of experience. So shall the wavering and inconstant emotions that now aspire to Him in the restless sea of our desires be led into the true light though understanding and love. Again, and for ever, my brother, the way is now before you; the gate can open now.

If the minutes of any previous meeting or other official business are to be taken in the Grade of Practicus, the temple must be reduced at this point to the Grade of Neophyte. By the power of his wand, the Master should close in the superior grade, open in the lower by fiat, and after the business has been discharged he should close similarly therein and re-open in the Grade of Practicus.

The Solemn Office of Closing The
Sacred Temple in the Grade of Practicus

Master of the Temple: (*Knocks*)

All rise.

Master of the Temple: To order, Fratres et Sorores. He has said unto us; Peace, be still. Assist me to close the temple in the grade of Practicus, remembering His coming. Frater Ostiarius, in the love of men and angels, and in the zeal of the secret doctrine, guard this sanctuary of the heart and the graces of consecration symbolized in the mystery of this grade.

The Frater Ostiarius, having seen that the door is secured:

Frater Ostiarius: Honorable Master of the Temple, the heart in its secret sanctuary is guarded surely.

Master of the Temple: Who keep the sacred precincts?

Frater Ostiarius: The invisible defenders of the mysteries.

Master of the Temple: Honorable Frater Theoreticus, who keeps the holy temple on the hither side?

Guide of the Paths: As ambassador of the Prince of Peace, I keep it for ever and ever till SHILOH comes.

Master of the Temple: Let Him be declared in the heart.

The Master and Warden descend from their thrones and face east, with wands uplifted. All present face east.

Master of the Temple: O ELOHIM TZABAOTH, O Lord of Hosts, ruler of the heart in man, King of the great Waters, about the sanctuary of the soul the world cries in vain. May the angel of Thy great council and the Prince of Thy perfect peace bring us into stillness of heart. Waters of life in understanding, renew the Waters of the soul. Fires of salvation in wisdom, save us by Holy Fire. Light of the crown, enlighten. Chesed, Geburah and Tiphereth, concur in the descent of the gifts ~ gifts from above, gifts of the supernal triad, inestimable gifts of grace.

The Master and Warden turn again to the west, and with his wand again uplifted:

WARDEN OF THE TEMPLE: Powers of the waters that are within us, sea unfathomable. In the deeps of the heart let us pray for the Sabbath that is to come, when there shall be harmony and equipoise in the outer worlds, and in that hidden world that is our own.

Then, with raised eyes and uplifted arms:

MASTER OF THE TEMPLE: The peace of Elohim be upon you, and the blessing of the Lord of Hosts. Depart in reconciliation; depart in light, O Brethren of the Rosy Cross. Go forth and carry the tidings, the glad tidings of peace in the inward stillness.

The Guide of the Paths turns westward, with arms outstretched.

GUIDE OF THE PATHS: Go, but return at your call to the work of consecrated hearts.

MASTER OF THE TEMPLE: Honorable Frater Practicus, the heart is the speaking witness, and the purified heart testifies to the practice of the work, that we may enter into the good things in the land of the living, which is the world of the second birth. The hour of the rite is over, and having attained our term therein, I direct you to close the temple in the grade of Practicus.

All members face as usual.

The Warden lifts up his wand.

WARDEN OF THE TEMPLE: Let purified hearts go forth, as vestals clothed in white, knowing that life in this world, and life in the world to come, is attained by the study of the doctrine. The doctrine is also the Tree. Fratres et Sorores, let us dwell with the Tree of Life and attain the Life of the Tree. In the name of the Lord of Hosts, I close this holy temple in the grade of Practicus.

WARDEN OF THE TEMPLE: (*Knocks Three Times*)

GUIDE OF THE PATHS: (*Knocks Three Times Rapidly*)

MASTER OF THE TEMPLE: (*Knocks Three Times at Intervals*)

HERE ENDS THE RITUAL OF THE GRADE OF PRACTICUS

The Second Order of the Rosy Cross

World of Formation

Part III

The Ceremony of Advancement
in the
Grade of Philosophus

4 = 7

Privately Printed

1916

The Fellowship of the Rosy Cross

—

Grade of Philosophus
4 = 7

—

The Solemn Ceremony of Opening The Temple in the Grade of Philosophus

—

The arrangement of the temple is hown in the official diagram of the First Point.

The celebrants or officers of this grade are the Master of the Temple, the Warden and Guide of the Paths, in addition to the Ostiarius, being the last candidate who has attained advancement therein.

If the temple should not have been opened previously in one of the lower grades, the ceremonial vesting of officers and members, the invocation or prayer at the east and the assoilment of the temple are performed as exhibited therein.

The Master of the Temple assumes his throne, holding the wand of his office. The other celebrants repair to their stations, and the ordinary brethren are ranged north and south, according to the precedence of their grades. All members are seated, and a short period of inward recollection follows.

MASTER OF THE TEMPLE: (*Knocks*)

All rise.

PHILOSOPHUS INITIATION

MASTER OF THE TEMPLE: To order, Fratres et Sorores, in the union of consecrated wills. The grace of the Lord be with us, the Light of the Lord be with us, the Holy Spirit of the most high God be with us henceforth and for ever. In His name who is King of the heavenly armies, assist me to open the temple that we have built for His service in the grade of Philosophus. Frater Ostiarius, in the spirit of conformity, I direct you to see that this house of the Rosy Cross is guarded against the spirit of the world.

The Frater Ostiarius opens the portal, inspects the immediate precincts in the accustomed manner, again secures the threshold and turns to the east, with uplifted wand.

FRATER OSTIARIUS: Against the will of the world and the will of unreconciled men, it is closed, O Master of the Temple.

MASTER OF THE TEMPLE: To the will of God and to those who are born of God, be it open for ever, my brethren. Honorable Guide of the Paths, assure yourself that all present have been established in the solemn dedication of this grade of wisdom.

The Guide of the Paths, standing in his place, lifts up his wand of office.

GUIDE OF THE PATHS: Fratres et Sorores, by the fourfold bond of our Fellowship and the yoke of the Rosy Cross, I demand the sign of a Philosophus.

He turns in succession to the four quarters and receives it from all present, the Master of the Temple excepted. The Guide turns to the Master, communicating it on his own part.

GUIDE OF THE PATHS: Honorable Master of the Temple, they have given me the sign of the will restored in purity.

The sign is repeated by the Master.

MASTER OF THE TEMPLE: Unto them be fruition therein, and the sacred Sephira Netzach declared in the spirit of the brotherhood. JEHOVAH TZABAOTH, God of the great armies, give us joy in the sign of Thy SHEKINAH.

This is said with raised eyes and uplifted wand. The pause of a moment follows.

WARDEN OF THE TEMPLE: May the gift of understanding in our symbols and the fullness of their inward meaning be renewed in the spirit of the Fellowship. Let us declare the mystery of this grade in the sacramental attributions thereof.

MASTER OF THE TEMPLE: The grade of Philosophus is the grade of the Sephira Netzach, and it is in correspondence ~ by symbolical attribution ~ with the macrocosmic element of Fire. But this is the Fire of brightness, symbolizing the will of man in its union with the Divine Will.

WARDEN OF THE TEMPLE: The star of the Philosophical grade is the planet Venus spiritualized, and great is the mystery thereof. EST OMNIS ANIMA VENUS, in which doctrine is the secret of the second birth and the science of union.

GUIDE OF THE PATHS: The way of attainment is the way of progression in the Tree by the path of Pe, even unto the victory that is Netzach and the presence of SHEKINAH therein as the white rose of our purpose, awaiting our rebirth in God.

MASTER OF THE TEMPLE: (*Knocks*) Open the gate, O Lord, by which we shall go out of our exile.

The Master and Warden descend from their thrones. All present face east. The Master lifts up his wand.

MASTER OF THE TEMPLE: We have worshipped Thee as ELOHIM TZABAOTH on the side of Thy justice, and we have seen Thy glory, which is Hod. We adore Thee as JEHOVAH TZABAOTH, for the victory of Thy mercy has been shown to us in the Sephira Netzach. Turn upon us the eye of Thy compassion, the eye of the world of life, the blessing of Thy people, Israel. Place us in Thy great assembly between Jehovah and Elohim, in the equilibrium of Thy mercy and Thy justice. The deliverance of Thine elect is hidden in the sacrament of Thy Holy Name.

The Master of the Temple turns westward with uplifted arms.

MASTER OF THE TEMPLE: My will is to do the will of Him that sent me. Take away my spirit of rebellion. Suffer Thou my will in Thy service.

The Master moves slowly southward, and says in his passing:

MASTER OF THE TEMPLE: Greater love than this no man has ⁓ that he should lay down his life for his friend. I loved my life and I have lost it. I laid it down in my desire for Thee, and it was dissolved in Thy love. I would live, but not I; live Thou, O Lord, in me.

The Master of the Temple halts in the middle south facing the tablet of the south. The Warden and Guide of the Paths occupy two points on the same line at a convenient distance behind him, so that the three form a triangle, having its apex upward. All present are now facing south. The Master of the Temple hands his wand to the Warden and takes up the thurible in front of the tablet of Fire. He traces the symbol of Fire in the air before him.

MASTER OF THE TEMPLE: Let there be lights in the firmament of heaven, in the microcosmic heaven within. Let the greater Light of the Spirit rule over the mind below; so shall it be as day therein ⁓ sunshine of Divine Will and transforming purpose. Let the lesser lights of the mind rule over our earthly part, in the night of material things. And God set them in the firmament, to rule therein. In the name of Elohim, who dispenses to the world in justice; in the name of Jehovah Tzabaoth, supernal grace, life of the world to come and minister of mercy, let the will of our natural manhood and its purpose shaping life, adore the Lord and God.

The master of the Temple offers incense, describing the sign of Leo.

MASTER OF THE TEMPLE: In the name of Michael, the great angel, whose mission is to kindle the sacred Fire on earth, as it is maintained in heaven, and in the mystical sign of the lion, ye living wills of men, adore your Lord and God.

Then, making the sign of the cosmic ✠ *with the thurible:*

MASTER OF THE TEMPLE: In the Holy and Divine names. Names about the quarter of the south, blazoned in a heaven of light, let the rectified will of man adore our Lord and God.

The Master replaces the thurible and resumes his wand. The three celebrants return with the sun to their places. All members face as usual. Standing at his throne, the Master uplifts his wand.

MASTER OF THE TEMPLE: In the sanctification of undivided self, in the utter dedication of our being, in the name of Jehovah Tzabaoth, mighty armies of our nature and the God who rules therein, I declare that the temple is open in the grade of Philosophus and of the will that is turned to Him.

MASTER OF THE TEMPLE: (*Knocks four times*)

WARDEN OF THE TEMPLE: (*Knocks four times*)

GUIDE OF THE PATHS: (*Knocks four times*)

The celebrants and members are seated.

This ends the solemn ceremony of opening the temple in the grade of Philosophus.

FIRST POINT
THE CEREMONIAL ADMISSION OF A
FRATER PRACTICUS IN THE PATH OF PE

The postulant is alone in the vestibule on a prie-dieu in full light, with a scroll in his hands, containing versicles proper to the grade.

MASTER OF THE TEMPLE: Fratres et Sorores, may we come by the study of the doctrine to know the ineffable name of our Master. May we see Him with our own eyes. May we hearken with our own ears to the utterance of the great voice. The Lord be with us until that day of unveiling, and the Lord be with us now in the work that we are about to perform for the glory of His manifested name. By the power to me committed under the dispensation of the Third Order, I open that gate that leads to the sanctuary in Netzach, through the sacred path of Pe, for the advancement of our beloved frater Adveniat Regnum (*vel nomen aliud*). He shall look upon the mysteries therein. Honorable Frater Theoreticus, you are the Guide of the Paths. Heaven and earth may pass away, but the mercy that you symbolize shall abide in the world within until God is All in all. Go therefore unto our postulant and brother. Say to him that we have heard his voice, crying in the watches of the night, and that God shall give him his desire in the presence of a chosen people.

The Guide rises in his place.

GUIDE OF THE PATHS: He shall know that the Reconciler is with us. I will proclaim the mystery of redemption and the time of salvation at hand. The heaven and the earth were created for Thine elect, O Lord. Their place is in Thy holy temple.

Taking with him the sacramental lavacrum from its place on the altar, the Guide of the Paths passes by south and west to the door of the temple and there gives the sign of the grade. The door is secured behind him.

N.B. The orientation of the temple is purely arbitrary and for purposes of convenience only in the path of Pe.

MASTER OF THE TEMPLE: Fratres et Sorores, our Frater Adveniat Regnum (*vel nomen aliud*) has beheld the light of our symbolism on the plane of material things. He has been purified in his earthly part. In the free spirit of the Air he has felt the wind of the Spirit and has been consecrated in his mind to God's service. We have hallowed the sea of his emotions and declared the presence of God in his psychic part. O Lord, save his soul. May he give unto Thee his will for ever. May he know that his path is in Thee. Take him, that he may be wholly Thine and that nothing may be left within him that does not belong to Thine union.

In the meantime, the Guide of the paths has greeted the postulant on the further side of the portal, saying:

GUIDE OF THE PATHS: I come in the purification of the will. Glory be to God in the highest and peace of fulfilled purpose to seekers for Divine union in the Light of the Rosy Cross.

The Guide of the Paths prepares the Frater Practicus by placing in his hands the vessel of sacramental Water and about his neck the Calvary cross of ten squares.

GUIDE OF THE PATHS: Purify the will, O Lord; redirect the hearts intention; sanctify the purposes of man. And remember on your part, my brother of the Rosy Cross, that it is the quest after God and His union that turns the whole nature. Herein is the second birth. I say unto you therefore, O Frater Adveniat Regnum (*vel nomen aliud*), be the quest of our end before you, and hallowed be your will.

The Guide of the Paths gives the battery of the grade (knocks three times, then one knock after a short pause).

When this has been done in the precincts, the Frater Ostiarius turns down the lights and opens the door. In the act of opening:

MASTER OF THE TEMPLE: In the name of the God of grace and captain of mercy: enter in the name of the Living God.

The Guide of the Paths brings in the postulant, saying:

GUIDE OF THE PATHS: Kindle in the soul and the heart the desire of the eternal hills. Show unto us the sun of righteousness, shining in the temple of the Most High.

The door is secured behind them. The Guide of the Paths pauses with the postulant at or near the entrance.

MASTER OF THE TEMPLE: In the darkness of nature, in the gloom of the winter tide, teach us, Thy children, to remember that life is in Thee, Amen, for ever and evermore. Give unto them the Life of life. Give unto Thy beloved the sleep that is sweet in Thy refuge and to awaken in the sun of Thy beauty.

The Guide of the Paths leads the postulant and places him between the pillars. As they are passing slowly forward:

GUIDE OF THE PATHS: We move in the shadow of light. We offer up the new light declared in the heart.

As they stand between the pillars, the Guide being a few inches behind the frater Practicus:

MASTER OF THE TEMPLE: Frater Adveniat Regnum (*vel nomen aliud*), testify concerning your titles. Give me the outward signs of the inward grace communicated to the purified heart in the mystery of Hod.

The Guide of the Paths has taken the vessel of Water from the hands of the postulant. He dictates the answer of the postulant in an undertone.

FRATER PRACTICUS: I received the sign of the grade as a testimony to the Tree of Life rooted in the heart of the postulant. (*He gives the sign.*) There were communicated to me the sacred words ELOHIM TZABAOTH, signifying Lord of Hosts. The password of the grade is ELOHA, which is also a name of God, formed by the letters Aleph, Lamed, and He. The mystical number drawn from this name, is 36. I was given the symbol of Water in the Hebrew word MAIM, and the title MONOKEROS DE ASTRIS, for the consecrated soul is a virgin and the daughter of the bright stars.

The Guide of the Paths replaces the vessel of Water in the hands of the postulant.

MASTER OF THE TEMPLE: Frater Adveniat Regnum (*vel nomen aliud*), earth and heaven are founded on the alliance of God with man. The mysteries of this temple are mysteries of a Divine covenant. Will you take them into your heart as such? Will you keep them as secrets of God? Will you enter the sanctuary, by the path that leads thereto, as into the inmost place of your spirit, and place upon its holy altar the oblation of your consecrated will in conformity with the Divine Will.

FRATER PRACTICUS (*who is prompted by the Guide of Paths*): As a fire upon the altar of God, I will purge the fire of the will. I place it in the hands of Michael, the great angel. Sacrifice me among the souls of the just. I will keep the mysteries of the path and the holy temple.

The Guide of the Paths takes the vessel of Water and moving behind him, raises it over the head of the postulant.

GUIDE OF THE PATHS: Fratres et Sorores in the Fellowship of the Rosy Cross, I testify that the purified desire of humanity is zeal of the city of God, and therein is the Water of life.

The Master of the Temple gives a battery of one knock, and rises in his place, with uplifted arms.

MASTER OF THE TEMPLE: By the fire in the heart that purifies, the fire of the mind that enlightens, and the fire of the will when the spirit is turned to God, may you be carried up the holy mountain. May you walk in the light of your fire.

He resumes his throne. The Guide of the Paths moves with the sun, deposits the vessel of Water on the northern side of the altar, and returns with the sacramental lamp, which he places in the hands of the postulant and then resumes his station behind the pillars.

MASTER OF THE TEMPLE: Frater Adveniat Regnum (*vel nomen aliud*), I now bid you kneel down (*the Guide assists the postulant*). Raise up the sacramental lamp with both hands, and say in a clear voice: I will consecrate the fire of the will. I seek after the will of God. Make me one with Thy Divine purpose, which moves through all the worlds; shape me to Thine ends, O Lord.

This is repeated by the postulant, following the Master.

MASTER OF THE TEMPLE: Rise, frater Practicus, an accepted postulant for advancement to the grade of Philosophus.

The postulant rises. The Guide of the Paths directs him in a low voice to lift up the sacramental lamp to the full height of his arms and say after him clearly:

FRATER PRACTICUS *(following the Guide):* Into Thy hands, O Lord, for the work of the Rosy Cross, I commend my life of will.

He lowers the lamp. The Guide of the Paths should perform this part of the ceremony so that attention is directed to the postulant rather than to his own prompting.

PHILOSOPHUS INITIATION

MASTER OF THE TEMPLE: May the victories of wisdom in the supernal world of Chokmah be reflected into the life of your being.

The Guide of the Paths moves round slowly with the sun and faces the postulant, whom he draws between the pillars.

GUIDE OF THE PATHS: I say unto you that the darkness grows toward morning and that the day of the Lord is nigh.

He takes his place on the right hand of the postulant. Both are facing the east.

MASTER OF THE TEMPLE: There is a mystery concerning the paths that lead from the Sephira Hod to the Sephiroth and grades that are beyond. It is indicated by the banners of the 23rd and 25th paths in the north west of the temple, inscribed respectively with the letters Mem and Samech. The heights loom about you as you advance further, under the obedience of the Rosy Cross; but - as on previous occasions - not every path on the threshold of which you stand is free for your traveling. The Sephira Hod is in communication with worlds beyond your ken and two of its gates of issue are in darkness of great darkness, which the eyes in this temple are not meant to penetrate. By the power to me deputed, I have opened before you the sacred path of Pe, as a lineal mode of communication between Hod and Netzach. The Guide of the Paths shall lead you, seeking a goal of quest, with all your will in the darkness directed toward things Divine.

The Guide of the Paths moves forward slowly, leading the postulant.

GUIDE OF THE PATHS: Let us enter this path of reconciliation, under a bond of compassion and judgment. The fire of Divine love is behind the universe, and the heart of justice is mercy.

MASTER OF THE TEMPLE: The life giving heat of Divine Love is revealed to the soul in its darkness. The saving will of the soul reaches up toward Divine ends.

WARDEN OF THE TEMPLE: The will of the soul is love, and this love can unite you with the Divine in the universe. The root of the soul is the root of the world, my brother.

GUIDE OF THE PATHS: If I dwell in the noon, I am with Thee. If I abide in the midnight, I shall see Thee. In the veiling of Thy light I will have faith in the coming of Thy perfect splendor. Thou art my glory and my star. My steps shall not falter. I shall behold the Light that is in Thee.

They have reached the western side of the altar, which stands between the thrones. The Master of the Temple has risen with uplifted arms.

MASTER OF THE TEMPLE: Let the sons of the priesthood put Fire upon the altar of the heart.

GUIDE OF THE PATHS: Plead with the Fire of our love. Plead with us in Thy Holy Fire. Give answer in heaven to our longing.

MASTER OF THE TEMPLE: Descend upon our mountain, O Master, and the bushes shall burn with fire. Come into our temple and consecrate the fires therein.

The Warden of the Temple has risen with uplifted arms.

WARDEN OF THE TEMPLE: The desire of the soul is to Thy Name and to the remembrance of Thee. Thy worship is a Tree of Life. We seek the knowledge of Thy ways.

The Frater Ostiarius turns up the lights of the temple. The Master raises his hands over the head of the postulant.

MASTER OF THE TEMPLE: Be unto us a consuming Fire and purge our grosser wills. Enter into our purpose and purify; come into the will and consecrate. Open thy temple, O brother of the Rosy Cross, and receive the will of the Holy One.

The Master and Warden of the Temple resume their thrones. The Guide of the Paths directs the postulant to deposit the sacramental lamp on the eastern side of the altar. The postulant is left standing at the western side and the Guide returns to his seat. While still erect thereat, he lifts up his wand, saying:

GUIDE OF THE PATHS: O glorious SHEKINAH, Holy, Holy spouse, bring us into the white rose of Thy presence, symbol of that Divine alliance that sustains the worlds.

WARDEN OF THE TEMPLE: Lead us, O Lord, in Thee to the union of Chokmah and Binah.

The Guide resumes his seat.

MASTER OF THE TEMPLE: Frater Adveniat Regnum (*vel nomen aliud*), between the pillars of severity and mercy, you have followed a path that leads to a place of mercy, because it signifies a state of union between the active intention of man and that law of eternal being that is understood as Divine Will. It is by such integration that the soul fulfils itself and attains the perfect fruition of its own being. The will that dies to itself, in the personal or separate sense, enters into true life. It does not therefore die but is changed by a new birth in time, and moves thereafter in concurrence with the purpose of the Cosmos. The pure all penetrating flame of that Divine purpose will transmute the fires of your nature and will permeate your whole being. The flame is also light, intelligible light of mind, a word speaking within and leading into all truth. He who listens in his heart and he who hears it within him becomes himself the true and the good. When it speaks in your heart, my brother, hearken to the voice of Fire.

There is here the pause of a moment.

MASTER OF THE TEMPLE: The cross that you bear on your breast, as one of your titles of admission to the path of Pe, is the unfolded form of the cube, and herein is a great mystery - not to be declared in this grade. When the cube is closed up it represents the altar of incense, upon the material correspondence of which, in the temple of the Rosy Cross, you have offered up yourself in sacrifice - signifying sanctification and self attainment in God. The Calvary cross is inscribed with the names of the Sephiroth. May the cross of your manifested personality, my brother, be written within and without by the graces and virtues that are signified by those titles. So shall there be a crown of your life and a kingdom of God within you.

WARDEN OF THE TEMPLE: The path by which you have traveled is that from which you will enter the holy sephira Netzach in the Second Point of the grade. It is called the 27th path and also the active intelligence, a spirit that informs all things and is the motion thereof. It is an allusion to the mystery of the will, and in the first place to that of the Divine Being, wherein is the root of activity, the perfection and consummation of all things; but in the second place to that of man as the native power ~ that under the eternal guidance ~ carries him through the paths of eternity. Its work is by the way of intentness, desire, and love. The banner of this path is displayed in the due east.

The Warden of the Temple rises with uplifted wand.

WARDEN OF THE TEMPLE: Give us, O God, recollection. Give unto us aspiration and desire. And give unto us a knowledge of those secret ways through which we shall pass behind material reason into the living sun of Thy truth.

He resumes his seat.

WARDEN OF THE TEMPLE: The 28th path of Tzaddi, which is a channel of communication between Netzach and Yesod, is called in our secret tradition the natural intelligence. It is said to perfect, after its own kind, the nature of every being under the orb of the sun. It refers more especially to the mind, which is allocated to the Sephira Yesod. The ascent into Netzach is not through the natural mind but by that directing power that works within it. There is also the 30th path of Resh, which connects Netzach and Malkuth. It is called the collective intelligence, and the tradition that we have received tells us that herein is the law of judgment concerning celestial signs and the stellar influences, SAPIENS DOMINABITUR ASTRIS, and such intelligence is for us the law of grace and loving kindness that obtains in all things. It is also an art of wisdom by which we overrule all things in virtue of that law.

The Warden has indicated the several banners at the proper points of his discourse.

MASTER OF THE TEMPLE: All these paths are in communication with the pillar of mercy, which is mystically on the masculine side of the Tree, and their meanings are explained and extended by the great pictorial symbols attached to the paths. Each of them illustrates the operation and influence of SHEKINAH, not only as the guide of the soul in the paths that are actually traveled but in those that are only passed by on the ascent of the holy mountain. The symbol that lies uppermost on the altar is that of the 27th path. It represents SHEKINAH as the Lady of Reconciliation and lady of the pillar of benignity, intermingling and reconciling the influences of Chesed and Geburah, regarding as cleansing water and saving fire. They are poured forth from two chalices, which have a meeting point at Yesod and descend thence as a river of life in Malkuth. In the ascent of the Tree this symbol signifies the will toward rebirth, being the last mystery unfolded by the grades of the Rosy Cross at that point where the world of formation merges in the world that is beyond. In the descent of the influences from above it signifies the virtues and graces of the pillars on the right and the left uniting with those that come down from the middle pillar, represented by SHEKINAH, who is herself the vesture of Messias. Her chalice is a chalice of salvation, a principle of sacramental life. Her cup is the cup of benedictions. It is an eternal cup of mercy, uplifted in the worlds of the Tree. It is also a well of cleansing, even as the laver of Moses, and a deep water of illumination, like the sea of Solomon. Open your heart, my brother, and its blessing shall descend upon you. It shall be as the cup of your consecrated being, hallowed by the desire of Kether, the crown and term of all.

The Master of the Temple exhibits the second symbol.

MASTER OF THE TEMPLE: The symbol of the 28th path represents SHEKINAH as the new moon on the side of Mercy, looking towards the glorious sun of Tiphereth and reflecting its sacred radiance. The animals below are the unregenerate instincts of the natural man in Malkuth, while the crayfish reaching up toward the land is the evil part of our nature. SHEKINAH is the soul-part shining in the region of material darkness, ignorance and savage fear. She reflects over the sad region of our suffering estate the Divine Light of the self-knowing spirit. The two towers signify the ramparts of the visible world, and the space between them is the issue into the unknown. In another and not less important aspect, the moon is the natural mind, the state of reflected and partial light, the illusion, the glamour and the uncertainties of the logical understanding in the presence of the great problems. I have said that the new moon is on the side of Chesed; in the waning it is on that of Geburah; and at the full it is said to reflect the sun of beauty and righteousness. These also are aspects of the mind, which in the glory of its fullness reflects the mind of Christ, thus corresponding to SHEKINAH, whom I have termed the vesture of Messias.

The Master of the Temple exhibits the third symbol.

MASTER OF THE TEMPLE: The symbol of the 30th path is an analogue of that which stands first in the present sequence. It is SHEKINAH again in the act of dispensing the powers and virtues from above. The pillars of mercy and severity are represented by their Sephiroth in the form of stars. Tiphereth is immediately above and appears as a star of six points, by reference to the Christ nature. She herself bears upon her breast the star that corresponds to Yesod, and at her feet is Malkuth, whereon her urns of life are emptied. They are urns of Water and of Fire ~ the rain of doctrine, the dew of Divine speech, the great Water of understanding; and the Fire of the Holy Spirit, the tongues of flame, the splendor of supernal wisdom.

The Guide of the Paths comes up direct from his seat and takes charge of the postulant.

MASTER OF THE TEMPLE: Frater Adveniat Regnum (*vel nomen aliud*), you have now passed in our symbolism through a complete consecration of personality. May the Divine Will rule henceforth therein and realize in your life itself the things that we have presented in ritual. You have traversed the path that leads to the victory, which is Netzach. I salute you as son of the path. I bid you go forth in peace, to contemplate its mysteries and to prepare for your final experience in the world of formation.

The Guide of the Paths leads the postulant to the door without passing through the pillars. The postulant leaves the temple. The door is secured behind him.

Here ends the ceremonial admission of a Frater Practicus into the path of Pe.

SECOND POINT
THE CEREMONIAL ADVANCEMENT OF A
FRATER PRACTICUS TO THE GRADE
OF PHILOSOPHUS, 4 = 7

The arrangement of the the temple is shown in the official diagram of the Second Point. The temple is in light.

MASTER OF THE TEMPLE: God save you, Fratres et Sorores. Our Frater Adveniat Regnum (*vel nomen aliud*) has offered up his willing sacrifice. That is the act of dedication on his own part. We have communicated to him the mystery of those paths of grace and enlightenment that lead from Sephira to Sephira and in fine to the sanctuary of Netzach. That is the consecration in symbolism that we have performed upon our part. Another phase of Rosicrucian doctrine will now be committed to his charge. Then will the worlds of action and formation have given to him that which is theirs - a light dawning in the darkness and the evidence of a light beyond. Honorable Guide of the Paths, as the priest of mediation in this holy temple, say unto our beloved brother that the time of the contemplation is over, that the mystical gate is open and the sanctuary awaits his presence.

As the Guide of the Paths rises from his seat and moves with the sun westward:

GUIDE OF THE PATHS: In the name of supernal wisdom, of the word that restores the worlds, prevailing from end to end, strongly and sweetly overruling all things, and in the perfect sanctification of will, he shall know the victory that is Netzach. I will teach him the way of prudence.

He has now reached the door, and - giving the sign of the grade - he leaves the temple. The door is secured behind him.

MASTER OF THE TEMPLE: There is a Water of the wise in Chesed. There is a Fire in the Water of the wise. That Sacred Fire is an influx from Chokmah, communicating to the purified will in Netzach the wisdom that is above understanding and preparing it toward the second birth. Fratres et Sorores, may that Fire descend upon us for the reintegration of our wills in God. May it descend upon him who is about to be received among us at this pregnant epoch of his progress. May he look toward the hidden sanctuary and the desire of the eyes in Tiphereth, as one who knows that his Redeemer lives and that after the captivity of Zion there is the freedom of the spiritual city. O wisdom from the mouth of the Most High, scepter of the house of Israel, Immanuel, our King and law giver, come and set us free in Thy mercy. Delay no longer.

While this takes place in the temple, the Guide of the Paths prepares the Frater Practicus in the precincts by decorating him with a badge or collar corresponding to that which is worn by a Warden of the Temple, but not with the other insignia belonging to this high office. While so doing:

GUIDE OF THE PATHS: Purified in the body and mind, consecrated in heart and will, O brother of the Rosy Cross, remember, I pray you, that the high mystery of the soul in union begins in a mystery of the will.

The Guide of the Paths directs the frater Practicus to give the battery of the grade on the outer side of the door, thus knocks four times in rapid succession.

The Ostiarius opens the door and the Guide leads in the Practicus

GUIDE OF THE PATHS: Beneath him are the everlasting arms, and the shadow of the wings is over him.

The Guide of the Paths pauses with the Practicus in the north west of the temple. The door is secured behind them.

MASTER OF THE TEMPLE: The Lord has heard his voice crying in the wilderness of material things.

GUIDE OF THE PATHS: The Lord has raised him up and brought him through a sacred gate into a holy place.

As the Guide of the Paths leads the Practicus and places him between the pillars:

WARDEN OF THE TEMPLE: We have opened the gate of Light, that in God he may see Light.

When the Guide and the Practicus stand between the pillars:

Master of the Temple: Frater Adveniat Regnum (*vel nomen aliud*), open your gates, open your spiritual portals; so shall the King of glory come in and abide in your secret temple. You heard in the grade of Practicus concerning a secret church and a higher state of soul, represented in our symbolism by the mystical garden of Eden. You are again on the threshold of that sanctuary and are called to enter therein, as one who would search more deeply into the hidden mysteries of union.

Warden of the Temple: By what sign do you enter this house of victory, O son of consecrated will?

Frater Practicus *(as prompted by the Guide):* It is borne on your own heart, O Honorable frater Practicus; it is borne also on mine. It is the symbol of the Sephira Hod; it is the sacred letter He and the sign of consecrated hearts.

Warden of the Temple: Remember, O Frater Adveniat Regnum (*vel nomen aliud*), that man doth not yield himself to God and the Divine purpose utterly, save only by the fortitude of his sanctified will.

The Master of the Temple descends from his throne and pauses before it, facing west.

Master of the Temple: By the dedicated will of the postulant, by his complete consecration of personality, and in the name of the all-hallowing God, bring him across the threshold.

Guide of the Paths: The will of man in redirection ascends like a pure fire toward the Supreme Being, whose essence is also will.

As the Master of the Temple approaches the western side of the altar:

Master of the Temple: The will of man in its union is of the substance of Divine Will.

The Guide of the Paths leads the postulant to the western side of the altar, where the Master is now standing, and then resumes his seat.

MASTER OF THE TEMPLE: The banner that overshadows the altar in this grade represents that Divine estate in paradise that preceded the condition depicted in the grade of Practicus. Some intimations of it have reached you already in the legend recited therein, and the two allegories – taken together under our mystical interpretation in the light of the Rosy Cross – offer lessons of deep importance. In the mystery that was unfolded on the severity side of the Tree you heard rumors also concerning the traditional fall of man, which brought about a separation between the Divine son and the Immaculate Bride who is SHEKINAH. That separation had its high purpose in the scheme of human redemption, as presented by the secret tradition of Israel; but one of its results was a division in the sacred name, for – as it is said – the He fell to earth; and it is only in the fulfillment of the scheme – or at the end of the redeeming process – that perfection will be restored to the name. But that which is to come is that which has also been, and in this great allegory of being and of states, the past depicts the future, while the future restores the past.

You see no longer before you a SHEKINAH in exile abiding in a desecrated kingdom of this world. She is now located in Tiphereth – that is to say, in the heart of her Eternal Spouse. She is again contained within Him, and the intercourse of this union is ineffably more perfect than when she was brought forth like Eve from Adam, so that she was face to face with her Spouse and dwelt with Him in the state delineated to you as that of mystical marriage. The latter is like moonlight in its contrast with the darkness and frustration of love in earthly intercourse. The former is like sunlight in its comparison with both and dissolves them in its own splendor. The Tree of Life is itself transfigured by the union, and the Divine Name is perfect in the depths, as it is also perfect in the heights. You will see that Malkuth carries the crown that is Kether, that mercy presides over judgment and that the names and titles of the Sephiroth are counterchanged everywhere. It is indeed a new heaven and a new earth, for He that sits upon the throne has said: Behold, I make all things new.

Were these things, my brother, but the bones of some old theosophy, they could have no place in our Rosicrucian inheritance, if that is to be accounted a house of living treasures. But we have told you already that SHEKINAH in our mystical allegory is the proclamator of unity and the guide of man therein. As the He final in Malkuth, she is in the state of separation or exile, and so also is the soul of man, apart from the Spouse of the soul. In the state of union, which is the state of the middle pillar above Malkuth, the He is in union with the Vau, as exhibited by the diagram before you and as represented, also traditionally, in Rabbinical Hebrew by the exclamation VAH, which expresses a state of joy. But this union, which begins in Yesod and is so symbolized therein, is perfected in Tiphereth, where the Lover and Beloved are no longer face to face, in simple union no longer, but in the condition that is called UNITAS, wherein there is no passage between subject and object, for all things that belong to love have been made one in the heart of love. But this, my brother, is not only the traditional history SHEKINAH; it is that of your own soul and all souls of election on the way of their return to God. In a most particular manner it is the scheme of your proper advancement through the grades of our Fellowship, and because this illustrates a real experience within, I have intimated that our secret house of initiation contains a living treasure and not the *disjecta membra* of dead theosophical lore. As an illustration out of due time of that which awaits you beyond the second world of Rosicrucian knowledge ~ and to mark its harmony with tradition and with mystical experience ~ those who enter Tiphereth find that the Guide of their Paths, who is the living symbol of SHEKINAH, no longer leads them on the visible way. At least for the time being, her work seems done. She has gone inward into the Christ state, and the Beloved is hidden in the Lover.

You were told in the grade of Practicus that we are concerned with Divine principles, not with personalities. SHEKINAH is not for us either a Person in the Godhead or a great emanated angel. She is a principle, in virtue of which we go back whence we came. We all come forth from the center and ~ because of this principle ~ the center draws us back. The name of this principle is Love, and Love is the power whereby the Will of God ~ that works toward union ~ is done on earth, even as it is done in heaven. When you were told ~ also in the grade of Practicus ~ that SHEKINAH is the soul in the universal sense, the same truth was intimated in synonymous words, for the soul is Love ~ Love in dereliction for most of us, Love in the night of divorce, Love in the paths of loss and a thousand morganatic marriages, but always and only Love.

Brother of the Rosy Cross, I give you the last message of this unfolded mystery. Your soul is itself SHEKINAH ascending towards Tiphereth, or union with the Divine son, who is called Messias in the tradition of Israel and Christ under the new law. Awaiting that hour of attainment in the realization of living experience, the portals of a symbolical Tiphereth may open in our order to receive you. Remember in both respects that when ~ according to the apocalypse ~ the Spirit and the Bride, say, Come, the answer of the faithful witness follows in a white flame of aspiration; even so, Come therefore ~ our Lord and our God.

The Master goes back to his throne. The Guide of the paths moves forward, places the postulant with his back to the north and assumes a position facing him.

GUIDE OF THE PATHS: Frater Adveniat Regnum (*vel nomen aliud*), the sign of this grade is given by raising the arms at full length above the head, with the palms of the hands outward and the thumbs joined at the tips. It refers to the ten sephiroth ruling over the whole personality and the direction of the will toward the heights of mystical attainment. The sacred words are JEHOVAH TZABAOTH, signifying God of armies, and they are the complement of ELOHIM TZABAOTH, referred in the secret tradition to SHEKINAH as Lady of Battles, allocated to the sephira Hod. The latter is on the feminine side of the Tree, while Netzach is on the male side. The password of the grade is CADAD, meaning sparks and alluding to the flight upward. Its numerical value is 28, and this is the mystical number. I invest you with the girdle of a Philosophus, the color of which is green, being that assigned to Netzach in the symbolism of the Rosy Cross. It has also an allusion to the planet Venus spiritualized, because the soul is in search of espousals though the path of the second birth and the growth of that life that is in God. The planet of the grade is Venus and it is traditionally a star of birth. In the spiritual mystery of the elements, the grade of Philosophus is in correspondence with Fire, symbolizing the will of man. It is this that we seek to reestablish in conformity with Divine Will. The four-square tablet that is placed in the middle south of the temple, containing Divine and angelical names referable to the southern quarter of the heavens, is in correspondence with the element of Fire, and is set up as a symbol in our temple for the sanctification of the will of man. The banners before you are symbolical banners of the paths leading from the grade of Philosophus to the mysteries of the Third Order. The banner in the due north represents the path by which you have entered Netzach. This sephira is called in the secret tradition a recondite or hidden intelligence, and it is so termed because it is the refulgent splendor of all the intellectual virtues that are perceived with the eyes of the mind and are attained in the ecstasy of faith.

The Guide turns the postulant so that he faces the east and then goes back to his place.

MASTER OF THE TEMPLE: You are entitled to receive in this grade and ~ by the power to me entrusted ~ I now confer upon you the mystical title of Pharos Illuminans, signifying a tower of Light. I give you also the symbol of Aesh, being the Hebrew name of Fire. Let them both be memorials of your inward dedication and your consecrated life henceforth. It is written, my brother, that the fourth river is PHRATH, or Euphrates. And because you have other worlds to conquer I give you that word, to keep green in your memory when the heart is athirst within you, when you long for the paradise that is above and listen in all the vistas for a voice that cries; whosoever will, let him drink the Waters of Life freely. Remember also that the waters were parted and became into four heads. Honorable Guide of the Paths, I bid you announce that he who was Frater Practicus in the Fellowship of the Rosy Cross has been advanced to the grade of Philosophus.

The Guide of the Paths comes forward and taking the postulant by the right hand leads him about the altar, where they turn to the west, so that he is in the general sight of the brethren.

GUIDE OF THE PATHS: In the name of JEHOVAH TZABAOTH, and by the ordinance of the Honorable Master of the Temple, I proclaim and testify that Frater Adveniat Regnum (*vel nomen aliud*) has been admitted to the grade of Philosophus in virtue of a lawful communication, that he is a son of the 27th path, and that he has received the mystical title of Pharos Illuminans, with the symbol of Aesh and the word PHRATH, being the fourth river of Eden.

The Guide of the Paths turns eastward with the postulant.

MASTER OF THE TEMPLE: As regards your further progress through the worlds and grades of our Fellowship I have neither counsel nor information to impart. The power to me entrusted reaches its term in Netzach, of which I am the representative and spokesman. The course of your advancement through the First and Second Orders should have taught you that the great secrets are under a great reservation, and that it is given to those only who keep themselves unspotted from the world to break the seals of the inner sanctuary or to open the Book of Life.

The Guide of the Paths leads the postulant with the sun to his proper place in the temple, being that of Ostiarius. He returns to his own seat.

The allocution of the grade follows and is delivered by the Imperator, but him failing by his substitute, or by the Master of the Temple.

THE ALLOCUTION OF THE GRADE OF PHILOSOPHUS

God's providence overtakes us in many places, that we may be directed into paths of Light, paths of intelligence and high paths of grace. In the following of these, we who at some time ~ when we know not, God knows ~ went forth upon the outward quest shall be drawn on the quest that is within, and He shall give us back unto Himself, after worlds of separation and exile. The soul and the Divine Spouse are both, meanwhile, in widowhood. Let us pray therefore that the grace of the centripetal attraction may continue to draw and draw, preventing the defending on all sides. May that grace also enlighten in the public thoroughfares of life, but us above all and with all ~ in the mystical ways of knowledge. Therein, by His special election, He has brought us already a certain distance in the quest that is ours and His. In this spirit, Fratres et Sorores, and realizing ~ as we are called to do ~ that for every step that we can take with our feet of desire, the Divine Lover advances on his own part through a world of distance, to meet and forestall us at the term of union ~ I invite you to lift up your hearts, to hear and accept therein the allocution belonging to the grade of Philosophus.

In the symbolism of this grade, the wings of the morning are uplifted already in the orient of mystical life. The clouds dissolve and the face of the Beloved begins to be reflected in the soul. It is but the image of the King in His beauty, yet the night and its shadows are over; a star in the east goes before us, and the vision of the sun of righteousness is at hand. The path of search is truly a path of consecration, but the language of our concern has suffered a certain change. The alliance between God and man is no longer a tongue of symbolism but a principle of work in common, an unity and integration of will and a marriage with the purpose of the worlds. The difficulty is not to do the will of God but to know it, for many earnest hearts in the world without. In the Fellowship of the Rosy Cross we have learned that Love is the key that opens every gate, and especially the gate of will. It has been said to you that will is Love. Marriage with divine purpose postulates antecedent love, and the purpose of God in the world is one at the root and one in development with that which obtains in respect of every soul. The end is union.

We are told in our secret tradition that the sole object for which man was sent into this world was to know that JEHOVAH is ELOHIM, or that God and His SHEKINAH are one. There are many deeps of meaning in the doctrine thus briefly formulated. It signifies that SHEKINAH is the Divine energy that sends out from the center and draws back thereto; that every soul come forth from God, in virtue of the principle of union, is by necessity on the quest of Him ~ through all its worlds of being and manifestation; and that it can attain true rest only in return to Him. But seeing that the principle, the need, the end are summed up in the word Love, the union with which they are concerned is formulated rightly and always in terms of marriage. SHEKINAH presides over marriage, is the Beloved in search of the Lover, the Bride joined to the Spouse and abiding in His heart.

All symbolism that can be derived from the cosmic and microcosmic world is taken to illustrate the path of advancement toward this end in the ritual sacramentalism of our Fellowship. From grade to grade the brother of the Rosy Cross is led through successive consecrations, ending in that of the will at the height of the Second Order. It signifies the conversion of his whole object in life and nature. He stands therefore now upon the threshold of a Second Birth, as if a change in the substance of his being. Frater Adveniat Regnum (*vel nomen aliud*), the Second Order delivers you, who have been advanced this day among us, to the keepers of the greater mysteries, as one who in the ritual sense has been make white within and without, even as the white rose of SHEKINAH in the sphere of Netzach. May you so work and so attain that our symbolism shall become life in you, and when in a yet deeper symbolism you are called to the Second Birth, may you be truly born again. So shall the recondite or hidden intelligence descend into your soul, my brother, and be realized by the consciousness of the soul in the ecstasy of faith.

If the minutes of any previous meeting or other official business are to be taken in the grade of Philosophus, the temple must be reduced at this point to the grade of Neophyte. By the power of his wand, the Master should close in the superior grade, open in the lower by fiat, and after the business has been discharged he should close similarly therein and reopen in the grade Philosophus.

The Solemn Office of Closing the Sacred Temple in the Grade of Philosophus

Master of the Temple: (*Knocks*)

All rise

Master of the Temple: To order, Fratres et Sorores. The Kingdom that is above sends down its perfect voice, and the kingdom that is below sends up its voice of gratitude, in the humility and reverence of which assist me to close this temple in the grade of Philosophus. Frater Ostiarius, guard our sanctuary of the will and the graces of dedication symbolized in the mystery of this grade.

The Frater Ostiarius, having seen that the door is secured:

Frater Ostiarius: Honorable Master of the Temple, where the will of the Lord is done, we are delivered from the will of our enemies. The temple is surely guarded.

Master of the Temple: Honorable Frater Theoreticus, Guide of the Paths and Grades, the secret law is Chokmah and its tradition is a Sabbath, the rest whereof is reflected into the Sephira Netzach. Assure yourself that all present have known its repose in their hearts.

The Guide of the Paths, standing in his place, lifts up his wand of office.

Guide of the Paths: Fratres et Sorores in the Fellowship of the Rosy Cross, give me the sign of dedication belonging to this grade of wisdom.

He turns in succession to the four quarters and receives the sign of the grade from all present, the Master of the Temple excepted. The Guide turns to the Master, giving it on his own part.

Guide of the Paths: Honorable Master of the Temple, the parts of our personality are as a chariot, and the will that cleaves to God is the Spirit that rides therein, prevailing as a victor over all things, and imposing peace on all. They have given me the sign of this Spirit.

The sign is repeated by the Master.

MASTER OF THE TEMPLE: It was said: Let there be light and the same is perfect love.

The Master and Warden descend from their thrones and face east, with wands uplifted. All present face east.

MASTER OF THE TEMPLE: May we who have incurred the judgment, lest we die therein, be saved by the name of thy mercy, JEHOVAH TZABAOTH. Thy word is the protection of those who are united by faith in Thee. Send down the ambassador of Thy mercy, send down Thy Holy SHEKINAH to abide in us, fill of celestial benediction. Man cannot enter her hidden palace and behold her glorious face until he is reborn in Thee. Grant that after such regeneration we may live in her Holy Light and may die by the kiss of Thy SHEKINAH, that we may enter into the mystery of Thine union.

The Master and Warden turn again to the west, and with his wand uplifted:

MASTER OF THE TEMPLE: Fire of the heart and fire of the mind, fire of the will that seeks in God for wisdom. May the Spirit descend upon us in tongues of flame, and ~ even as flame leaps upward ~ so on the wings of purpose may we ascend to Him.

Then, with raised eyes and both arms uplifted:

MASTER OF THE TEMPLE: The peace of Messias be upon you and the blessing of the King of Peace. Depart in the fire of foreknowledge concerning His coming.

WARDEN OF THE TEMPLE: Go, but return at your call to the work of consecrated wills.

The Master and Warden return to their thrones, but remain standing.

MASTER OF THE TEMPLE: Fratres et Sorores, the palace of SHEKINAH is open to all prayers. Pray, therefore, for ever in our hearts; seek in our wills for ever the coming of the King. In the name of JEHOVAH TZABAOTH, in the name of Glorious Messias, I close this holy temple in the grade of Philosophus.

MASTER OF THE TEMPLE: (*Knocks four times rapidly*)

WARDEN OF THE TEMPLE: (*Knocks four times at a moderate pace*)

GUIDE OF THE PATHS: (*Knocks four times, pausing after each one*)

HERE ENDS THE RITUAL OF THE GRADE OF PHILOSOPHUS, AND HERE ENDS THE SECOND ORDER OF THE ROSY CROSS.

The Third Order of the Rosy Cross

World of Creation

Part I

The Ceremony of Reception

in the

Portal of the Third Order

Being

The Second Portal Grade

Privately Printed

1916

The Fellowship of the Rosy Cross

—

The Ceremony of Reception in the Portal of the Third Order

—

THE HIGH OFFICE OF OPENING THE HOLY PORTAL

—

The temple is arranged for the opening and for the first point as follows: The banners of the 25th, 26th and 24th paths are displayed in the east, in the order here given. The banner of the 26th path is immediately behind and above the throne of the Celebrant. The great symbols of the paths are suspended beneath the banners from the poles on which they are elevated. The diagram of the paths and grades is laid upon the altar, which is immediately in front of the Celebrant. The four elemental symbols are grouped about the diagram in their proper quarters thus:

- *The rose on the eastern side;*
- *The lamp on that of the south;*
- *The bowl of Earth on the west; and*
- *The vessel of sacramental Water on the north side.*

The pillars are towards the west, and on the floor between them is a square frame containing the four elemental tablets, with the Tablet of Union in their center.

The throne of the east is occupied by the Celebrant of the grade, who is saluted in the ceremony by the title of Master of the Portal. He is either the Imperator of the rite or his appointed substitute. He wears the vestments of the third celebrant in the grade of Adeptus Minor, namely, an orange cassock and cloak, and the proper jewel of the rose-cross, depending from a ribbon of blue silk. He carries the ordinary wand of the Imperator.

The officers of the inferior grades, wearing all vestments and insignia, are seated thus: The Auxiliary Frater Zelator in the farthest west, with Fratres Thurificans et Aquarius on his right and left respectively. They represent the position of Malkuth on the Tree, and they correspond to the grade of Zelator, in which the earth part or body of man is purified. The Guide of the Paths is seated in front of the Auxiliary Frater Zelator, and is thus at a short distance behind the pillars. He corresponds to the grade of Theoricus, located in the Sephira Yesod, and to the purification of the natural mind. The Master and Warden of the temple are seated in front of their respective pillars, and answer, as always, to the grades of Philosophus in Netzach and of Practicus in Hod respectively, as also to the will and the emotions. The Aquarius has the lustral water and aspergillus of his office. The Thurificans has charge of the thuribulum, from which incense issues freely. The officers of the inferior grades are all facing east.

If the temple should not have been opened previously in any grade of the First or Second Order, the ceremonial clothing of officers and members takes place in the manner prescribed by the Ritual of the Neophyte Grade, and the assoilment follows as usual. It is performed by the Master of the Portal. It should be noted that as technically and sometimes actually the officers of the First and Second Orders are not all of the 5 = 6 Grade, so therefore in this ceremony, which cannot be witnessed by anyone below the Portal of the Third Order, they are not all of necessity those appointed at the last Equinox and holding positions therefrom.

The prayer at the east having been recited, if necessary, the Celebrant turns to the west before the altar, and is thus at a short distance in front of his throne. The frater Aquarius comes up, following the course of the Sun, and lifts up his vessel for consecration, according to the prescribed form of the Neophyte grade, unless so consecrated already. Thereafter the Celebrant turns to the east, having frater Aquarius on his left, from whom he takes the vessel and aspergillus in exchange for his wand. He makes the sign of the cross with the aspergillus, and sprinkles water in the east.

CELEBRANT: Pure waters and holy waters; wells of the waters of life. In the name of the living Waters.

The Frater Aquarius goes before him, bearing his wand, and they circumambulate the temple. The Celebrant pauses and turns in the middle south, where he makes the sign of the cross with the aspergillus, and sprinkles thrice.

CELEBRANT: Cool waters and still waters; silent wells of soul. In the name of the waters of union.

He performs the same ceremony in the west.

CELEBRANT: Waters of creation; waters flowing back to their source. In the name of the waters of sanctification.

He performs the same ceremony in the north.

CELEBRANT: Influx descending from BINAH; waters of understanding. In the name of the waters of compassion.

He reaches the east for the second time, and there turning westward, lifts up the vessel of Water.

CELEBRANT: Behold, I have purified with Water.

Receiving his wand, he gives back the vessel and aspergillus. The Aquarius returns with the sun to his seat. The Frater Thurificans has risen and following the course of the sun, brings up his vessel of incense, which he elevates before the Celebrant, who consecrates it according to the prescribed form of the Neophyte grade, unless so consecrated already. The Celebrant turns to the east, having Frater Thurificans on his left, from whom he takes the thurible in exchange for his wand, makes the sign of the cross therewith, and offers incense in the east.

CELEBRANT: Fire which comes down from above; fire in the supernal world; In the name of that fire which enkindles.

The Frater Thurificans goes before the Celebrant, bearing his wand, as both circumambulate the temple. The Celebrant pauses and turns in the middle south, where he makes the sign of the cross with his thurible, and offers incense thrice.

CELEBRANT: Fire which rises upward; fire of the soul's aspiration. In the name of our fire of longing.

He performs the same ceremony in the west.

CELEBRANT: Fire of the outward splendor; fire of the indwelling glory. In the name of that glory which is Shekinah.

He performs the same ceremony in the north.

CELEBRANT: Fire of purgation in GEBURAH; holy fire of judgment. In the name of transmuting fire.

Again he reaches the east and there, facing westward, lifts up the thurible.

CELEBRANT: Behold, I have consecrated with Fire.

He returns the thurible and receives his wand. He takes his place at the throne of the east, but remains standing. There is now the pause of a moment. Frater Thurificans has resumed his proper place.

CELEBRANT: Fratres et Sorores in the Fellowship of the Rosy Cross, brethren of the concealed sanctuary, I say unto you that the sun has risen, with light and healing in its wings. Assist me, I pray you, to open that secret path which leads from the grade of Theoricus to the hidden portal in Tiphereth and the sanctuary of the Third Order.

All rise

CELEBRANT: Honorable Frater Theoreticus, Guide of the Paths and Grades, assure yourself that those who are present have known the offices of mercy which abide in the middle path and have passed in our sacred symbolism through the mystery of the second birth.

The Guide of the Paths comes up with the sun to the western side of the altar and there faces west.

GUIDE OF THE PATHS: Fratres et Sorores in the Fellowship of the Rosy Cross, give me the sign of the portal.

It is so done accordingly.

GUIDE OF THE PATHS: This is the answering sign.

It is given accordingly. The Guide of the Paths turns eastward, falling back in so doing towards the middle place of the temple, and there pausing:

GUIDE OF THE PATHS: Master of the Portal, they have made their dwelling in the mystic city, and are children of the second birth in the hidden temple of the heavenly school.

He returns to his place with the sun.

CELEBRANT: Honorable Frater Philosophicus, Master of the Lower Temple and expounder of the lesser mysteries communicated therein, your station heretofore has been ever on a throne of the east. Why are you located at the western end, with the officers under your charge?

MASTER OF THE TEMPLE: On the threshold of the path of Ayin, I am seated by the pillar of Light, at the southern side, to signify the sacramental element of Fire and the consecration of the will of man. I am the grace of the Sephira Netzach. I am in correspondence with the letter Yod.

CELEBRANT: Honorable Frater Practicus, Warden of the Lower Temple, why are you placed in the west, on the northern side?

WARDEN OF THE TEMPLE: On the threshold of the path of Ayin I am seated by the pillar of Darkness, to signify the sacramental element of Water and the consecration of the desires of man. I am the power of the Sephira Hod. I am in correspondence with the letter He.

CELEBRANT: Honorable Frater Theoreticus, Guide of the Paths and Grades, what is your symbolical situation in the precincts of the Portal?

GUIDE OF THE PATHS: On the threshold of the path of Ayin, with my fellow ministers and co-heirs of the Order, I await the opening of the path, that he whom I have brought so far in our mysteries may be directed by the middle way, even to the portal of Tiphereth. I signify the sacramental element of Air and the consecration of the mind of man. I am in correspondence with the letter Vau.

PORTAL INITIATION

CELEBRANT: Auxiliary Frater Zelator, what is your station in the temple?

FRATER ZELATOR: Most Honorable Master of the Portal, my place is in the nethermost west. I stand in the sphere of Malkuth, signifying the element of Earth and the consecration of the body of man. The Thurificans and Aquarius are beside me, bearing their mystical elements as symbols of the work of sanctity. Beyond Malkuth we have no part or office in the task of preparing the candidate. I am in correspondence with the final letter He.

CELEBRANT: Yod, He, Vau, He. Herein and herewith I communicate the sacred Name which is the synthesis of our research in the lower temples of the Fellowship. I have come forth from a sanctuary that is within, bearing the Rosy Cross upon my breast, and I testify that its sacred mystery is written in my heart. I stand before the portal of the Third Order, as the witness and the messenger thereof. I am the form which the door gives up. I convey the tidings of Tiphereth. Now, therefore, my brethren in the Fellowship of the Rosy Cross, assist me to form the sacred and worshipful Name which is entrusted in the path of Ayin to those who have entered therein.

MASTER OF THE TEMPLE: Yod

WARDEN OF THE TEMPLE: He

CELEBRANT: Shin

GUIDE OF THE PATHS: Vau

FRATER ZELATOR: He

MASTER OF THE TEMPLE: The Name is Yeheshua, the savior revealed within and the Life of the world to come.

CELEBRANT: It is the veil of a great mystery, which is opened to the purified man at the epoch of the second birth. By the sacred Name and the secret veil, I open the path of Ayin.

CELEBRANT: *Knocks*

MASTER OF THE TEMPLE: *Knocks*

Warden of the Temple: *Knocks*

Guide of the Paths: *Knocks*

Frater Zelator: *Knocks*

All are seated.

Here ends the solemn ceremony of opening the temple in the portal of the third order.

First Point
The Ritual of the 26ᵀᴴ Path

The Postulant is alone in the vestibule on a prie-dieu, in full light, with a scroll in his hands containing versicles proper to the time.

Celebrant: Fratres et Sorores, there is a door which opens from Tiphereth, and the grace of the sphere of beauty is communicated to the Sephiroth that are below. By the power in me vested as Chief of this sacred rite [**But in the case of a substitute**: By the power to me committed as a messenger of the Third Order], I have opened that door and have entered the temple which is below. Health and benediction, my brethren; light from the Rosy Cross; glory from the sun of Tiphereth. I testify also that the door opens inward for the reception of those who have been prepared in the outer ways, who carry the grace of the heights in their inmost hearts, who have turned their wills to God. I come as a herald from beyond, and my tidings are glad tidings. The time of probation is over; the days of strife are ended; and in all the parts and regions of his natural personality the dedication of our beloved Frater Adveniat Regnum (*vel nomen aliud*) is complete within the measures thereof. I have opened therefore the path of Ayin for his decreed advancement therein, and that he may receive the annunciation of his election at the Portal of the Third Order. Honorable Guide of the Paths, you have my authority to exercise your office of Mediator for the last time in respect of our Frater Frater Adveniat Regnum (*vel nomen aliud*). Seek him in the precincts without; bring him within our holy temple; place him at the western end, before the pillars of the path of Ayin, at the extremity of the Sephira Yesod.

PORTAL INITIATION

The Guide of the Paths rises in his place and gives the first sign of the Portal. Proceeding to the east, he takes the lamp from the altar and passes with the sun to the door.

GUIDE OF THE PATHS: I will show forth tidings of good. I will publish salvation. The ends of the earth shall see it. I will go forth in the brightness thereof, as a lamp that burneth.

He gives the closing sign and retires from the temple. The acting Ostiarius secures the door behind him. The seat of the Guide is removed.

CELEBRANT: Fratres et Sorores, may the vivifying rain of the secret doctrine refresh us in the wastes of time. May the Shekinah, which is an indwelling presence, bring us with both hands the bread of life. May we pass over the holy hills of incense and sacred mountains of myrrh. May the yoke of the kingdom be upon us, even the heavenly kingdom, the world to come, which is the world of the Holy One.

In the meantime, the Guide of the Paths has greeted the Postulant on the further side of the door, uplifting the lamp which he bears, as a sign of fire and light, and a sign of will.

GUIDE OF THE PATHS: I come in the light of life; I come in the life of light, the Light of the Christ-Life; and this is the life of rebirth. Glory be to God in the highest, and peace of the world to come for all who seek after God in the way of the Rosy Cross.

The Guide of the Paths prepares the Postulant by placing in his hands the lamp of sacramental Fire and about his neck the cross with equal arms, inscribed with the letters Yod-He-Vau-He and the letter Shin in the center.

GUIDE OF THE PATHS: The years of our spiritual life on earth are as certain moons following conception, during which the form of divine desire grows up within our manifest part. In a due season, clothed with this spiritual body, we shall issue forth and shall see with our own eyes that which all things now foreshadow, all faiths make evident.

The Guide of the Paths gives the battery of the Portal in the following form: Knocks four times in quick succession, pauses, knocks once.

The acting Ostiarius opens the door. The Guide of the Paths brings in the Postulant.

GUIDE OF THE PATHS: The mysteries are a singing voice. Let us enter the place of song. Let us hearken to the daughter of the voice.

The door is secured behind them.

CELEBRANT: He shall enter in peace. The secret doctrine is the Tree of Life for those who cultivate it. He shall enter the Kingdom of God. The law is the Tree of Life. He shall come forth with joy and be welcomed with gladness. The law is the waters of life.

The Guide leads the Philosophus to the western side of the temple, between the pillars.

CELEBRANT: Frater Adveniat Regnum (*vel nomen aliud*), I salute you by the mystical title of Pharos Illuminans, conferred on you in the grade of Philosophus. May your presence be as a tower of light in the midst of your peers. I have come from the secret places through a hidden Portal, bearing the titles of your advancement in a world unknown. Give me the symbol which you received in the 4=7 grade.

FRATER PHILOSOPHUS *(who is prompted by the Guide):* Master of the Portal, they gave me the symbol of Phrath, which is the fourth river of Eden.

CELEBRANT: I testify that it is the path of Ayin, by which you are called to ascend from the world of formation to that of Creation in God and the threshold of the Third Order. It is prolonged from the grade of Theoreticus, and from Yesod, wherein you stand, to the Holy Sephira Tiphereth. It is the path of a river of Light, and the temple is therefore in light. In front of you are the four tablets which have been bound about your personality, by the consecrations of the First and Second Orders. In the midst of them there now lies the tablet of union. It represents that which binds all parts of the personality together by a great act of dedication. I bid you therefore kneel down. (*The Philosophus is assisted by the Guide.*) Place both hands on the tablet of union. (*The Philosophus is assisted by the Guide.*) Bow your head reverently, as a token of humility and the will that is turned to God. Repeat your sacramental name, and say after me (*knocks*).

PORTAL INITIATION

All rise. The Guide takes charge of the lamp.

The Obligation

Celebrant: I, Frater Adveniat Regnum (*vel nomen aliud*), most solemnly swear that I will never communicate the secrets of this path and of the Portal of the Third Order, save only in the manner wherein and with the high authority whereby I here and now receive them. I undertake to maintain the veils between the Second and Third Orders. I invoke the four parts of my consecrated personality, the body by which I am manifested, the mind which is the seat of consciousness, the emotions and desires which uplift me, and the will which rules in all. May they bear witness to this my pledge. Deal with me in the righteousness of my intention, O just and righteous God. With all the powers of my being, hereby and hereon, I consecrate and dedicate myself to Thy service in the grades of the second birth. Send down on me, I pray Thee, the Light of the Spiritual Consciousness, that I may be truly reborn in Thee.

There is here a short pause.

Celebrant: Rise, searcher of the path, in the Portal of the Third Order.

The Guide of the Paths assists the Philosophus. He raises the tablets from their place between the pillars, and moving with the sun, restores them to their proper points in the temple. The tablet of union is fixed vertically to the western side of the altar. He returns to the right hand of the Postulant. The Celebrant and the brethren are seated, the Guide and his charge excepted. The lamp is restored to the Postulant.

Celebrant: There is a door which opens outward from each Sephira, and those who issue thereby enter the mystical path which leads to the next grade. There is a door which opens inward to each Sephira by a path of lawful traveling. There are three modes of communication upward with Tiphereth, but two of the doors are sealed. They open only from within, for the descent of influences.

The Guide of the Paths places the Philosophus in the middle way, between the pillars.

CELEBRANT: You bear in your hands the sacramental lamp, which is one of the characteristic symbols belonging to the Philosophical grade. Raise it to your forehead, my brother, to signify the lifting up of the will as an eternal sacrifice.

It is so done accordingly.

CELEBRANT: You stand now symbolically on the threshold of the 26th Path.

The Guide moves round the pillars with the sun, and faces the Postulant.

CELEBRANT: Honorable Guide of the Paths, as a minister of mercy and high priest of redemption, I bid you bring forth the Postulant. I bid the Postulant lift up his eyes eastward, looking toward the supernal heights or opposite to the world of Malkuth, wherein is the generation of the flesh.

Taking him by his two arms, the Guide of the Paths draws the Postulant through the pillars.

GUIDE OF THE PATHS: There is a river, the waters whereof shall make glad the City of God.

The Guide of the Paths is now standing by the side of the Philosophus, both looking toward the east, with the pillars immediately behind them.

MASTER OF THE TEMPLE: The shadow of the supernal hypostases is on you. You have dwelt beneath the wings of Shekinah. You are Israel, passing out of exile, and the great gates open to receive you.

WARDEN OF THE TEMPLE: Remember, O Pharos Illuminans, that gate which is the synthesis of all gates, the grade which is a crown of grades. By such gate and grade does man enter into the knowledge of the Holy One.

As the Guide moves forward, leading the Philosophus, and again pauses:
CELEBRANT: Who enters the middle path and the path of love, which is also the path of union? Who testifies concerning him?

PORTAL INITIATION

The Auxiliary frater Zelator rises with his assistants in the far west.

FRATER ZELATOR: With all the voices of the earth and in all its silence, I testify concerning him, our beloved frater Adveniat Regnum (*vel nomen aliud*). He knows that Divine Love is an eternal holocaust.

They are again seated, and the Guide again moves forward, leading the Philosophus, very slowly and reverently.

GUIDE OF THE PATHS: The path of spiritual consciousness is the path of the study of the secret doctrine. But those who would study the law must also keep it. The law is understood only in the intercourse of Holy Union.

In the middle part of the temple they are brought again to a pause by the voice of the Celebrant. The Philosophus is still holding the lamp near his forehead.

CELEBRANT: Wells of doctrine; deep wells; wells of Divine Doctrine; wells of love. Enter into the wells of doctrine. The study of the doctrine is the work among all works, the worship above all worship, the prayer of prayers.

The Guide again moves forward, leading the Philosophus, and they arrive at the western side of the altar. Taking the sacramental lamp from the hands of its bearer, and moving behind him, the Guide raises it over the head of the Philosophus.

GUIDE OF THE PATHS: Master of the Portal, I testify that the Postulant has traversed all the paths and dwelt in all the Sephiroth of the First and Second Orders; that the Divine Name ～ Yod, He, Vau, He has been restored in a sacrament within him; that with the zeal of his whole being he looks towards the second birth and the sacred letter of the spirit which completes the Divine Name. He bears it on the cosmic cross, which is the badge of his admission.

The Guide restores the lamp to the southern side of the altar. His seat has been replaced in the middle west beyond the pillars, and he returns thereto. The Celebrant rises and extends his hands above the Postulant's head.

CELEBRANT: Be thou therefore as one born among us into the mystery of God.

He resumes his seat. The pause of a moment follows.

CELEBRANT: Through whatever grades of our Order the Postulant may pass in this life, they are all symbolical stages of the ascent to the height, or otherwise of his return to the center. The diagram of paths and Sephiroth which lies before you on the altar depicts these stages. It delineates also the mystery of descent into manifestation, when the Soul had come forth from God. We are concerned with it in the former aspect, and you will see that the Sephirotic scheme has four chief divisions, corresponding to the Orders in our Fellowship. With two of these you are already familiar, having passed through the grades therein. You stand on the threshold of the Third, corresponding to Tiphereth, Geburah, and Chesed, the 5=6 grade of Adeptus Minor, the 6=5 grade of Adeptus Major, and the exalted grade of 7=4, being that of Adeptus Exemptus. Above these spheres there is the Supernal Triad, which involves the conception of a Fourth Order, subsisting in uttermost concealment ‑ like the Sephiroth to which it is referred. In symbolical advancement through the grades and worlds of our Fellowship, there is no point of entrance thereto or way of communication therewith, except in the great mystery of Daath. The four-fold division which I have indicated offers a perfect correspondence with the four worlds of the secret tradition in Israel. In Malkuth is the world of Assiah, to which the life of the body corresponds, and it is called the world of action. In our scheme of degrees, it is not the material world except in an individual sense, or so far as the Postulant is concerned. It is the world of his material purification. It is natural life and the light of outward things communicated through sacraments of sense. It contains the two grades of Neophyte and Zelator. Yetzirah is the world of formation, wherein are the three Sephiroth ‑ Netzach, Hod, and Yesod, corresponding to three inward parts of the natural man ‑ his will, emotions, and mind. The grades of Theoreticus, Practicus, and Philosophus are allocated to these sephiroth, and the world of Yetzirah in our system is that of formation in God, leading to rebirth in Him. Yesod is the source and cause of the second birth, and for this reason you have returned thereto in this sub-grade of the Portal. Hod is the reflected glory of the world to come, or the transmutation of outward things which corresponds to conversion within. Netzach is victory over the forces which impede rebirth. In the grade of Theoreticus, the purified mind conceives the theory of the world. In that of Practicus, the heart is the speaking witness, and beholds in its purified state the consequence of desire diverted from the true ends. The grade of Philosophus is that of the will in union. The Postulant stands symbolically on the threshold of a great experience, an opening of the spiritual mind, and has all desire thereof, all purpose turned thereto. It is the purpose of the new man. Briah is the world of creation, the place of those reborn in the likeness of Christ, and its three grades are mysteries of mystical life, death, and resurrection. Beyond these things is the world of Atziluth, being that of withdrawal in God.

There is here a short pause.

CELEBRANT: The banners before you represent the several paths which connect the grades and Sephiroth in the Second Order of the Rosy Cross with Tiphereth in the Order that is beyond. By the hypothesis of the paths and the Tree, as delineated in the altar diagram, you will observe that it is possible to proceed from the 4=7 grade of Netzach to that of 7=4 in Chesed (*The Celebrant here indicates the path of Lamed in the diagram*); but there is no ascent to the heights along this path, either in the Second or Third Order. It seems possible also to advance from the 3=8 grade of Hod to the 6=5 of Geburah (*The Celebrant indicates the path of Mem*); but this mode of progress is closed for ever to the Practicus. There remain, however, the 24th, 25th, and 26th Paths (*these also are indicated*), by which Tiphereth communicates with Netzach, Hod, and Yesod, or the grade of Adeptus Minor with the grades that are below. The threshold of this exalted sphere is reached by the vertical or middle path of Ayin (*it is indicated*), which you have just traversed symbolically. It was by a vertical path that you passed from the Sephira Malkuth, at the beginning of your journey upward. It is by the corresponding vertical path that you enter the Third Order. The path of Tau is the only vertical path traveled in the lower worlds, and it symbolizes the making of a good beginning. At this entrance or vestibule of the Third Order, you mark a definite and vital stage in your further progress. I commend to you the saving sense of another, a most new beginning. See that it is good and true within you, as it is true and holy without, in the world of symbols. So shall you be prepared to follow henceforth the perfect rule of the reborn.

The Celebrant descends from his throne and faces the east, by the altar, on the right side of the Philosophus.

CELEBRANT: The great symbols of the paths, displayed beneath their banners, reveal to you that in the nature of things there was no other path of ascent open than that which you have followed, namely, the 26th Path. The path of Nun, governed by the symbol of the sun, and leading from Netzach to Tiphereth, is forbidden to the Philosophus, though it would seem a direct way from the Sephira in which he has dwelt under the rule of purified will. But this symbol is one of attainment at the apex of the Christ Life, when he who in your person ~ the prototypical adept ~ is seeking the true light on the paths of return to God, shall have become an abider in light, a freeman of the Holy City and the eternal kingdom. The sun is the Cosmic Christ, the Christ Spirit, depicted as the light of the universe. The human figure immediately beneath it, with uplifted arms, is in the act of drawing down the Divine Light and diffusing it with extended healing hands, while it penetrates his own being. The solar image is therefore emblazoned on his breast. He has become, within his own measures, a prince of heaven and a manifestation of the Christ Spirit. The symbol ~ as a whole ~ reveals how the power and the majesty, the grace and glory of God encompass the whole creation, how that which came forth from Him, but fell away from its first perfection, is reinvested with the Light of His eternal beauty, through which, as through paths of sanctification, it is drawn again to Him and is a mediator of His Light to the world.

The symbol is shown to you at this stage of your progress as a glory of the unknown future which awaits you in the fulfillment of the great work of your rebirth. The path of Samech, governed by the symbol of Lucifer, and leading from Hod to Tiphereth, is forbidden by the laws of the hierarchy. The path is sealed to the Practicus, who has no title as such to enter the grade of Adeptus Minor, and it offers no means of progress to him who is already a Philosophus, for he does not return to Hod.

Remember, my brother, that you are following the path of liberation, but liberation is according to law. It is for this reason that there is a seal upon the path of Samech, and this seal is not broken. You will observe that the symbol beneath the banner of the path is in the likeness of him who was called the Son of the Morning and Light Bearer, rather than of Diabolus, or Satan. He is the Prince of this World, and the antithesis of the Christ Spirit, represented by the other symbol. It is for this reason that they are contrasted together in the paths. The Lucifer of this diagram is the desire after spiritual things, to empower the life of sense and to equip the mind in separation. He is the magus opposed to the saint, and the path of occult science in its contrast to the science of the mystics. The end of these things is bondage, represented by the chained figures shown beneath his altar in the symbol.

PORTAL INITIATION

Celebrant: That path of the secret tradition which corresponds to the letter Nun is in analogy with the gates of Light, of which the Keeper is said to be God, and with the heaven of the sun, which, in Christian tradition, is Christ, the sun of justice and of righteousness. It is held to be the ground of similitude in the likeness of beings and of things, and this is the sense in which the followers of Christ become partakers with Him, the Sons of God and the heirs of glory.

On the other hand, the path of Samech is that of temptation or of trial, and that which is our symbolism stands at the gate thereof to forbid our quest therein is called the sustaining God, while the obedience exacted is a test of mind applied to those whom God calls to his service.

And now, as to the *via media*, that path of Ayin which you have traversed, and the great symbol which it discovers for your instruction and support: you know that the middle paths, which are our way of ascent to the heights, are connected by their Sephiroth, and in these binds of union may be called a single path, which is the central pillar of benignity in the Tree of Life. The left-hand pillar is female and corresponds to severity in the symbolism. The right-hand pillar is male and corresponds to mercy. The middle pillar is bi-sexual, being the conjunction of right and left. The paths are the nexus which binds male and female together.

These things are to be understood, my brother, in the grace of the spirit and not according to the flesh, for I speak of Divine Mysteries. The key-note of our entire grade sequence is that earthly and heavenly life are both a work of marriages. At the beginning of his progress, the Neophyte was married to the quest. Male or female on the physical plane, the end of us each is union, or espousals within of the male and female sides in the Christ nature. But the Postulant must forget all sex-differentiations which belong to the body of things, because the union that he seeks is spiritual. It is only after rebirth that there can be new life, new, perfect and real nuptials.

Beneath the banner of the middle path is a symbol representing marriage. You were told in the 4=7 Grade that Shekinah is the feminine and Messiah is the male aspect of the Divine in manifestation. The union of both must be attained in us, and it is this which you see before you, the wedlock of the soul and the Christ natures, under the wings of Shekinah. The ascent into union by way of the middle pillar is the path to your own marriage. At the beginning it is like the upward breathing of a pure spirit, and the breath of the Spirit comes down. And till the great day of consummation the Spirit and the bride say, Come. The benign and gracious being who officiates at the espousals before you is also a symbol of the second birth in spiritual consciousness. She presides over marriages and births.

173

He who has attained to this state of regeneration in God shall draw, my brother, all parts of his personality into the redemption of the higher nature. He shall raise up his fallen Sephiroth, including Malkuth.

The Guide of the Paths comes up to the Philosophus. The Celebrant returns to his throne and standing with uplifted wand, continues:

CELEBRANT: Fratres et Sorores, it is within ourselves, and so only, that the Sephiroth which fall in us are in us also raised. And seeing that in the progress of our mystery we leave Malkuth to abide for a season in Tiphereth, it is indubitable that we take the lower Sephiroth into exaltation. And so all things shall be one, for the immemorial miracle of the one great work of the soul. Hereunto I pray that we who have been called of old, seeing that we are chosen also, may be dedicated, now and henceforward, world without end.

The Celebrant resumes his seat.

CELEBRANT: Honorable Guide of the Paths, you have my command to lead our beloved brother to the court of this temple. Leave him to meditate therein, praying for light and guidance, aspiring to that inward change which alone can open the portal of mystic life. He has traversed the middle path, and the analogical portal of our symbolism shall be revealed to him on his return.

The Guide conducts the Philosophus by south and west to the door, without passing through the pillars. They leave the temple. The Guide returns immediately, proceeds to his seat and says, standing thereat:

GUIDE OF THE PATHS: Lord, now lettest thou thy servants depart in peace, for our eyes have seen thy salvation in the union of Tiphereth and Malkuth.

The Celebrant rises in his place, with uplifted arms.

CELEBRANT: To the glory of thine elect, would without end; in the light which is perfect love; and this is the love of perfection.

He resumes his seat.

CELEBRANT: It is written that the princes shall lay away their robes.

In reverent and perfect silence, the officers of the First and Second Orders disrobe, putting away their vestments and insignia. The banners of the paths are removed and placed in the west. The altar is placed in the middle of the temple, and the pillars are set on either side of the throne in the east. The Banners of the East and West are on either side of the pillars. The seats of the other officers are removed, and they repair to their proper places among the ordinary members.

Here ends the ceremonial admission of a Frater Philosophicus into the path of Ayin.

SECOND POINT
THE PORTAL OF TIPHARETH

The Postulant is alone in the vestibule on a prie-deieu, in full light, with a scroll in his hands containing versicles on the mystery of the second birth.

The Guide again leaves the temple and stands for a few moments on the threshold with arms crossed upon his heart. In complete silence he proceeds to prepare the Postulant by placing about his neck the collar of a Master of the Temple, and putting into his hands the sacred symbol peculiar to the second point.

The Guide gives the battery of the grade of Adeptus Minor on the door of the temple, thus knocks four times in quick succession, pauses, then knocks once.

The Acting Ostiarius opens the door and admits them, after which it is again secured. As they pause within the threshold:

CELEBRANT: It is written, Thou art my Son, and this day have I begotten Thee.

The Guide of the Paths leads the Philosophus to a seat in the far west of the temple and then takes his own place among the unofficial brethren. That which follows lies solely between the Celebrant and the Postulant.

CELEBRANT: There is a door in Tiphereth which shall open for you, my brother. The emblazonment of visible signs does not appear thereon, but it is full of spiritual inscriptions. My throne is between the pillars thereof, and I symbolize the opening of the gate. In this sense I am the gate and way of your advancement. May it be unto you the spiritual portal of a path which leads to God. Through moons of probation, passed amidst purifying rites, through moons of quest and reflection, you have reached this stage in your pilgrimage, and it is here that the veil divides.

The Portal sub grade leading to the Third Order is a grade of rebirth in symbolism. May it be unto you an efficacious sacrament communicating the living experience within. So shall your consciousness enter into the state of union reflected from Tiphereth. So shall the Portal of the Adepts, by which you now stand, give entrance into new life, which is that of Christ in His Kingdom. You have reached it by that middle way which ~ as you were told in the 4=7 grade ~ is the path of return into unity. It was said to you in that grade that the sun of righteousness should rise. You had carried your cross previously through many paths of darkness, and now another has been given you to bear through a path of light. You took up that cross as directed and went in search of the sun. In this manner you have traversed the path of Ayin and have laid it down in purity.

Another title of admission has been granted in the symbol which you now bear. It shall be unto you a sign that the wings of the morning are uplifted in the orient of life. You will observe that in this symbol ~ to which I direct your attention in a special manner ~ the four living creatures of Ezekiel's vision are grouped together in correspondence with the inward meaning of your progress through the lower grades of our Fellowship. Leo at the summit signifies the grade of Philosophus and the dedication of your natural will. The bull at the lowermost point represents Malkuth and the consecration of your earthly body in the grade of Zelator. The man corresponds to Yesod, the grade of Theoreticus and the purification of your natural mind. The eagle has referenced to Hod, to the 3=8 grade of Practicus, and to the human emotions and desires which are hallowed therein. In the center of all is the white wheel of the spirit, the sign of the cosmic Christ, of the second birth and the Christ life in man. The four living creatures correspond in the secret tradition to the angels of the four quarters, and to the Divine names emblazoned thereon. They are the synthesis of the elemental tablets, and the wheel of the Ogdoad corresponds to the tablet of union. We learn also that the four sacramental elements of which man is said to have been made ~ which were gathered by the Elohim from the four quarters of heaven, and are analogous to the parts of our personality ~ will be ruled as a kingdom by those who obey the law, or ~ in other words ~ that man is detached by sanctity from the bondage of elemental life. But that by which he is liberated is the wheel of the spirit, dwelling in the center of his personality.

The cross which you carried in the path of Ayin and have now laid down at the threshold of the sacred Portal, will hereafter carry you. One of its correspondences is now shown to you in the east, borne upon the heart of the messenger who has come to you from the grades beyond. I am sealed with the Rosy Cross, and you should know that the rose in its highest understanding is a symbol of the Divine Principle operating in you and in humanity, so that the evil which is scarlet in our nature may become whiter than snow, and that the whiteness of regenerated life may be incarnadined by Divine Fire. How is that Fire communicated? It is an operation of the second birth, and the experience therein constitutes a secret doctrine, the students of which are themselves compared to roses. In this sense the rose is the Israel of God, the chosen souls of the sanctuary, and the thorns which encompass the rose form a purifying cross, from the midst of which springs up the perfect flower of election. The five petals correspond to the five virtues which lead to perfection, namely, love of God, chastity, charity, humility, and steadfastness in the experience which is called a study of the secret doctrine. But these virtues are great mystical paths. They are also five manners of wounding, by which the Adept is crucified to his lower self-center, and to that which is perishable in the world, for the manifestation of the Divine within him.

The rose is also a chalice, and its mystery is that of the chalice of salvation. It is lastly the cup of benedictions. These modes of interpretation, with many others, their seeming divergence notwithstanding, are one at the root, as a branch of many roses springing from a single stem. Except in a secondary sense, or in the world of simple images, the rose does not typify material desire immolated on the cross of suffering. On the deep personal side it represents the beatific vision, which only unfolds on the cross, though it is formulated in this temple from very far away. Those who attain the vision ~ thereby and thereon ~ bow their heads and say: It is finished. Thereafter is the indrawn state in which consciousness enters into union. You should understand further that the vision ~ as the banner of the east exhibits ~ is manifested on a background of purity. It is the simplicity and singleness and detachment and continence, concerning which it may be said that he who is sealed therewith shall be opened to Divine secrets, even as the Lamb slain from the foundation of the world opened the book of life. Love and understanding are the keys, the motive and the harmony of that world.

We have spoken to you of many hallowings, and I invite you, at this stage more especially, to remember the will in union, which is the deeper meaning of its consecration in the grade of Philosophus. This is the state in which the sons and daughters of the doctrine, who have become familiar by experience with the mysteries of the way, the truth and the life, are declared to be little children. They have graduated in conformity, in that union of the human with the Divine will which is an earnest of the ineffable union. It is the condition of the opening of the eyes, so that the eyes see and the heart realizes the eternal subject of research.

What is it that dawns upon the soul in the Neophyte grade? The blind sense of want, a great desire, some deeper sense of want, a longing for reality, the burden of darkness, and thereafter a first suggestion of twilight before morning. The path of search becomes a path of dedication, and this has brought you to the threshold of higher light, where in place of the desire of the Spirit there should be realization of Its abiding presence.

As a son of the paths, you have traversed the path of love. I now bid you arise. Lift up the symbol you carry. Let it rest on your forehead, supported by the two hands. Go up to the altar of God. Place the symbol on the altar. Retire into your inward self. Think well of the parts of your personality, united and made perfect in the presence of the abiding Spirit, as the Life of the life therein. I call upon you now to depose your nature, thus completed, on the supernal altar of burnt offerings before the Divine Will.

While the Postulant bends over the altar, there is silence for some moments, and thereafter the Celebrant rises with uplifted arms.

CELEBRANT: O Frater Pharos Illuminans, the Lord Himself enlighten thee. This is thine offering. The Lord thy God accept thee. This is conformity.

The Celebrant resumes his seat.

CELEBRANT: It is by such unreserved dedication in all stages of the work that those who are called on earth to an experimental knowledge of the Life of life become elect thereto; those who are chosen become heirs at law; and the heirs enter into their heritage. You have now made your offering on the threshold of the inner temple. This is the court of its tabernacle. The years of strife are ended. I have prayed for peace in all your habitations. The price is paid. May the peace that is signed in Heaven be declared also on earth. The time of probation is over. I have come through a gate of peace. Behold, I have come quickly, lest your steps should err in the paths. Come hither. The door is behind me. I have opened the ways thereto. You shall enter and go in.

The Postulant has approached as directed, and is now standing opposite the throne in the east.

CELEBRANT: May you enter, by the practice of the presence of God, into consciousness of God in the spirit, of God who is within. Let your heart be filled with holy expectation, and you shall hear in a high symbolism the Divine Voice speaking in the universe, the Christ-Spirit giving testimony concerning Itself, and concerning the path of your attainment.

The Celebrant rises, and still standing on the dais of his throne, speaks.

CELEBRANT: By the power in me vested, as Master of the Portal (or *in the case of a substitute*: By the power to me committed), I testify that the veil of the inner temple opens on the cross, and I give you the opening sign.

This is done with extended arms and open palms. The sign is repeated by the Postulant.

CELEBRANT: It is the Sign of Messias extended on the Sephirotic cross, with the head resting on Daath, the arms reaching to Gedulah and Geburah, and the feet established on Malkuth. There is represented in this manner the descent of the Divine Influences from the three supernals through the temples of the Rosy Cross, their members, and the postulant passing through the various grades. There is also a closing sign, which is given thus, by crossing the arms upon the breast. (*The postulant repeats the sign after the Celebrant*). It signifies the reception of the influences into the heart of the postulant, in common with the whole Brotherhood of the Rosy Cross. The word of the Portal is Yeheshuah, which is at once a Divine Name in the personal and universal sense, signifying the Christ manifest in life and time, and the cosmic Christ. It is formed by placing the sacred letter Shin in the center of the four letters Yod, He, Vau,. He, which are read by us as Jehovah. You know that these letters are inscribed on the laminae of the officers in the worlds of symbolism through which you have passed, under the obedience of the Rosy Cross. They signify the purified state of the four parts of personality, to which the officers correspond. The Third Order is concerned with the quest and attainment of that state which is symbolized by the letter Shin. Therefore, this sacred letter is emblazoned in the center of the rose on the Rosy Cross which I bear. I invest you with the corresponding jewel of the Third Order. See that you keep it in purity and remember the quest that you follow, being that of the Christ-state. Brother of the Rosy Cross, I look to your creation in God.

The Celebrant takes the hand of the Postulant and draws him round, so that he faces to the west. While still holding him by the hand:

CELEBRANT: To all who have entered the Portal, to the Fratres et Sorores in all grades of Adeptship, I proclaim that our Frater Adveniat Regnum (*vel nomen aliud*) is a son of the path of love, and that he stands on the threshold of Tiphereth.

The Celebrant resumes his seat.

CELEBRANT: You will now take your place among the brethren of the Third Order, toward the east of the temple.

The Postulant is directed accordingly and takes his seat.

CELEBRANT: Fratres et Sorores, when the veil of the temple is parted by reverent and holy hands, moving from within, the Holy Voice says unto each as he enters: Come in peace. The offices of our Fellowship are therefore offices of mercy, reflected from the supreme Crown. Kether is a world of mercy, the place where there is neither sorrow nor wrath, neither separation, but glory and splendor, grace, and joy. It is also supernal loving kindness, which is communicated to Chokmah as the beginning and end of all, and Chokmah is the door by which there is entrance to the King of heaven. It is good pleasure and benevolence, and in the Sephira Chesed it passes into manifested love. But by Chesed the world was made, and all the Sephiroth below are saturated with benignity therefrom. The four worlds of the Rosy Cross are therefore worlds of love, and the grades of the Third Order are high palaces thereof. Holiness, love, the works by which we are judged, the goodwill that consecrates works, the Divine intention which is their substance, the repose that remains for all who have turned to God in their hearts, the purity which is the quintessence of moral life, and God as all in all; hereof is our sum of perfection. And hereof also, O Frater Adveniat Regnum (*vel nomen aliud*), is the prospect extending before you. Searcher of the great secret, that stone of the wise which we pray to attain in this Order ~ I testify that the white stone, the true medicine thereof, and the Divine tincture, are in our inward nature. Was it not said to you of old that God is within? When the Divine Spirit is declared in our consciousness, then is the secret found. This is the doctrine of Light, and where is that Light, my Brother? Our tradition tells us that it is in the center of the Holy Cross; but this is an allegory of our own nature and another formulation of that work to which you are called henceforth. Innocent of hands and clean of heart, you will go up the mountain of the Lord in the following of that work. Remember, the temple on its summit and the aspiration of the sons and daughters of desire which beats about its golden gates. This is the last message which I deliver from the throne of the Portal. It takes us where we should be always in spirit ~ to the throne of God. But, Fratres et Sorores, and all ye chosen hearts ~ this is Atziluth.

This ends the ceremony of admission to the Portal of the Third Order.

THE HIGH OFFICE OF CLOSING THE HOLY PORTAL

The minutes of receptions into the Portal of the Third Order are read in the grade of Adeptus Minor. The temple cannot be reduced from the grade of the Portal to that of Neophyte, and no official business is therefore transacted.

CELEBRANT: Fratres et Sorores, assist me to close this holy temple according to the ritual of the 26th Path, and in the grade appertaining to the Portal of the Third Order.

All Rise.

CELEBRANT: (*Knocks Once*) To order, Fratres et Sorores.

He descends from the throne and faces east, with arms extended in the opening sign of the grade.

CELEBRANT: I have entered, O merciful Father, behind the veil of the temple. I have seen the glorious sun of Tiphereth. But I know that there is another world of splendor, another and more glorious sun. O, after all the radiance of the natural world, after the golden dawn and the noonday radiance, after Thy sunset lights, and behind the spiritual transfiguration of outward things, give unto us Thine own light, the true illumination that is within, the inexpressible splendor of Thy presence, and the Glory of Thy Perfect Union.

The Celebrant returns to his throne, but remains standing.

CELEBRANT: Fratres et Sorores, I declare that the word is Yeheshuah, the salvation of Christ manifest.
He gives the closing sign.

CELEBRANT: In and by that name, and in accordance with the mystic sign, I close this holy temple.

He gives the battery of the grade, knocks four times in quick succession, pauses, knocks once.

HERE ENDS THE RITUAL OF THE PORTAL OF THE THIRD ORDER.

The Third Order of the Rosy Cross

World of Creation

Part II

The Pontifical Ceremony of Admission
to the Grade of Adeptus Minor

5 = 6

Privately Printed

1917

The Celebrants of the Grade

The Chief Adept: *Holding by investiture the august grade of 7=4, being that of an authorized teacher. He is the living symbol of the Sephira Chesed and is the spokesman of the highest grade in the Third Order. His title of nobility is Merciful Exempt Adept.*

The Second Adept: *Holding by institution the most secret grade of 6=5. He represents the Sephira Geburah and is the spokesman of the mystery therein. His title of honor is Mighty Adeptus Major.*

The Third Adept: *Who is preferably a senior member in the grade of 5=6. He is a living symbol of the Sephira Tiphereth and is the spokesman of Adepti Minores. His official title is Auxiliary Frater Adeptus.*

In addition to the Celebrants there is a Servient Frater who acts as Keeper of the Threshold and Usher of the Grade. He is the last admitted therein, and the postulant is more especially in his charge. His proper title is Honorable Frater Custos Liminis.

Unofficial members are addressed as honorable Fratres et Sorores.

THE ROBES AND JEWELS OF CELEBRANTS AND MEMBERS

THE MERCIFUL EXEMPT ADEPT: *Wears a cassock and robe of violet. He is girt about the waist with a citrine girdle, with which color the hood of his robe is lined. His biretta is of violet, having the square of Chesed on the front, emblazoned in gold. The symbol of salt is embroidered on the left side of his robe. His collar is of citrine silk, from which depends the Symbolum Magnum of the Rose-Cross, which he alone is entitled to wear ~ in virtue of his office. He carries a wand surmounted by the figure of the risen Christ.*

THE MIGHTY ADEPTUS MAJOR: *Wears a cassock and robe of red. He is girt about the waist with a green girdle, with which color the hood of his robe is lined. His biretta is of red, having the pentagram of Geburah on the front, emblazoned in gold. The symbol of sulphur is embroidered on the left side of his robe. His collar is of green silk, from which depends a golden pentagram, having a red rose of five petals in the center. He bears a wand surmounted by a white double cube, inscribed on the four sides with the letters Yod, He, Vau, He, and on the summit a Shin, all in pure gold.*

THE AUXILIARY FRATER ADEPTUS: *Wears a cassock and robe of orange color. He is girt about the waist with a blue girdle, with which color the hood of his robe is lined. His biretta is of orange, having the hexagram of Tiphereth in the front, emblazoned in gold. The symbol of mercury is embroidered on the left side of his robe. His collar is of blue silk, from which depends the particular symbol of the Rose-Cross belonging to the grade of Adeptus Minor. He bears a wand surmounted by a crucifix.*

THE HONORABLE FRATER CUSTOS LIMINIS: *Wears the ordinary clothing of the Adepti Minores, which is a white cassock with an orange scarf or girdle and a collar of blue silk, from which depends a gold Calvary cross, having a red rose of five petals at the meeting point of the arms. He carries a wand surmounted by a dove of peace, similar to that of an Ostiarius in the worlds below Tiphereth.*

The colors of the robes worn by the three Celebrants represent: solar orange ~ the sun of righteousness in Christ, the splendor of mind, when illuminated by a certain grade of consciousness in God; red ~ the victory of the soul, which overcomes death in love; violet ~ royalty of the risen life and the will perfected in God.

The unofficial clothing worn by the Imperator of the order in the grades of the Third Order is the ordinary white cassock and orange girdle, with the addition of a collar of white silk, from which depends a gold lamina having the sacred Ogdoad emblazoned within its circle also in gold.

N.B. The crown of the biretta is cruciform, with a rose of five petals at the meeting point of the arms, but this rose is of the same color as the biretta itself.

The Fellowship of the Rosy Cross

—

THE SOLEMN OFFICE OF OPENING THE
HOUSE AND SANCTUARY OF ADEPTS

—

The arrangement of house and sanctuary follows the unwritten precedents. The veil is before the sanctuary. The brethren of the house have assembled, wearing their white robes, the scarf or girdle of the grade to which they belong and the Rose Cross of Tiphereth. The three Celebrants have assumed their vestments and insignia. They take up the wands of the rite and repair to their invariable stations, as guardians of the veil. The proper seat of the Servient Frater Adeptus is by the door of the holy house, as Keeper of the Threshold. All brethren are seated in silence and recollection.

ADEPTUS EXEMPTUS: *Knocks three times.*

ADEPTUS MAJOR: *Knocks once.*

ADEPTUS MINOR: *Knocks once.*

All Rise.

ADEPTUS EXEMPTUS: Salvete, Fratres et Sorores Roseae et Aureae Crucis.

ADEPTUS MAJOR: Health and benediction in the Lord.

AUXILIARY FRATER ADEPTUS: Vigilate, Fratres et Sorores.

ADEPTUS EXEMPTUS: Honorable and Adept brethren, assist me to open the house of the Holy Spirit, in the heart and the inmost heart, in the manifest life of nature and in spiritual consciousness as the sun of the life of life.

There is here the pause of a moment.

ADEPTUS EXEMPTUS: Honorable Frater Custos Liminis, see that the door of the house is sealed against all intrusion with the watchword: God is within.

This is done accordingly, and thereafter the Keeper of the Threshold bends in salute, with arms crossed upon his breast.

FRATER CUSTOS LIMINIS: Merciful Exempt Adept, the seal is on the threshold of the house, and I testify that the sacred watchword is held in everlasting remembrance.

ADEPTUS EXEMPTUS: Mighty Adeptus Major, by what sign do we open the house of the spirit and its holy sanctuary?

ADEPTUS MAJOR: By the sign of Messias extended on the Sephirotic cross.

He has given the opening sign.

ADEPTUS EXEMPTUS: Auxiliary Frater Adeptus, what is its inward meaning?

AUXILIARY FRATER ADEPTUS: It is the sign of dividing the veil, signifying the dissolution of the veils of matter for the revelation of the life of the Spirit and the opening of the holy sanctuary for the admission of the postulant therein.

ADEPTUS EXEMPTUS: Mighty Adeptus Major, what is the deeper meaning?

ADEPTUS MAJOR: Merciful Exempt Adept, the symbolic veil is that of the holy of holies, and I testify that the veil is Christ, manifest to eyes of flesh.

ADEPTUS EXEMPTUS: Auxiliary Frater Adeptus, by what sign do we close the house of the spirit and its holy sanctuary?

AUXILIARY FRATER ADEPTUS: By the sign of the Spirit received and abiding in the heart of the brotherhood.

He has given the closing sign.

ADEPTUS EXEMPTUS: Mighty Adeptus Major, what is its inward meaning?

ADEPTUS MAJOR: This also is twofold. It signifies the closing of the veils of matter behind the postulant when he has entered and gone in. But according to the deeper sense, it testifies to the necessity and perpetuity of Christ manifest as the tabernacle of Christ mystical. The veil of this temple opens, but the veil is not rent. It dissolves, and again is fixed. It is neither changed nor removed.

ADEPTUS EXEMPTUS: Yod

ADEPTUS MAJOR: He

AUXILIARY FRATER ADEPTUS: Shin

ADEPTUS MAJOR: Vau

AUXILIARY FRATER ADEPTUS: He

ADEPTUS EXEMPTUS: Yeheshuah

AUXILIARY FRATER ADEPTUS: Holy, holy, holy ~ the veil of the Sanctum Sanctorum.

ADEPTUS EXEMPTUS: Mighty Adeptus Major, what is that sacred word that keeps the threshold of the house on the hither side of the portal?

ADEPTUS MAJOR: It is the affirmation of absolute being ~ Aleph, He, Yod, He ~ reflected from the crown of the three. It signifies I am, and every brother of the Rosy Cross who can utter it in the true sense, or in God who is all in all, has attained the term of our research.

ADEPTUS EXEMPTUS: Auxiliary Frater Adeptus, what is the mystical number of this grade, derived from that sacred word?

AUXILIARY FRATER ADEPTUS: In the sequence of orders and of rites, the number is twenty-one.

ADEPTUS EXEMPTUS: Mighty Adeptus Major, what is the house of the Holy Spirit?

ADEPTUS MAJOR: A ghostly palace, a secret church of the elect, a school of mystical love.

ADEPTUS EXEMPTUS: Auxiliary Frater Adeptus, where is the holy house symbolically situated, and on what is it built?

AUXILIARY FRATER ADEPTUS: On the place of holy mysteries, the invisible mountain of the wise. Its foundation is the corner stone, and that stone is Christ mystical.

ADEPTUS EXEMPTUS: Mighty Adeptus Major, how was this secret mountain designated by the elder stewards of the mysteries?

ADEPTUS MAJOR: As Mons Abiegnus, the mount of firs, but the reference is more especially to the sacred fir-cone, the symbolical cone of the ancient mysteries. It is the place of reception, progression and final attainment. In its most withdrawn sense, the cone signifies the enfolded meanings and symbols of the written word, the manifold interpretation of things signified without. And the mountain is the place of ascent, the scale of perfection and the journey of the soul in God. On the summit thereof we look to greet in peace at the term of quest, when the desire of the eyes and the heart is at length attained by the soul.

ADEPTUS EXEMPTUS: Auxiliary Frater Adeptus, how is the mountain designated in the tradition of the Rosy Cross?

AUXILIARY FRATER ADEPTUS: It is the true Horeb and Calvary, whereon is the true Zion, a house of living bread.

ADEPTUS EXEMPTUS: Mighty Adeptus Major, what is the sanctuary of the house?

ADEPTUS MAJOR: It is the most sacred place of the mystery, revealed in the Third Order and attained by the soul in Christ.

ADEPTUS EXEMPTUS: What are the modes of this mystery, as shown forth in the holy grade of Adeptus Minor?

ADEPTUS MAJOR: Life, death and resurrection ‒ the life that follows re-birth, mystical and divine death, and the glory of those who come forth from the great darkness, restored in union.

ADEPTUS EXEMPTUS: Auxiliary Frater Adeptus, how is the sanctuary of the house delineated on the external side of our tradition?

AUXILIARY FRATER ADEPTUS: It is the sepulcher of our beloved found-er, Christian Rosy Cross, which he made in the likeness of the universe, as a door that is entered at birth and a temple opening from earthly into spiritual life. It is said that he reposed at the center, because this is the point of perfect rest at the seat of activity.

ADEPTUS EXEMPTUS: Mighty Adeptus Major, what is implied by the name of our mystical Founder?

ADEPTUS MAJOR: The rose of Christ manifested on the cross of human personality.

ADEPTUS EXEMPTUS: Auxiliary Frater Adeptus, of what configuration is the sanctuary?

AUXILIARY FRATER ADEPTUS: It is a figure of seven equal sides, signify-ing the life of nature and the grace that is behind nature.

ADEPTUS EXEMPTUS: Mighty Adeptus Major, to what are these seven sides referred in their deepest sense by the law of correspondence between things above and below?

ADEPTUS MAJOR: To the seven operations of grace in the holy spirit of man; to the seven days of our creation in the likeness of God, who is our end; to the lower Sephiroth, which are seven; to the planets, which are also seven; and to the seven maxims of the golden rule by which they are spiritualized in the grades of the Rosy Cross. For the great mystical number prevails in the height above, even as in the depth beneath, and in the lesser as in the greater world.

ADEPTUS EXEMPTUS: Auxiliary Frater Adeptus, by what gate do we enter the holy sanctuary?

AUXILIARY FRATER ADEPTUS: Est Omnis Anima Venus. It is entered through the gate of the mystical planet Venus, and a spouse is promised to the soul.

ADEPTUS EXEMPTUS: Mighty Adeptus Major, what is the presence in the sanctuary?

ADEPTUS MAJOR: It is the eternal love, in virtue of which God is immanent in nature, the lamb is slain from the foundation of the world and Christ abides within us.

ADEPTUS EXEMPTUS: Auxiliary Frater Adeptus, what is the office of the postulant?

AUXILIARY FRATER ADEPTUS: To pass within the veil and by his own love and desire to awaken that which is within.

ADEPTUS EXEMPTUS: Mighty Adeptus Major, what is the outward sign that I wear here on my heart, and what is its inward meaning?

ADEPTUS MAJOR: It is the Sacramentum Magnum of the Rose-Cross, typifying the eternal word that is hidden in nature and the manifestation of the expounded word. It is the harmony and development of all Rose-Cross symbolism, and it has many meanings belonging to the greater mysteries.

ADEPTUS EXEMPTUS: Auxiliary Frater Adeptus, what is the wand of office that you bear in your right hand?

AUXILIARY FRATER ADEPTUS: The sign of the word made flesh and manifested in human life. It is for this reason that man is the key of all things and the cross is the sign of glory. The letters emblazoned thereon are I...N...R...I... containing the mystery of the key. It is a great mystery of being.

ADEPTUS EXEMPTUS: Mighty Adeptus Major, what is the message implied by your wand of office?

ADEPTUS MAJOR: It is that which goes before and comes after, life in the hidden state, the unspoken word and the silence of the word withdrawn. The cubic altar of incense unfolds as a cross of life. The Christ life is a sacrifice, as an incense offered on the altar of God. But after the perfect oblation, the cross of life folds up its arms in sanctity, and life is withdrawn in God. The cross returns into the cube, and the word make flesh is hidden in the rock-hewn sepulcher. The letters emblazoned hereon are Yod, He, Shin, Vau, He and I testify that there is no other name given unto man whereby he shall be saved. It is therefore the grand word of the grade.

ADEPTUS EXEMPTUS: The sign of resurrection is uplifted on my wand of office. I am He who testifies thereto from the height of the Third Order, and I bear faithful witness, in the mystery of the risen word, which overcomes death and is clothed with power and glory. The letters of this mystery are LVX, and this is the Light of the world.

There is here the pause of a moment.

ADEPTUS EXEMPTUS: Auxiliary Frater Adeptus, what are the words inscribed on the door of the holy sanctuary, and how is it guarded?

AUXILIARY FRATER ADEPTUS: The words are: Post Centum Viginti Annos Patebo. The door is guarded by the sacred letter Shin, which is that of the Christ Spirit. It is written; his days shall be 120 years. And it is during this symbolical period that the spirit of Christ strives with the spirit of man. When man has completed his age, the number 120 is reduced to the mystical ogdoad by an operation of three and five, producing the Christ number and the number of rebirth. The triad rules in all things, and the grace of the pentad is declared in the spirit of man, that Christ may be all in all.

The Honorable Frater Custos Liminis, as Usher of the Grade, gives a battery of one knock. The veil is parted by the Second and Third Celebrants.

The Celebrant in Chief opens the door of the sanctuary to its full extent. He passes between the other Celebrants, who face inward with uplifted wands. He enters the sanctuary and proceeds with the sun to the due east, where he turns and faces west. The Second Celebrant proceeds to the south of the altar and the Third Celebrant to the north. They face inwards. The three Celebrants are standing erect, with wands uplifted in their right hands, and with their left hands placed upon the heart.

ADEPTUS EXEMPTUS: Aleph, He

ADEPTUS MAJOR: Yod, He

AUXILIARY FRATER ADEPTUS: Ehyeh

ADEPTUS EXEMPTUS: It is written; Before Abraham was, I am.

ADEPTUS MAJOR: Whom say ye that I the Son of Man am?

AUXILIARY FRATER ADEPTUS: Christ, the power of God and the wisdom of God.

ADEPTUS EXEMPTUS: I, N

ADEPTUS MAJOR: R

AUXILIARY FRATER ADEPTUS: I

ADEPTUS EXEMPTUS: Yeheshua

ADEPTUS MAJOR: Nazaraeus

AUXILIARY FRATER ADEPTUS: Rex Judaeorum

ADEPTUS EXEMPTUS: LUX, the Light of the world.

The Second and Third Celebrants proceed direct to the door and stand on either side, facing inward.

The Celebrant in Chief comes round with the sun and passes through, saying:

ADEPTUS EXEMPTUS: May we who are many be one body in Christ, one mind and a soul that is one in his union.

The door being now ajar and the Celebrants standing in their places:

AUXILIARY FRATER ADEPTUS: Fratres et Sorores, in the name of our great master and by the titles of the Christhood, I open this house of the spirit (*knocks once*).

ADEPTUS MAJOR: (*Knocks Once*)

ADEPTUS EXEMPTUS: I have opened its holy sanctuary (*knocks three times*).

The opening sign of the grade is given by all present.

Here ends the solemn office of opening the house and sanctuary of the Adepts.

THE FIRST POINT

The altar is removed from the sanctuary and placed in the center of the temple. The Rose-Crucifix, lamp, cup, poniard and chain are left upon the sacred symbols to which they appertain. The holy cross of obligation has been erected in the center of the sanctuary. The door of the sanctuary is shut and the veil is drawn across it. The Celebrants take their seats and also the Honorable Frater Custos Liminis.

The candidate is alone on a prie-dieu in the vestibule, in full light, with a scroll in his hands containing versicles on crucified life.

The Merciful Exempt Adept gives a battery of one knock.

ADEPTUS EXEMPTUS: Honorable Fratres et Sorores, blessed is he who cometh in the name of the Lord, looking for the Light of His glory.

The Keeper of the Threshold rises, with the opening sign of the grades.

FRATER CUSTOS LIMINIS: I testify concerning our frater Adveniat Regnum (*vel nomen aliud*) who stands on the threshold of Tiphereth. He has been prepared in the outer ways and the temple of inward grace has been made ready to receive him.

ADEPTUS EXEMPTUS: Honorable Frater Custos Liminis, go forth and admonish the aspirant that now is the accepted time and that the sun of salvation shines in the house of beauty. As procurator of the temple, prepare him on your part and bring him to the holy precincts.

The Keeper of the Threshold gives the closing sign of the grade and leaves the temple, securing the door behind him.

ADEPTUS EXEMPTUS: Auxiliary Frater Adeptus, guard the hither side of the portal. By the power to me committed, and in accordance with faithful testimony, open to those who knock.

The Auxiliary Frater Adeptus rises with the signs of the grade and takes his place by the door, where he remains standing.

ADEPTUS MINOR INITIATION

ADEPTUS EXEMPTUS: Fratres et Sorores, the holy mysteries do ever recall us to that one way that has been known and declared from of old.

ADEPTUS MAJOR: Many lights show forth the Father of Lights, and the darkness testifies concerning Him.

ADEPTUS EXEMPTUS: We confess that we have aspired to the crown, seeing that we are children of the King, and we look for the glory of God, praying that it shall be made manifest.

ADEPTUS MAJOR: From the natural life of man there extends a certain narrow path, even unto the crown of all, and this path is called magnanimity.

ADEPTUS EXEMPTUS: The middle place therein is adorned by the title of beauty, and the sun of beauty shines in the zenith thereof.

ADEPTUS MAJOR: It is made known that the light of the soul is even as the light of the sun. Let us therefore look up, because salvation is near.

These versicles should be recited clearly and somewhat slowly, with certain pauses between, as they are designed to occupy the time during which the candidate is prepared.

While this takes place in the temple, the Usher of the Grade has greeted the postulant in the vestibule, saying:

FRATER CUSTOS LIMINIS: Man enters into his true self as a priest into the holy place.

The Usher of the Grade prepares the postulant, who should already have assumed his cassock, by clothing him with the robe and collar belonging to a Master of the Temple in the grades below the portal of the Third Order. While doing so:

FRATER CUSTOS LIMINIS: We desire to put off imperfection and to be clothed in God.

Thereafter the Usher of the Grade leads the postulant to the door of the temple and sounds the battery of the grade with a certain force and distinction, thus: knocks three times, pauses, knocks twice.

The Auxiliary Frater Adeptus opens the door saying:

AUXILIARY FRATER ADEPTUS: Blessed and holy is he who shall enter into real knowledge. Wisdom and understanding meet to pour their influx upon him.

The Usher of the Grade has entered leading the postulant. The door is secured behind them. The Auxiliary Frater Adeptus returns to his seat. The Usher of the Grade conducts the postulant to an open space on the eastern side of the altar, and faces him toward the east.

FRATER CUSTOS LIMINIS: Merciful Exempt Adept, I present to you our beloved Frater Adveniat Regnum (*vel nomen aliud*), who places his perfect trust in God Who is our end, desiring the life of Tiphereth and the Grace of Christ Who is within. He has traversed the paths and grades of the inferior orders. He has been purified and consecrated therein, even in the four parts of his natural personality. He has turned his will to God, as one who in the darkness of night-time has set his face toward Jerusalem. He has seen the darkness kindle beyond the eternal hill, the light breaking in the east. The remembrance of that light is within him. It has shown him the straight and narrow way by which the spirit of the aspirant ascends to Tiphereth. At the portal thereof, at the point where the veil divides, he has passed through the second birth in the symbolism of our Holy Fellowship. He has been told that the door shall open; it has opened already in his heart. He has offered up his whole nature on the supernal altar of burnt offerings, in the presence of the Divine Will. It has been said that by such an oblation those who have been called are chosen for the knowledge of the Life of life. It has been said also that he shall enter and go in. Born in the spiritual Bethlehem, presented in the temple under the aegis of the old law in the Second Point of the Portal, give unto him the desire of his heart on the quest of the Divine within him, in the place of purified life, the life that follows rebirth. In virtue of my faithful testimony, he prays to be received among you.

The Usher of the Grade now returns to his seat.

ADEPTUS EXEMPTUS: Blessed are those who in the paths and Sephiroth of the Fellowship of the Rosy Cross have come to be reborn in heart and have dedicated all life therein. Frater Adveniat Regnum (*vel nomen aliud*), we acknowledge your titles and the claims embodied by these. The covenants of our authorized Messenger, speaking on the threshold of Tiphereth, are also faithful and true, Amen, for ever and evermore. But you who have been initiated and advanced from grade to grade amidst the lights and shadows of our more external sodalities have yet another lesson to learn. It is the glory of the cross of Christ. The cubical altar on which you were pledged in the first grade of our order is that of your own personality, and this cube must open as a cross to Divine Life.

ADEPTUS MAJOR: He who has been made pure and has been consecrated; he who in will and understanding has turned to God as to his end; he who has offered up his entire nature, that it may be brought into conformity with Divine purpose in the universe, and henceforth and for ever may be part of the Will of God, is thereby on the threshold of Tiphereth; but the regenerated life of that grade, wherein you have asked to enter, is a life of crucifixion in respect of all that is below.

AUXILIARY FRATER ADEPTUS: The cross is the sign of sacrifice and therefore also of victory, the realization of self in sanctity. That suffering of which it is a symbol according to the law of nature is replaced or transmuted by the glory of which it is an image according to the law of grace. Its inward meaning contains the secret of liberation.

ADEPTUS EXEMPTUS: May yours be the mystic Rose and yours the golden cross. May this, our symbolical convention, bring you to the life of light, even the Light of the cross and the Life in the Rose therein.

The Usher of the Grade rises in his place, passes to the circular altar, removes the silver chain and stands by the side of the postulant.

AUXILIARY FRATER ADEPTUS: Take therefore this chain, O Frater Adveniat Regnum (*vel nomen aliud*). Raise it in your right hand, saying: I accept the binds of service in the law of Light.

The Usher of the Grade has laid the chain in the hand of the postulant, who repeats the formula, suiting the action to the words. The Usher replaces the chain and again returns to his seat.

AUXILIARY FRATER ADEPTUS: When the chain is placed upon the altar it reposes on the bull of earth, and this is in correspondence with the material part of your personality, which has been purified by the rites of our Order. Once it was lead, my brother, and once a burden of grief. Now it has suffered conversion, and the chain is therefore of silver, a bond of spiritual obedience, of holy devotion and ministry imposed by love. The yoke is therefore light. You have raised it in testimony to the great law of attainment ruling in the body of the Adept.

There is here the pause of a moment.

ADEPTUS EXEMPTUS: Mighty Adeptus Major, what is the symbolical age of our beloved postulant?

ADEPTUS MAJOR: Merciful Exempt Adept, his days are 120 years.

ADEPTUS EXEMPTUS: It is written; my spirit shall not always strive with man, seeing that he also is flesh; yet his days shall be 120 years. Auxiliary Frater Adeptus, to what does this age refer that we ascribe symbolically to the postulant?

AUXILIARY FRATER ADEPTUS: It is the period of his life in nature before God is declared in the heart. It ends in stillness of heart, when that which has been purified and consecrated enters into rebirth in God.

ADEPTUS EXEMPTUS: Frater Adveniat Regnum (*vel nomen aliud*), may you know the peace of that stillness and receive the gift of understanding in the holy light. This is the house of the Spirit, built upon the secret mountain, which ~ seeing that all things are within ~ is said mystically to be situated at the center of the earth. Here also is the sanctuary of the Adepts, where the pledges of your perfect dedication must be uttered upon the cross of our mystery. Are you willing in this manner to ratify your election by the Order?

The Usher of the Grade has come up to the altar and taking the altar lamp places it in the hands of the postulant.

The postulant having signified assent in his own language:

ADEPTUS EXEMPTUS: Raise therefore that lamp to your forehead, holding it in your two hands, and say after me; In the Name of God who is my help, and looking on the cross of life for the Light of the cross.

This is done accordingly, and the postulant remains holding the lamp upraised. The Second and Third Celebrants rise in their places and silently remove the veil from the door of the sanctuary. The Merciful Exempt Adept gives a battery of one knock and rises with all present. The Merciful Exempt Adept sets open the door of the sanctuary to its full extent. The rose-light in the ceiling is veiled with red crepe, and the cross in the center of the sanctuary looms dimly.

ADEPTUS EXEMPTUS: The glorious sun of Tiphereth shall shine on the summit of Calvary.

The Merciful Exempt Adept stands at the threshold of the sanctuary facing west. The Second and Third Celebrants kneel on either side of him, looking toward the east. The unofficial brethren kneel down, the Usher of the Grade directing the postulant. The Merciful Exempt Adept extends his arms in the form of a cross.

ADEPTUS EXEMPTUS: Fratres et Sorores, let us offer up our solemn worship to the Lord of goodness, who has sent the secret Light into the world and desires only that it shall be made manifest.

The Merciful Exempt Adept folds his arms upon his breast, making thus the second sign of the grade, and turns eastward, but remains standing.

THE PRAYER OF THE CELEBRANT IN CHIEF

All truth, Most High Father, comes down from Thee; the greater blessings and graces dost Thou dispense continually. Thou hast in particular emblazoned the symbolical characters of nature and hast established that Divine school that imparts their true interpretation. Take us by its leading behind all forms of expression, all pageants of the manifested world, into the state out of place and time, into the still, unspoken peace and the loving silence, where the meaning of all is Thou. In Thee is our help alone; in Thee are our stay and strength through the days of our questing. All has its source in Thee, and to the consolation of Thy great deeps must all in fine return. With the whole aspiration of our hearts, we look to be reintegrated in Thy love. Receive us, we beseech Thee; aid us still in our necessity; and do Thou, the throne of Whose majesty is exalted in heavens inaccessible, so purify and transmute Thy children of the second birth, the poor brothers of this Thy lowly sodality, that Thy place may be also in our hearts. Come to us in the Life of the cross; come to us in the death of the mystic; bring us to the Resurrection that is in Thee. And through all the grades of the Christhood, give unto us the realization of the union, that we may attain that self that is in Thee. So shall we come into our own, in the kingdom that is ours and Thine; and those who have been separate in manifestation shall know themselves one spirit in Thee, who art All in all.

Those who are on their knees rise up. The Second and Third Celebrants are seated, with the unofficial brethren. The Usher of the Grade brings the Rose-Crucifix from the altar and presents it to the Celebrant in Chief. The Usher of the Grade goes to the western side of the altar, where he faces east. The postulant has his back to the altar on the eastern side. The Merciful Exempt Adept elevates the Rose-Crucifix before the assembled Fratres et Sorores, as he approaches the postulant, saying:

ADEPTUS EXEMPTUS: In Hoc Signo Vinces.

When he reaches the postulant, the Merciful Exempt Adept raises the Rose-Crucifix over the bowed head of the postulant, and says:

ADEPTUS EXEMPTUS: May the Lord God lift up the light of His glorious presence within you.

Having assisted the postulant to rise, the Usher of the Grade receives the Rose-Crucifix and replaces it on the altar. He hands the dagger of the rite to the Merciful and Exempt Adept and stands on his right side holding the cup of wine.

ADEPTUS EXEMPTUS: Frater Adveniat Regnum (*vel nomen aliud*), give me the first sign that you received on the threshold of Tiphereth in the Portal of the Third Order.

There is no prompting, as the postulant has been tested previously. He gives and maintains thereafter the sign of the opening of the veil.

The merciful Exempt Adept dips the dagger in the wine and cross-marks the postulant on his forehead.

ADEPTUS EXEMPTUS: There are three that bear record in Heaven, the Father, the Word, and the Holy Ghost. These three are One.

He dips the dagger in the wine and cross-marks the feet of the postulant.

ADEPTUS EXEMPTUS: There are three that bear witness on earth, the spirit, and the water, and the blood; and these three agree in one.

He dips the dagger in the wine and cross-marks the postulant in the palm of the right hand.

ADEPTUS EXEMPTUS: Except a man be born again of water and the Holy Spirit, he cannot enter into the Kingdom of God.

He dips the dagger in the wine and cross-marks the postulant in the palm of the left hand.

ADEPTUS EXEMPTUS: If we be crucified with Christ, we shall also reign with Him.

There is here the pause of a moment.

ADEPTUS EXEMPTUS: Frater Adveniat Regnum (*vel nomen aliud*), give me the closing sign that you received on the threshold of Tiphereth in the Portal of the Third Order.

The postulant gives and maintains the sign of the closing of the veil. The Merciful Exempt Adept dips the dagger in the wine and cross-marks the postulant on his breast, above his folded arms.

ADEPTUS EXEMPTUS: The Lord abide within thee, an Everlasting Presence.

The postulant maintains the sign. The Usher of the Grade receives the dagger and replaces it with the cup on the altar. He then returns to his seat and stands thereat. The Second and Third Celebrants advance, and take up a position on either side of the postulant, facing east. The Merciful Exempt

Adept turns eastward and draws slowly toward the sanctuary, with wand uplifted. The Guides follow with the postulant, keeping at some distance from the Celebrant in Chief. The Merciful Exempt Adept enters the sanctuary. He pauses at a due distance within and turns westward. The Guides and the postulant reach the threshold of the sanctuary and pause.

The Guides face inward, with wands uplifted. The Merciful Exempt Adept draws the postulant over the threshold saying:

ADEPTUS EXEMPTUS: The counsel of peace is between us. Come in peace.

He has brought the postulant with these words to the foot of the cross. He withdraws behind the cross and turns westward, while the Second and Third Celebrants advance and bind the postulant to the cross. Thereafter they go back to their positions on either side of the threshold, facing inward. The Usher of the Grade gives a battery of one knock and the unofficial brethren rise and remain standing. The Merciful Exempt Adept comes forward, confronting the postulant. He raises his face and hands.

ADEPTUS EXEMPTUS: Spirit of the Height, look down; guardian of our Holy Sodality; virgin soul of the Christhood; guide of the elect in God. By the glorious name of Shekinah, abiding Presence in the sanctuary, hear Thou the solemn pledge. Receive the perfect oblation of this brother of the Rosy Cross.

Then in tones that are audible to the postulant only:

ADEPTUS EXEMPTUS: Repeat your sacramental name and say after me:

The Merciful Exempt Adept imposes in a clear voice

THE PLEDGE OF THE GRADE

I, Frater Adveniat Regnum (*vel nomen aliud*), an aspirant after the life of the Spirit, who have been prepared, purified and consecrated by the Light of the Rosy Cross, and thereafter brought in the Portal of the Third Order to a second birth in symbolism, do offer up my life in sanctity on the

204

mystical cross of the Christhood, for the Divine end declared in the heart and the soul. I desire consciousness in the Spirit, knowledge of eternal things and the realization of God abiding in that sanctuary that is within. I testify that from this day forward, so far as in me lies, I will look unto the supreme crown and the supernal unity in Kether; that I will ever seek my perfection through the mystery of wisdom in Chokmah, which is supernal wisdom, where severity is transformed into mercy, and will build my house therein as a temple of the Holy Spirit. That I aspire to the spirit of understanding, spirit of counsel and strength, spirit of knowledge and truth, and the consolation of its gifts and fruits in the sea of Binah, which is supernal understanding, wherein is the communion of the elect. That I look for the resurrection of the Adept, the body of redemption, the mystical life of union and the world declared in Chesed. That when my call comes I will make ready to enter the Sabbath, desiring the soul's bridal, the word received in the stillness, the sacred release of Geburah, in the halls of compassion and judgment, where death is by the mouth of the Lord and not by the serpent. I promise solemnly that, looking toward that day when I shall enter into the rewards of the spirit, I will, to the best of my ability, and with a full sense of dedication, lead the life of adoption in Tiphereth, wherein is the Ark of the Covenant, as one who has been born again of water and of the Holy Spirit. I will abide in conformity of will, the consecration of desire, dedication of mind and the purification of my bodily part, preparing the garments of the soul, as one who has been betrothed in God and is seeking the word of union. I testify that, as here and now in symbolism, I will accept the cross in Christ, that I may descend afterwards with Him into the valley of silence and may arise in the glory of His union. The veil of the sanctuary has been parted in my respect. I know that the veil is sacred. I will keep its secrets, which are mysteries of holy knowledge, as I have kept and will maintain for ever the first and sacred trust committed to my charge in the lower grades of the Fellowship. I will observe the laws of the sanctuary in faith, honor, and obedience.

I renew hereby and hereon the pledges of fraternity and fellowship, with the other obligations by which I have been bound previously. The law is a law of solidarity. I will preserve, with my peers and co-heirs of the Third Order, a perfect union in the mystery of faith. My desire is the Divine union, and seeing that it rests within my own acts and will whether the Tree of Knowledge shall in me be the Tree of Life, I testify that neither death nor life shall separate me henceforth from the love and the service of God.

This is my pledge in purity, by which I look to be uplifted in my higher part above the sphere of those elements wherein I once abode; and I will seek to draw after me the lower Sephiroth of my nature into the realization of the Eternal presence. After Chesed, Geburah, and Tiphereth, draw me, my Lord and my God, in my imperishable soul, within the peace of Thy center, that as I came forth at Thy bidding into the manifest world, so I may return at Thy will into the world unmanifest. May the light of the Indwelling Glory abide with me in the kingdom of this world, that I may belong to the world no more but to that which comes down from Thee with the life of grace into the heart and bears up those who receive it into the land of the living, even the kingdom of Heaven, world without end.

The Merciful Exempt Adept moves aside from the cross and turns west-ward. He lifts up his arms to their fullest height. The unofficial brethren are seated.

ADEPTUS EXEMPTUS: Fratres et Sorores, behold the son of the cross, our most faithful and beloved brother, brother of the Rosy Cross, Frater Adveniat Regnum (*vel nomen aliud*), suspended on the mystical Tree. He represents thereon the Divine Son of the secret tradition, first begotten of the Mighty Ones, Whose head rests upon Daath, Whose arms stretch to Chesed and Geburah, Who has Tiphereth over the region of the heart, and Whose feet stand on Malkuth. As the Divine Son came into manifestation for a work of election through the universe, so is our brother in God mani-fested this day out of material life, within the sanctuary of our holy assem-bly. The double cube of his natural personality has become the cross. May it be unto him the Tree of Life for the healing of all his principles. May he realize in its highest sense that the life of Tiphereth is truly the life of the cross. May he find at the end thereof after what manner the cross of this life folds up and becomes that white stone, in the hidden center of which is written a new name, which no man knows, save he that receives it.

There follows a short space of perfect silence.

The Second Celebrant lifts up his arms.

ADEPTUS MAJOR: I testify that the end is God and that the end is like the beginning.

The Third Celebrant lifts up his arms.

AUXILIARY FRATER ADEPTUS: I testify that the sun of justice, shining above the cross, is also the sun of love and that love is the life of Tiphereth.

The Merciful Exempt Adept points solemnly to the postulant.

ADEPTUS EXEMPTUS: Hic Pendet Frater Fidelissimus, Frater Roseae Crucis.

The Second and Third Celebrants close the door of the sanctuary and draw the veil before it.

The Merciful Exempt Adept unbinds the postulant and gives him his own wand of office.

ADEPTUS EXEMPTUS: Frater Adveniat Regnum (*vel nomen aliud*), go in peace and sin no more. Remember now and henceforward that you have become the cross. May you be also the Rose thereon.

He points the way to the postulant, who opens the door. The Second and Third Celebrants raise the veil to permit of his passing through and no more. The Usher of the Grade comes forward and leads the postulant from the temple

Here ends the First Point

The Second Point

The cross of obligation is removed, and the bier is placed in the sanctuary. The Celebrant in Chief takes his place thereon, in an attitude of repose. The red veil of Geburah is laid over him, covering him from head to foot, so that his outlines are concealed. The altar is restored to the sanctuary. The light therein is extinguished, except for the obscure red lamp, which burns on the altar. The door of the sanctuary is closed, and the veil is drawn. The lights are subdued in the temple. The Second and Third Celebrants are seated on either side of the sanctuary door. The officers and brethren remain the complete silence.

Meanwhile the Usher of the Grade has conducted the postulant to the vestibule, where his clothing and insignia, as a Master of the lower temple, are removed. He is vested in white, with the orange girdle and Rose-Cross appropriate to an Adeptus Minor. While this is being done:

Frater Custos Liminis: Be thou clothed with the garment of regeneration and with the life renewed in God. May God Himself engird thee with the righteousness of saints. And remember on your part, o brother of the Rosy Cross, that the life of Tiphereth prepares the bridal garments that clothe the soul against the day of her mystical marriage.

The postulant is instructed in the battery of the grade, knocking three times in rapid succession, pausing, knocking twice, and when the silence within is broken by the battery without, the Third Celebrant goes to the door of the temple and admits those who have knocked. The door is secured behind them by the Usher of the Grade, who takes the wand of the Celebrant in Chief that the postulant has carried. Then, as they stand on the hither side of the door:

Third Celebrant: Frater Adveniat Regnum (*vel nomen aliud*), receive at my hands the sacred grip of this grade.

It is given by placing the left hand on the breast, with all fingers extended, mutually raising the right hand, also with extended fingers, interlacing the fingers mutually, at first still extended and then clasped upon the hand, at the same time exchanging the salutation as follows: Ave, Frater, [*vel Soror*], which is answered by: Roseae et Aureae Crucis. *The words* Pax Christi

Tecum *are then repeated simultaneously.*

The Third Celebrant returns to his place. The Usher of the Grade leads the postulant to a seat in front of the unofficial members and facing the door of the sanctuary. The Auxiliary Frater Adeptus recites:

THE LEGEND OF THE ROSY CROSS

AUXILIARY FRATER ADEPTUS: Well beloved postulant and brother, the particular mysteries exhibited and the knowledge communicated in symbolism by the Order of the Rosy Cross have been shadowed forth under various veils from time immemorial. The sanctuaries of hidden tradition have been established among many nations, and as there was never a period when the ordinances of initiation were not in the world, so there was never a time and there was never a place when the greater mysteries had any object of research but that one and inevitable object that alone concerns every man who has entered into the consciousness of election. Under whatever names, and with whatsoever varieties of pageant and established form, all true rites and mysteries, in respect of their intention, have been ever but one rite expounding one mystery, which ~ to summarize it in all brevity ~ has been the re-integration of man in God. There is every multiplicity of official dogma; there is every emblazonment of symbolism; but, from neophyte to epopt, every postulant who has attained the knowledge of his source knows also that his perfect end is a conscious return therein.

The old rites are dead, while the records that remain of most are insufficient memorials and often mere vestiges or rumors. But the truths embodied by initiation are alive for evermore. By a dispensation given from above, as from a great and holy assembly, abiding in a sanctuary not made with hands, hidden within the veil, the hierarchic mystery of Christ was declared in space and time, by the manifestation of our Lord and Savior. He is to us in an especial manner the Great Exemplar of initiation ~ its way, its truth and its life. He exhibited the path and term, no longer in rites and symbols, but in the form of life, and has made partakers thereof, heirs and co-heirs with him, all those who have learned the great secret that His story is also theirs and must be reenacted in every soul. The second birth, my brother, through which you have passed in symbolism, corresponds to the nativity in Bethlehem. The life of the cross in Tiphereth, under the rule of Tiphereth, shall be unto you as the Christ Life. Thereafter comes a mystery of death and resurrection in God, which is hidden in the grades beyond.

When the things that now and hereafter you suffer and share in symbolism have become native inwardly and outwardly in your entire being, you also will have entered into Christhood, or that which is called figuratively the state of heirship and brotherhood in the Lord. The most secret science of the soul is here formulated and the life of initiation through all its stages, even to the goal of all, according to the doctrine and practice of the Rosy Cross. You will observe that it differs generically from the official and conventional secrecy of the lesser mysteries, for it does not consist in verbal and occult formulae. In its presentation it is the story at large of the chief annals of sanctity; but in its inward practice and understanding it is a mystery of experience. It is really secret because it can be announced everywhere but can be understood and realized only in the hearts of those who have entered into the experience within.

In addition to such open memorials as are records of saints and adepts in all churches and schools of Christendom, there is the secret tradition of Christian times enshrined in cryptic literatures, of which alchemy on its spiritual side offers a notable instance. The early history of the Rosy Cross is connected more especially with this aspect of the great subject, though it has known many dedications and has suffered many changes in its passage through the centuries and various countries of Europe. It reaches here and now its final evolution in the sacred rites of our Fellowship. Antiquity, my brother, is not regarded among us as essentially a test of value, and we confess that we have separated ourselves from much that was of false-seeming and disordered enthusiasm. While continuing therefore to preserve the symbolism of the past and to unfold it from its proper root, we have invoked upon it a new spirit and have set it to grow in grace and truth under the Light of God.

The legend in chief of the original Rosy Cross is concerned with the life and experiences of a particular German Adept; but herein the historical personality counts, mystically speaking, as nothing, while its symbolism is all in all. In things of the eternal spirit we do not derive from a Germanic revival of learning but by succession from the starry heavens. At the same time we respect the traditions of our Order, and we interpret them in their true sense. Mighty Adeptus Major and honorable Fratres et Sorores, under these exalted reserves, I present the legend of Christian Rosy-Cross ~ a poor brother of the Spirit, the friend of truth and a man of God ~ as an adumbration in part of the soul's legend in its search and attainment of the Christhood. The story itself has been drawn into many languages and does not call for recitation at length on the external and familiar side. It is said that the chief and originator of our fraternity belonged to the fourteenth century, much as the master-builder in another school of initiation is referred to the land of Israel and the period of Solomon the King. In respect of the immemorial origin and royal lineage of the soul, he is affirmed to have been of noble birth, as a son of the house of God. But in respect of spiritual poverty ~ while abiding in a house of flesh ~ he was accounted as of mean estate and was put to school in a cloister, a house of official religion, where he was instructed in the duties of faith and in knowledge of the logical understanding. These things are sealed with sanctity after their own manner, and we are told that he was sent eastward on a time-long journey to a land that is called holy. It was a pilgrimage of the soul in God, a return journey toward the center. He tarried at other houses of assembly, where it might be said that he came unto his own and that his own received him. As he had been taught according to the letter within the convent gate, so did he learn otherwise according to the grace of the inward meaning. That which opened at his knocking was of things within and without; of God, man and the universe; Macrocosm ad Minutum Mundum; the travels and metamorphoses of the soul; and the soul's rest in the union. Hereof is his ascent toward Kether, through the paths and worlds of the Tree.

He returned at length to the world, as one who comes back from Chesed for the healing of nations. But it was to be despised and rejected of men, more especially by the wise in their wisdom. It was only in his own cloister that he found a few of the elect, with whom he abode in a house of the Holy Spirit. Such was the beginning of our Fraternity of the Rosy Cross, incorporating at first four persons only, being the number of our natural humanity, but afterwards increased to eight, the number of the Christhood. It was agreed that the brotherhood as such should remain secret one hundred and twenty years, or for that symbolical period that answers to the earthly age of the postulant ~ when he stands on the threshold of Tiphereth, awaiting the second birth, the new age and the life of regeneration therein. Subsequently some of the brethren were scattered through various countries on works of ministry. They appointed successors in accordance with the laws of the Order, and these arose in this manner that second circle of initiates that is mentioned in the original memorials. The years had elapsed, and the loving frater C:. R:.C:. had passed from the house of the Holy Spirit in Tiphereth to the secret church in Daath. The members of the first circle had been dissolved also in their day. Those who came after them knew little of the sodality in its beginning, and ~ as it is hinted in the records ~ had not been admitted to all things. They were in fact philosophical brethren, awaiting in the Sephira Netzach for the end of the allotted period, namely, 120 years.

ADEPTUS MAJOR: It came, in our reading of the legend. Having passed through the mystical experience of that second birth that is illustrated in symbolism by the Portal of the Third Order, a solemn assembly of adepts was convened in the house of the Holy Spirit, the children of the portal were admitted and the veil was removed from the sanctuary.

The Second and Third Celebrants rise in their places and draw the veil. Afterwards they resume their seats.

ADEPTUS MAJOR: In this manner there was uncovered the door of entrance, bearing the inscription: POST CENTUM VIGINTI ANNOS PATEBO, written about the sacred letter Shin, encompassed by the four living creatures and crowned by the wheel of the Spirit. It represented then as now the transmutation of human personality by the Christhood immanent within and overshadowed by the cosmic Christ.

The Second Celebrant has pointed to the door of the sanctuary and the words emblazoned thereon. He now rises in his place, as does also the Third Celebrant.

ADEPTUS MAJOR: Frater Adveniat Regnum (*vel nomen aliud*), I testify that the door was opened by the Mighty Adeptus Major, Non Nobis, Domine, and that those who have been called and chosen beheld that mystery within, over which the records of the past have laid a heavy drapery of images. That which they saw and heard concerned an epoch to come in their own life of adeptship. After the same manner you also shall hear and see, if yours be the gifts of the spirit, as I now open this door.

The Honorable Frater Custos Liminis, at these concluding words, shuts off all lights in the temple, and the door of the sanctuary is opened. The dim red lamp on the altar alone enlightens the sanctuary. The Celebrant in Chief, beneath the great red veil, betrays no certain outline. The wavering shadows are everywhere.

ADEPTUS MAJOR: Having come so far in our journey, by God's most Holy Grace, let us lift up our hands on the threshold of His glorious sanctuary.

AUXILIARY FRATER ADEPTUS: In Artiis Tuis, O Hierusalem, Flectamus Genua.

ADEPTUS MINOR INITIATION

The Celebrants and all present kneel down. The Second Celebrant Recites:

THE PRAYER OF THE PRECINCTS

We worship Thee in the hiddenness of Thy presence, in the darkness and light of worlds, in the silent temple of the soul. Let Thy word speak in the hiddenness, and Thy glory shall be declared therein. In the heart's stillness we shall hear Thee; we shall behold Thee with inward eyes; the light of Thy sanctuary within shall transform the light without; the light without shall be even as the light within - Thou only in life and time; in death and resurrection Thou; and in the world to come - that is the world of ascension - we shall attain our end in Thee, O end and crown of all. Thou hast called and chosen this postulant, who kneels here within the precincts of Thy greater mysteries. Show unto him the secrets of Thy sanctuary, the life and death that are in Thee. Show unto him the Glory that is to come. Raise up this son of man to the Divine Sonship in Thee, an heir and co-heir in Christhood, O Father of worlds.

The Celebrants rise. The unofficial brethren resume their seats. The postulant remains on his knees.

ADEPTUS MAJOR: He who would be master in Israel must watch more than one hour; but hereof is the soul's vigil.

AUXILIARY FRATER ADEPTUS: The day for deeds and the night for contemplation; but out of this succession comes the great quest and the end attained therein.

ADEPTUS MAJOR: It is written that He gives His beloved sleep, and herein is a mystery of God.

AUXILIARY FRATER ADEPTUS: The sleep of thought is attained in a great suspension; and the sleep of mystical death is the shadow of the eternal Sabbath.

The postulant is assisted to rise by the two Celebrants. He is drawn across the threshold and is left standing at the western side of the altar. The Second and Third Celebrants proceed direct, and respectively to the southern and northern sides. The postulant can now discern in the obscurity the veiled and silent form of the Chief Celebrant.

ADEPTUS MAJOR: Behold a sanctuary of seven sides and seven angles, every side of five feet broad and the height of eight feet. No earthly sun can shine herein, but the glimmering ray of an altar lamp serves to make darkness visible. That shrouded figurative gleam seems only to express the gloom that rests on the prospect before you. In the middle part of the crypt there stands this circular altar, covered with a plate of gold and variously graven and inscribed. About the first circle or margin is written the central maxim in the true life of adeptship: Yeheshua Mihi Omnia.

The second circle contains in cipher the characteristic motto of the order, or A∴G∴R∴C∴. ~ Ad Gloriam Roseae Crucis. The inscription within the third circle is Hoc Arcanissimae Claustrum Deitatis Mihi Sepulchrum Feci. The interior space contains a great cosmic cross, having four circles at the extremities, enclosing the traditional emblems of the four living creatures and these four inscriptions, proceeding with the sun from the south:

> Nequaquam Vacuum
> Legis Jugum
> Libertas Evangelii
> Dei Gloria Intacta*

*Should it seem desirable for the instruction of the postulate to elucidate the Latin inscriptions, they may be translated literally thus: (1) Jesus is all things unto me; (2) To the Glory of the Rosy Cross; (3) I have made this inner sanctuary of the Most Hidden God a sepulcher for myself; (4) No Void; (5) The Yoke of the Law; (6) The freedom of the Gospel; (7) The Glory of God Inviolate.

They are in correspondence with the Divine Names Yod, He, Vau, He, and Aleph, He, Yod, He, read crosswise from the south and east respectively; with the Divine name ADNI, understood as a title of Shekinah and read from the east against the sun; and with the secret word AGLA, beginning at the south and following the course of the sun. At the meeting point of the arms ~ in the middle of the cosmic cross ~ is placed the wheel or circle of the Spirit, having eight radii, proceeding from the sacred letter Shin. The doctrine of the Rosy Cross in the grade of Adeptus Minor is here formulated and symbolized, with intimations of mysteries that lie beyond the grade. It is a doctrine based upon experience, the experience of Christ realized in the four parts of our personality, in virtue of which ~ at the term of adept sanctity ~ our human elements, like the four mystical creatures, encompass the great white Throne of God, Who is within.

Frater Adveniat Regnum (*vel nomen aliud*), the emblems of your consecrated personality are beside their correspondences on the altar. Symbolum ad symbolum loquitur, as heart unto heart in the silence. Take up the silver chain, which represents your material part transformed in the life of rebirth. Raise it in your right hand, as one who affirms God in all that manifests his being. Remember now and henceforward that there is a tincturing spirit within which transmutes our earth of life. Lay down the mystic chain, as one who has found that the silver cord is loosed in all that concerns bondage. Take up the dagger of gold and raise it in your right hand; so may Eternal Mind lift up your mind of manhood. Remember the sword of the Spirit and that purified mind has talents of gold within, gifts of the Spirit sent down. Be thou a buyer, my brother, of gold tried in the furnace, and when thou art tried therein come forth like gold refined. Be transformed therefore by renewing of the mind, and thou shalt not see corruption. Replace the golden dagger, and take up the cup of benedictions, for transmuted desire is exalted above all blessing. Partake of the cup in charity, and receive the wine of the kingdom. Set it again upon the altar and lift up the lamp on high. Be thou light in the place of light, and having been born of man, according to the will of flesh, but afterwards reborn of God, according to His holy will, work out thine end therein. Stand steadfast in the purpose of the Lord. Restore the lamp to its altar, and in the midst of speaking symbols, remember the things signified. So shall the types dissolve, but thou shalt be their life; for that which the wheel of the Spirit shews forth, at the center of the altar-circle, shall be Life of life within thee. And death shall be no more.

The Celebrants turn to the east.

ADEPTUS MAJOR: Pater Æternus Deus, Dona Nobis Vitam.

AUXILIARY FRATER ADEPTUS: Vitam Æternam Tuam Dona Nobis, Domine.

ADEPTUS MAJOR: Fili Redemptor Mundi Deus, Dona Nobis Verbum.

AUXILIARY FRATER ADEPTUS: Et Verbum Caro Factum Erit.

ADEPTUS MAJOR: Spiritus Sancte Deus, Lumen Dona Nobis.

AUXILIARY FRATER ADEPTUS: Lumen Veritatis Tuae, et in te Resurgamus Nos.

After these versicles there is a hush of complete silence.

The Celebrant in Chief speaks from within the veil.

ADEPTUS EXEMPTUS: In six days of his life is material man created, and thereafter cometh a Jubilee. The natural man is complete in his own degree, but above this there is the manhood of the sacred temple. From the life of man in nature, from the death that ensues thereon and opens the further prospects, we who have been called of the spirit have sought a path of elevation toward a more perfect mode. It is in losing that which the natural man holds most desirable that the spiritual man, after six days, shall find himself. We have looked for life in God and have been crucified in Him to all that here below interposes between Life Divine and the free way of the quest. We have stripped off the old vestures, praying to be clothed in God. We have found that the quest is love and that is also the end ~ in the paths of contemplation, and these are paths of love; in the rule of sacrifice, which is love made holy; we have found that life is love. Opened to Divine Love on the threshold of the life of Tiphereth, we have been born by love into true life for ever. We have laid bare our whole being to the sacred influx of love, and this is the life of the cross. We have become the mystic Rose in the center of the Holy cross. But the secret of death is also the secret of love. We have died upon the cross of Tiphereth. It is the mystic death of the kiss. There is a desire that kills, and the same also makes alive, Amen, for ever and evermore.

The voice dies away within the veil, and again there is complete silence. Afterwards the voice speaks.

ADEPTUS EXEMPTUS: Once it was the day of our espousals, for the second birth is betrothal. We have prepared our wedding garments. This also is life in Tiphereth. We have desired to be dissolved and to be with Christ. This is the death of the cross. Then is it great darkness, as of a rock-hewn sepulcher. But He Who stands at the door and knocks enters and comes in. This is the marriage of the soul.

The voice dies away within the veil, and yet again there is complete silence. But afterwards the voice speaks.

ADEPTUS EXEMPTUS: Brother of the Rosy Cross, it is not from man to man that the great gifts are communicated, for that which he can devise to another is that only which has been lent to the man himself. It is for this reason that, after solidarity and brotherhood, each of us stands alone. Stand therefore, my brother, maintaining with your peers and co-heirs a perfect union in the mystery of faith. But remember, a night cometh, and so stand, as one awaiting his call to enter the darkness. He who is reborn is he who shall die also and pass into the valley of silence. The sanctuary of your tomb is hollowed in the rock of ages, and your time is at hand.

The voice ceases within the veil, and the silence that follows is for a brief space only.

The Celebrants have taken up their places side by side with the postulant, whom they draw backward to the threshold, but are still facing east.

ADEPTUS MAJOR: I certify that Frater Non Nobis, Domine, and those who were with him, heard in the house of the Spirit and its Holy sanctuary the voice of the master, testifying concerning Divine Darkness and union with the Divine therein. It is an opening of the inward world and plenary realization of the Presence in the conscious soul, though it is told after another manner in the records that remain among us. There it is said firstly that they discovered the body of the founder, who bore the book of the mysteries on his breast, a treasure to be hidden from the world. But it is said also that this book contained by way of colophon the inscription: Ex Deo Nascimur, In Jesu Morimur, Per Spiritum Sanctum Reviviscimus. And this is a summary in brief of the Rosy Cross in all its grades of evolution. Take it into your heart, my brother, having prepared the heart as earth of the mystical kingdom. Let it dwell as a seed therein; the letter of the words shall die; the flower of the inward sense shall spring therefrom. The counsel is always to lose the symbols in their meaning. The material part should dissolve in the light of its spiritual significance, and this is what is meant among us by getting behind the symbol. There is no object in nature, no memorial in the written word of grace that cannot be used in this manner. There is above all no conception, whether of Divine Things and persons, or of saints also and angels, which will not open to us great vistas of secret knowledge by this philosophical solution.

AUXILIARY FRATER ADEPTUS: We know in this manner that our founder Christian Rosy Cross, being dead, yet speaketh ~ in the hidden church of the Adepts ~ concerning life, death and resurrection in God. In fine therefore, having heard and seen in the spirit, Frater Non Nobis, Domine, and his companions made fast the door of the sanctuary ad interiora terrae and setting seals thereon, recited their solemn closing in this point of our Christian mystery.

The Celebrants leave the sanctuary, together with the postulant. The door of the sanctuary is closed. The Second Celebrant lays his wand against the door. He takes the postulant by his two hands and looks earnestly upon him.

ADEPTUS MAJOR: I say unto you, Frater Adveniat Regnum (*vel nomen aliud*), that this also is your own story.

The Usher of the Grade comes forward and leads the postulant from the temple.

Here ends the Second Point.

THE THIRD POINT

There is light everywhere, in the temple and inner sanctuary. It is fuller and brighter than in the First Point. The door of the sanctuary stands partly open, but the veil is drawn across the threshold. The chairs of the Second and Third Celebrants are placed at a considerable distance westward, toward the middle part of the temple, and the Celebrants are seated facing east. There is a vacant point behind them for the postulant. The Celebrant in Chief is standing within the sanctuary, erect on the eastern side of the altar; but the intervening door conceals him from those who are without. These are seated in expectation and in silence.

Meanwhile the Usher of the Grade has conducted the postulant to the vestibule, where he rests for a period. While the two are seated together:

FRATER CUSTOS LIMINIS: Beloved brother, you have heard ~ and how often ~ of a light that shines in the darkness and that the darkness comprehends it not. It is light of the mystic end and the Life of life. In its absence the natural man is said to be complete within his own measures, but he has no conscious part in eternity, and he reigns only as the leader of the animal world. A desire of the true end that is set before all being may begin to awaken within him, as a kindling of the higher light. He sets out on the great quest. The light within him is also a light before him, and the desire of the holy house burns in his heart. So is he brought to our sanctuary and learns to comprehend the light that shines from the Rosy Cross. It is for him to remember therein that no initiation and no advancement can confer the light automatically. They remain within their law and their order, and operate only in symbolism. May you who are reborn in ritual be regenerated in the life of the soul, and may life, death and resurrection be stages of your inward experience, not merely an eloquent pageant performed in ceremony.

The Usher of the Grade again leads the postulant to the door of the temple. The battery of the grade is given, three knocks in succession, a pause, then two more knocks, and they enter unannounced. The door is secured behind them. As they move forward through the temple:

FRATER CUSTOS LIMINIS: He who puts aside the folds of the senses, as linen cloths laid by themselves, and the fleshly mind, as a napkin from about the head, shall arise in his spiritual part by a resurrection into divine life.

The postulant is now standing behind the seats of the Second and Third Celebrant, in the middle place between them, looking toward the door of the sanctuary. The Usher of the Grade has returned to his own place.

ADEPTUS MAJOR: When he who has been advanced into the mysteries of Divine experience goes forth again into the world, the memorial within him is like the letter of the sacred books.

AUXILIARY FRATER ADEPTUS: The spirit communicated in his temple is reserved to the temple.

ADEPTUS MAJOR: So also the letter alone can be used outside the sanctuary of the Rosy Cross.

Auxiliary Frater Adeptus: There is a shadow of light only beyond the lodge of the adepts.

Adeptus Major: The letter also is used within the sanctuary, but there is the sense of many meanings behind it.

Auxiliary Frater Adeptus: All degrees, however, end in expectation; all foreshadow something greater than themselves, by which the postulant of figurative mysteries should arise to experience in the real order.

Adeptus Major: But the initiations of the mysteries are true and efficacious, because they convey in circumstantial signs and tokens the living end of adeptship; and those signs can therefore be channels of life.

Auxiliary Frater Adeptus: May all the sacramental channels be opened and the Word that is life be spoken.

Adeptus Major: It is in stillness of thought that we shall hear the Word of Life.

The Celebrant in Chief speaks form within the sanctuary.

Adeptus Exemptus: I am the Resurrection and the Life. He that believes in Me, though he were dead, yet shall he live, and whosoever lives and believes in Me shall never die.

The Frater Custos Liminis moves quietly to the door of the sanctuary and drawns back the veil, saying:

Frater Custos Liminis: The angel of the lord descended from heaven, and came and rolled back the stone from the door.

The Celebrant in Chief speaks from within the sanctuary.

Adeptus Exemptus: I am Alpha and Omega, the first and the last. I am he that lives and was dead, and behold, I am alive for evermore, Amen; and have the keys of hell and of death.

The Usher of the Grade passes round to the postulant, whom he leads to the threshold of the sanctuary and there directs him to kneel. He sets the door of the sanctuary open to its full extent. The Second and Third Celebrants, and all members stand up. The postulant sees the Celebrant in Chief erect, with his arms extended in the form of a cross. The Usher of the Grade moves to one side of the entrance.

FRATER CUSTOS LIMINIS: I know that my Redeemer lives, and that he shall stand at the latter day upon the earth. I shall see him for myself, and mine eyes shall behold, and not another. My veins within me are consumed with earnest desire for that day.

He remains silently at his place.

ADEPTUS EXEMPTUS: I am the faithful witness, the first-begotten of the dead and the prince of kings of the earth. I am the way, the truth and the life. No man comes unto the Father but by me. Peace be unto you. I have finished the work. I know whence I came and whither I go. He that believes in me, believes not in me but in Him that sent me. I go my way to Him that sent me. I ascend unto my Father, and your Father; and to my God, and your God. I am the Light of the world. He that followeth Me shall not walk in darkness, but shall have the Light of Life.

The merciful Exempt Adept lifts up his hands and face.

ADEPTUS MAJOR: He that has an ear to hear, let him hear what the Spirit says unto the churches.

AUXILIARY FRATER ADEPTUS: Now is Christ risen from the dead, and become the first fruits of them that slept.

The Usher of the Grade moves forward, and as the postulant sees and hears the risen adept, directs him to say with him:

FRATER CUSTOS LIMINIS *(speaking on the part of the postulant):* One thing I know, that, whereas I was blind, now I see.

ADEPTUS EXEMPTUS: My peace I leave with you, my peace I give unto you. The Spirit of Truth abide with you for ever and teach you all things. May the great white glory of the Divine Spirit come down.

The Usher of the Grade has retired silently to his own seat and stands thereat.

The Celebrant in Chief comes round the altar to the threshold of the sanctuary and lays his hands upon the head of the postulant, having placed his wand aside.

ADEPTUS EXEMPTUS: This is also thine own story. Look to it therefore, beloved.

The Celebrant in Chief raises the postulant.

ADEPTUS EXEMPTUS: I raise you into the company of adepts in the house of the Holy Spirit.

The Celebrant in Chief seals the postulant on his forehead.

ADEPTUS EXEMPTUS: May your mind be opened to the realization that is above knowledge.

He seals the postulant on the heart.

ADEPTUS EXEMPTUS: May your heart become a sanctuary of light.

He seals the postulant on the hips.

ADEPTUS EXEMPTUS: May your body be the temple of the Rosy Cross.

He lifts up his hands.

ADEPTUS EXEMPTUS: May the glory of the Lord fill this house of the Lord.

All resume their seats, with the exception of the Celebrant in Chief and the postulant. The Celebrant in Chief turns to the east with the postulant and leads him to the western side of the altar. Having resumed his wand he proceeds himself to the east, and turns westward.

ADEPTUS EXEMPTUS: The Third Order of the Rosy Cross presents in symbolism three stages of experience in the realization of the Divine, and this realization is within. These stages are summarized in the Three Points of the grade Tiphereth, into which you have now entered, and it is therefore a synthesis of the Third Order at large, even as the grade of Neophyte offers at the beginning of our sacred mystery a compendium of the work performed in the worlds of action and formation. In the grade of Adeptus Minor the postulant is put definitely on the path of attainment, understood as the Way, the Truth and the Life that are in Christ ‒ the regenerated life of the soul, the state of mystical death and the risen life of union. The holy sanctuary of the adepts depicts in symbolism the ascent of the soul in God, from the deeps even to the heights, through the paths of the Christhood. There is firstly the dark ground whereon we now stand, being that out of which we have risen, the things of material sense and the absorption of the soul therein. Beneath the golden altar of our dedication and sacrifice there lies an inverted triangle, inscribed within a heptagram, to both of which are referred the Sephiroth of the shadow, as opposed to those of the light. After this manner do we in the sanctuary of the adepts, by virtue of dedication and sacrifice, symbolically over-rule and enchain the malign forces of our nature. Super Aspidem Et Basiliscum Ambulavi, Et Conculcavi Leonem Et Draconem.

In the middle of the black triangle there is placed for this reason the releasing symbol of the golden cross emblazoned with a red rose of 49 petals, being the rose of the gates of Light. Round about it are written the four pregnant words: He Descended Into Hell. They allude to the Divine Immanence within us through all phases of our being, in our darkness as well as in our light, amidst the bondage of the evil law and in the freedom of the Sons of God. We have come out of the evil law, and therefore the shadows of the things left are depicted below us.

The seven walls of the sanctuary represent the cosmos summarized in the planetary system, the sacramental grace signified to us by the universe, the glory of the world seen in the light of adeptship, sub specie aeternitatis. It is the world from the standpoint of the sanctuary. It is seen in that light that never was on land or sea for those who are without consciousness of God; but it is the light that is always present for those who look at the world from the summit of Patmos, who know what it is to have been in the spirit on the Lord's day, and who have heard the voice that says unto all who have ears: Behold I come quickly. The light is therefore communicated from within the adept of the Rosy Cross. There is a dual transfiguration ‒ that of the man and his world. It is not that he changes the world; but for him, with him and in him there is a change in its mode of manifestation.

The consciousness of the immanence within reacts upon things without, and then the Divine Immanence shines through the whole universe. It is the transmutation of regenerated life, of the Christ-Life on earth. This is the way in which sanctity transfigures all things, and the adept becomes a tingeing stone. The world is transmuted in the Christhood. But the seven walls are also indicative of states within the postulant, and they are seven stages of his progress from world to world in the Order of the Rosy Cross. From this point of view each wall is a gate, and you have entered the holy sanctuary by the gate of Venus, even as in your previous progress you passed through the gate of Earth to attain the Sephira Yesod, through that of the Moon in order to enter Hod, and finally through the gate of Mercury on your transit from Hod to Netzach. That you have yet other gates to open is shown by the walls emblazoned with the astronomical sights of the Sun, Mars, Jupiter, and Saturn.

Beyond these there lies the supreme mystery of the Rosy Cross. It is, however, only by analogy that the seven walls are attributed to the material planets, for the true stars are within you, and you know already that in our sacramental system the Moon has reference to the reflected light of mind, Mercury to the state of our desires, which must be fixed in God, and Venus to the conversion of redirection of will and purpose, by which only the soul can become a Venus and having been reborn in God is the conceiver and bearer henceforth of the Divine within it. The seven walls are also the Sephiroth from Yesod to Daath inclusive, it being understood that the last lies within the mystical decade but is not computed therewith in our secret tradition. It is the threshold of the supernals. In the middle place on the summit of each wall is the white wheel or sign of the Christ-Spirit, referring to the Divine Immanence that is present in all creation and operates in all the stages of grace and attainment experienced by the soul of man. The sign of the planet itself occupies the center of the wall, enclosed within the circle of the Sephira to which it belongs, while about it are the Divine Names and Sephirotic titles referred to each numeration. The ground of each wall is on the rainbow or spectrum color ascribed to the particular planet, while its spiritual counterpart is that of the sacred Sephira. And because there is a mystery herein that is formulated in the various scales of color connected with this grade, I confer upon you the sacramental name of Frater Hodos Chameleontis, meaning the Path of the Chameleon. The colors symbolize graces; may you pass from grace to grace and from glory to glory.

The Supernal Sephiroth are represented by the triangle on the ceiling, and within this triad is placed a rose of 22 petals, similar to that which I wear here on my heart. The light in the center is that of the Christ-Spirit, and it flows over the whole sanctuary. The petals are the paths of the

Christhood, the paths of the Tree of Life, through some of which you have traveled. The rose is placed in the center of the triangle representing the three supernals, because the Christ is the Way, the Truth and the Life, and no man comes to the Father but by Him, through Whom we look in fine to be withdrawn in God, as this sacred rose in the roof of our holy sanctuary is withdrawn into the sacred Delta.

Frater Adveniat Regnum (*vel nomen aliud*), look to that which you are and remember ever the vocation of the Christ-Life. May you know like Christ whence you came and whither you are going. The Christ-Life in our order ~ as in all the annals of sanctity ~ is only in broad analogy with the Divine Life in Palestine, but it is exact within its own measures. The state of mystical death, which is intimated by the Second Point of the grade of Tiphereth, is only in broad analogy with the death on Calvary; and the adept risen in symbolism who testifies in the Third Point is in no sense taking the part of the great manifested master in a dramatic pageant; but he bears witness to resurrection in the spirit, which is a mystery of experience awaiting those who have been brought into Divine Union.

The Celebrant in Chief moves round by the south and leads the postulant from the sanctuary, closing but not sealing the door behind them. The Second and Third Celebrants come up from their places.

ADEPTUS EXEMPTUS: The sacred and mystical number of this grade is 21, and the root thereof is in the triad. It is derived from the first of the sacred names and words that will now be communicated to you. Follow them on your own part in the heart and mind.

ADEPTUS EXEMPTUS: Aleph, He.

ADEPTUS MAJOR: Yod, He.

AUXILIARY FRATER ADEPTUS: Ehyeh.

ADEPTUS EXEMPTUS: It is written; Before Abraham was I AM.

ADEPTUS MAJOR: Whom say ye that I the Son Man am?

AUXILIARY FRATER ADEPTUS: Christ the power of God and the wisdom of God.

Adeptus Exemptus: I, N.

Adeptus Major: R.

Auxiliary Frater Adeptus: I.

Adeptus Exemptus: Yeheshua.

Adeptus Major: Nazaræus.

Auxiliary Frater Adeptus: Rex Judæorum.

Adeptus Exemptus: Lux, the Light of the cross.

Auxiliary Frater Adeptus: Remember that Tiphereth is called in the secret tradition the mediating intelligence.

Here ends the Third Point.

The High Office of Closing
the House and Sanctuary of Adepts

The Celebrants of the rite are seated as guardians of the veil. The door of the sanctuary is ajar, but the veil is drawn before it. The new adeptus has been led to a seat by Frater Custos Liminis.

Adeptus Exemptus: (*Knocks three times*)

Adeptus Major: (*Knocks once*)

Auxiliary Frater Adeptus: (*Knocks once*)

Adeptus Exemptus: Valete, Fratres et Sorores Roseae et Aureae Crucis.

ADEPTUS MAJOR: May the good pleasure of the Lord of mercy, prevailing in the height and deep, pour down on us the gifts of the Spirit and the fruits thereof.

AUXILIARY FRATER ADEPTUS: Orate, Fratres et Sorores. Glory be to God in the highest, who has visited and redeemed his people.

ADEPTUS EXEMPTUS: Honorable and adept brethren, assist me to close the house and its holy sanctuary in the fullness of spiritual life declared in the Holy of Holies, and in the gracious, the glorious, the divine intimations of this august ceremony. Auxiliary Frater Adeptus, how many years does the Spirit of God strive with the spirit of man?

AUXILIARY FRATER ADEPTUS: Merciful Exempt Adept, it is written that the Most Holy Spirit shall plead the cause of the union for 120 years.

ADEPTUS EXEMPTUS: Mighty Adeptus Major, what does this number mean?

ADEPTUS MAJOR: The tetrad of our natural humanity becomes the pentad, and by an operation of four and five the number 120 is reduced to the hexad, which is the number of life in Tiphereth.

AUXILIARY FRATER ADEPTUS: When the age of 120 years has been attained by the postulant.

ADEPTUS EXEMPTUS: Mighty Adeptus Major, for what period do we close it?

ADEPTUS MAJOR: Merciful Exempt Adept, it is closed in expectation and the silence of grade desire while the Spirit of God strives with the spirit of man.

ADEPTUS EXEMPTUS: Post centum viginti annos patebo (*He shuts and secures the door.*) Looking therefore towards the grades that go up to the height, toward the height itself and the summit, O brethren of the Rose and Cross, in the recollection of the mind, in the devotion of the heart, in the great love and the great desire that past all space and time alone can find their object, I have closed the sanctuary of the adepts.

AUXILIARY FRATER ADEPTUS: I close this house of the Holy Spirit on the mystic mountain of the wise.

AUXILIARY FRATER ADEPTUS: Ex Deo nascimur (*knocks once*)

ADEPTUS MAJOR: In Yeheshuah morimur (*knocks once*)

ADEPTUS EXEMPTUS: Per Spiritum Sanctum reviviscimus (*knocks three times*)

The closing sign is given by all present.

HERE ENDS THE HIGH OFFICE OF CLOSING THE HOUSE AND SANCTUARY OF THE ADEPTS.

The Third Order of the Rosy Cross

World of Creation

Part III

The Ceremony of Admission
to the
Grade of Adeptus Major

6 = 5

Being the Most Holy Grade of Geburah
Id Est
Mysterium Shekinah

Privately Printed

1917

The Pontifical Officers of the Grade

The Celebrant in Chief: id est, Adeptus Exemptus, 7=4, legate of the house of resurrection.

The Second Celebrant: id est, Mighty Adeptus Major, lord of the halls of judgment, 6=5.

The Most Holy Priestess of the Rite: representing in living symbolism the glorious Shekinah, in her character of Matrona in Binah and leader of the elect on the path of their return to Him.

The Usher of the Grade: id est, the keeper of the threshold, id est, frater Peregrinus Vallis, 6=5. He has the first care of the postulant.

The Auxiliary Frater Adeptus: 5=6, being the postulant on the threshold of judgment, is, in a certain sense, an officer of the grade, in a rank corresponding to that of third Celebrant in the grade of Tiphereth.

As the clothing of the Celebrant-in-Chief and the Second Celebrant corresponds to their grade of adeptship in the world of Creation, it remains the same as in Tiphereth. The postulant wears vestments of the Auxiliary Frater Adeptus. The Most Holy Priestess wears the white habit of the Third Order and the girdle and veil of Binah. The Usher of the Grade and the unofficial members are clothed in the white habit, with the girdle of Geburah and the Rose-Cross belonging to that Sephira. The Usher carries a wand, surmounted by a dove of peace, similar to that of an Ostiarius in the worlds below Tiphereth.

The Fellowship of the Rosy Cross

—

Grade of Adeptus Major
6=5

—

THE SOLEMN CEREMONY OF OPENING THE
HOUSE AND SANCTUARY OF ADEPTS
IN THE GRADE OF GEBURAH

—

The arrangement of house and sanctuary follows the unwritten precedents. The door of the sanctuary is open to its fullest extent, and the sanctuary itself is draped according to the scale of colors complementary to those of Tiphereth; that is to say, in the scale of the Great Mother. The funeral litter and catafalque fill the center, having red draperies and hangings. The candles of the dead are placed about the litter. There is a veil drawn before the symbol of the setting sun on the outer side of the door, and this veil is red. The cross of obligation in Tiphereth is erected at the western end of the temple, facing the door of the sanctuary, and is covered by a red curtain. The altar of the grade is placed in the middle way of the temple, and is draped in red. It is in the form of a double cube. The sacred pictorial symbols of Kaph and Mem are turned westward on the altar and lie on either side of a human skull, turned eastward and covered with red crape. Between the altar and the western end of the temple are the pillars of the Rosy Cross, each having a great light similarly veiled. If there are other lights in the temple, these also are draped with red. The seats of the Celebrants are set facing west, by the altar, that of the Merciful Exempt Adept being on the southern and that of the Mighty Adeptus Major on the northern side. The Celebrant-in-Chief, having assumed his vestments and insignia in advance of the other brethren, proceeds from the vestibule to the temple and passes behind the sanctuary into that place of concealment which represents the region of the Supernals. When there is sufficient space in a temple it consists of a very small apartment, draped in the color of Binah in the scale of the Great Mother and provided with two seats; one for the Celebrant-in-Chief and one for the Priestess of the Rite, who should preferably remain in seclusion when not serving in the temple.

The Second Celebrant, the Honorable frater Peregrinus Vallis and the unofficial members being assembled and clothed in the vestibule, they pass in procession to the temple and take their places in silence. The Usher of the Grade is seated by the door and has charge of the pot of incense. The Second Celebrant proceeds to the western end of the catafalque and there faces westward. He opens the sacred ceremony with a battery of one knock and proceeds as follows:

ADEPTUS MAJOR: Fratres et Sorores, having come so far in our journey from the circumference to the center, let us abide here for a period, since the day is far spent.

There is here the pause of a moment.

ADEPTUS MAJOR: Faithful companions of our common exile, I pray you, remember the center.

There is here the pause of a moment.

ADEPTUS MAJOR: It is known that this is also the height, whereunto many voices summon us.

There is here the pause of a moment.

ADEPTUS MAJOR: It is well that those who are called should go before their election; it is well that those who come after should find the path more smooth, since others have gone up first.

There is here the pause of a moment.

ADEPTUS MAJOR: I testify therefore that, seeking the height or the center, we do not stand alone.

There is here the pause of a moment.

ADEPTUS MAJOR: A memorial is always with us, behind the door of this sanctuary. We have found herein a house of rest upon the way; and the solemn task devolves upon us to open its secret place unto other travelers whose knocking is heard without.

There is here the pause of a moment.

ADEPTUS MAJOR: Fratres et Sorores, what manner of place is this?

There is here the pause of a moment.

ADEPTUS MAJOR: It is the house of love, of the soul going to its bridal; but it is also a house of judgment.

There is here the pause of a moment.

ADEPTUS MAJOR: The sign of the house is that of the mystical Rose, which is the sign of mercy and judgment on the right and left of the Tree, the sign of union with Christ in the central pillar of benignity, the sign of Messias in the work of redeeming souls and the symbol of the Great Mother.

There is here the pause of a moment.

ADEPTUS MAJOR: Let us kneel therefore, O Fratres et Sorores, for here is the holy place.

The Second Celebrant turns eastward and kneels. All present kneel down.

THE PRAYER AT OPENING

ADEPTUS MAJOR: We, who are the stewards of the mysteries in this little kingdom of Thy love, do beseech Thee, in the bond of our union, that the saving grace of Thy guidance may be with us now and to the end. By the great names of Thy love, even by Taboonah and Matrona, holy sister. holy spouse, virgin and mother in transcendence, encompass us on every side. Thou hast suffered with the elect in all ages. Thou dost lead us on the path of our return. We have seen the beauty of Thy face, O angel of liberation.

Thou has drawn us into sacred halls in the realm of mystical death, O Indwelling Glory. Thou hast visited us in the kingdoms which are below. Thou doest remember us in the palace which is above. Keep us under the shadow of Thy wings. Give unto us the nourishment of the elect ~ red wine of Thy rapture in Geburah, white milk of Thy mercy in Chesed. Bring us ~ in the temple of holy espousals ~ into the joy of Thy nuptial union, O sacrifice of the Holy One, O endless love of the Highest. We have dwelt, our Lady and Mother, under many dispensations, in worlds of derived light, of sorrow which does not lead and joy which diverts from the way. But the call came by which we were brought to Thy knowledge, enkindled with the fire from Thee; and seeing that it has been given us in fine to lead others on the road which Thou hast opened before us, we ask Thee in Thy great justice for the light to guide them well. It is written that Thy house is a house of prayer. Matrona, Shekinah, first of all that is, Mera Benignitas, Beneplacitum termino carens; give unto them as to us that they shall see Thy glory in the death which is life from Thee.

There is here another pause. The Celebrant in Chief opens the secret door and issues from behind the sanctuary, bearing all his insignia. The door closes behind him. He raises both arms, holding his wand of office in his right hand.

ADEPTUS EXEMPTUS: Salvete, Fratres et Sorores; health and resurrection in the Lord, union declared in triplicity, the body of redemption for those who are redeemed in the spirit, and the wealth of the knowledge of God.

He lowers his arms and wand. He is standing behind the lighted candles, facing westward. The Second Celebrant is still kneeling at the western end of the catafalque, looking toward the Celebrant in Chief.

ADEPTUS MAJOR: And hail unto thee, O Prince of Chesed, Merciful and Exempt Adept, who comest in the name of our salvation, bearing the signs thereof, and clothed with holy sacraments.

ADEPTUS EXEMPTUS: Peace be with you, O Mighty Adeptus Major, Lord of the halls of judgment. And from the house of resurrection to you, O Fratres et peace Sorores, dwelling in the grade of Geburah, at the heart of the mystical Rose.

ADEPTUS MAJOR: By the mystery of the secret mountain, in a middle place of the earth; by its inwardness of all the hiddenness; by the sun which shines therein; by the setting of that sun in splendor; by the great and holy darkness; by the figurative death therein, which is the passage of life for ever; by the conformity and brotherhood with Christ, in whom is the hope of our resurrection; bring us into the light of Chesed.

ADEPTUS EXEMPTUS: I am he who bears witness to the light and the risen life in Christ. For this I have entered Geburah, the house of the holy Rose. For this I descend into Tiphereth, as a beautiful house of life. For this I open the Portal which leads to the Sephiroth below; and I call the children of men to the royal heritage and sonship of those who are born in God.

The Celebrant in Chief passes with the sun to the western end of the cata-falque. The Second Celebrant rises. The Usher of the Grade signifies to the Fratres et Sorores, who rise and remain standing. The Celebrants leave the sanctuary together and take up their places at or near the threshold. When this has been done:

ADEPTUS EXEMPTUS: (*Knocks once*) Fratres et Sorores, Adepti Majores, I invite you to join your intention with mine in the solemn act of opening this holy house of the spirit in the grade of Geburah, wherein is the mystery of death.

ADEPTUS MAJOR: The sacred Name is Taboonah, on the left hand side of the Tree, and it signifies an influx from Binah, the desire of the Eternal Days. We invoke under this title the Great Mother in God, Who is love and benignity in the Great Father of all.

ADEPTUS EXEMPTUS: But on the right hand side of the Tree, which is the male side, the sacred Name is Yah, and this signifies an influx from Chok-mah, which is in union with Binah for ever, both cleaving unto Kether, where Jehovah is united to Elohim, the purpose and love of God which flow over the whole creation. In virtue of this union we return whence we came.

ADEPTUS MAJOR: I testify therefore that Yah is the name of mercy, and thence is derived the mystical Number of this grade, which is 15; but the synthesis of the same is 6, being the time of life in Tiphereth, while the analogy is 33, being that of Divine life.

ADEPTUS EXEMPTUS: The mystery of redemption is comprehended by these numbers, and the over-ruling of evil things, for the number 15 is that also of the evil governors.

ADEPTUS MAJOR: They are numbers of mercy and judgment, the meeting of which opens a path to the Crown, and this path is called Magnanimity.

ADEPTUS EXEMPTUS: If the pillar of mercy were separated from that of judgment the vault of the temple would fall.

ADEPTUS MAJOR: I have entered the halls of judgment; I have found a place of peace; I have heard the Voice of the Stillness.

ADEPTUS EXEMPTUS: I have traversed the path of Teth; I have dwelt in the Palace of mercy; I have heard the Risen Voice.

ADEPTUS MAJOR: Geburah is a rite of Nuptials, the marriage night of the soul, the secret of death therein, and resurrection in the Rose.

ADEPTUS EXEMPTUS: It is a union in still consciousness, and the epoch is three days.

ADEPTUS MAJOR: Give unto us, O Master of All, the espoused life thereafter, and the risen glory therein.

ADEPTUS EXEMPTUS: In the spirit hereof, I call upon you to declare that this holy house is open for the work that we are deputed to perform, by the power to us commissioned.

ADEPTUS MAJOR: O house of many graces; I open the house of the spirit in the grade of Geburah, where death is by the mouth of the Lord and not by the serpent (*knocks three times, pauses, knocks twice, pauses, knocks once.*)
ADEPTUS EXEMPTUS: (*Knocks three times, pauses, knocks twice, pauses, knocks once.*)

Here ends the solemn ceremony of opening the house and sanctuary of adepts in the Grade of Geburah.

THE FIRST POINT,
BEING THE RITUAL OF OBLIGATION

The Celebrants repair to their places. The Usher of the Grade closes the door of the sanctuary and sees that the curtain is drawn to conceal the symbol in chief and inscriptions. The Celebrants and Members are seated. A short pause follows.

ADEPTUS EXEMPTUS: It is written in faithful words that those who are guides of the perplexed are true leaders of me. At the beginning of this high celebration I testify that we are wardens of death and that in virtue of such office we are deputed to bring many out of great tribulation into cool and sacred chambers.

ADEPTUS MAJOR: So high a duty now devolves upon us. Therefore, in your perfect compassion, I beseech you to have mercy on the soul of our faithful associate, the Auxiliary Frater Adeptus, Frater Adveniat Regnum (*vel nomen aliud*), on whom the necessity of this time exhorts us to confer the benefit of holy sepulture.

ADEPTUS EXEMPTUS: Do you certify, Mighty Adeptus Major, that now is the accepted time?

ADEPTUS MAJOR: It is known that the spirit is willing and that those who oppose are weak.

ADEPTUS EXEMPTUS: Fratres et Sorores, I call upon you therefore to assist me with loving hearts, here seeking the higher direction.

ADEPTUS MAJOR: It is well, brother. Amen.

ADEPTUS EXEMPTUS: Honorable Frater Peregrinus Vallis, you have my command to ascertain the dispositions of the postulant, to see that he is prepared properly and to present him in due form.

The Usher of the Grade rises with crossed arms.

FRATER PEREGRINUS VALLIS: Merciful Exempt Adept, I obey your behests.

He leaves the temple and goes to prepare the postulant, who is alone in one of the vestibules, isolated from all interruption. He is kneeling on a Prie-Dieu in sufficient light to read the scroll which has been placed in his hands. It contains versciles on mystical death and the union of the lover and Beloved. He is greeted by the Usher of the Grade saying:

FRATER PEREGRINUS VALLIS: Salve, Frater. Sub umbra alarum tuarum, Yeheshua, Domine noster, protégé et custodi nos.

He prepares the postulant by clothing him in the full vestments and insignia of an Auxiliary Frater Adeptus in the grade of Tiphereth. While this is being done:

FRATER PEREGINUS VALLIS: I pray that the shadow of death be turned for thee into morning, and that the light within be greater than light without. But without and within I wish thee all white brightness, when ~ after Calvary and Sepulture ~ there cometh thine Easter-tide. Behold, the purified soul goeth through the gates of death, as a virgin goeth to her bridal; and having great hope in thy death, I cloth thee not for the grave, but for the day of thy marriage, with vestures of gold, even with a golden girdle, and I give unto thee a wand of power.

His preparation being finished, the postulant is led, by the Usher of the Grade, from the vestibule to the door of the temple. Meanwhile the watchwords of the time have been exchanged as follows therein.

ADEPTUS EXEMPTUS: Fratres et Sorores, we are in fine called back to the house of the Father. Let us fear not therefore those waters which intervene, though they are cold to the simple senses.

ADEPTUS MAJOR: If it were not for cool, restful and wholesome death, we should never have part in the resurrection.

ADEPTUS EXEMPTUS: It is the call of every man ultimately to stand alone ~ that is to say, independently of the rest of his kind.

ADEPTUS MAJOR: But when a man is alone for far as the world is concerned, he is the nearer to the Presence of God.

ADEPTUS EXEMPTUS: Herein is the Divine Help which remains always with us; and the soul in the realization of that Presence enters Eternal life.

ADEPTUS MAJOR: Fratres et Sorores, we also have slept in the deep enchantment of the senses. We have paid the price of our exile.

ADEPTUS EXEMPTUS: Blessed by those whose sleep is taken away, who awaken and behold his glory.

Thereafter is silence, till the Usher of the Grade sounds his battery of one knock without. The answer within the temple is the solemn striking of a gong six times. The Usher of the Grade enters slowly with the postulant, and the door is tyled immediately. The entrance is so ordered that the following colloquy is heard by the postulant.

ADEPTUS EXEMPTUS: Mighty Adeptus Major, what is that?

ADEPTUS MAJOR: Merciful Exempt Adept, it is the hour of sunset.

ADEPTUS EXEMPTUS: I say that it is the hour of the rite.

ADEPTUS MAJOR: The night cometh and the darkness. The day is worn to evening. The season of stars is at hand.

ADEPTUS EXEMPTUS: Till He giveth His beloved sleep, it is meet and just that we should zealously redeem the time.

The Usher of the Grade leads the postulant within the sun to the western end of the temple, immediately behind the pillars. As they pass in the south:

ADEPTUS EXEMPTUS: Welcome, brother, in the names of those who are with us, a great Company, keeping the place of our mystery.

The Usher of the Grade and the postulant face east.

ADEPTUS EXEMPTUS: Honorable Frater Peregrinus Vallis, who is he that has followed you?

FRATER PEREGRINUS VALLIS: He is the Auxiliary Frater Adeptus, Frater Adveniat Regnum (*vel nomen aliud*), who ~ being well known among us ~ has come in the fullness of time seeking the benefit of sanctuary.

ADEPTUS EXEMPTUS: What is the age of our beloved brother?

FRATER PEREGRINUS VALLIS: It is thirty-three years.

ADEPTUS EXEMPTUS: Do you testify, Frater Peregrinus Vallis, that he has fulfilled the covenants of Tiphereth and has been heard in the holy Assemblies, bearing witness on his own part to the great day of the Lord and the glory of His coming.

FRATER PEREGRINUS VALLIS: He has led the hidden life in the house of the Holy Spirit, and on the threshold of its mystical sanctuary. He has fulfilled his time of ministry as Auxiliary Frater Adeptus in the rite of the grade of Tiphereth, and he has born faithful witness concerning the Life of life and the Advent of Messias the King.

ADEPTUS EXEMPTUS: Auxiliary Frater Adeptus, what is your own testimony?

The Usher of the Grade falls a little behind the postulant and directs him in an undertone.

AUXILIARY FRATER ADEPTUS: I look within this temple for the coming of the Peacemaker.

He has lifted up his wand solemnly and now lowers it.

ADEPTUS EXEMPTUS: Give me the signs of the temple.

The Auxiliary Frater Adeptus, still instructed by the Usher of the Grade, gives the opening and closing signs of the 5 = 6 grade and says:

AUXILIARY FRATER ADEPTUS: The kingdom of God is within.

ADEPTUS EXEMPTUS: Do you firmly and fully believe that beyond your present grade and the experience obtained therein are further sacramental mysteries delineating deeper states, and that the closed veil is not an unknown darkness?

AUXILIARY FRATER ADEPTUS: It is written that in a day to come the Lord will take away the veils.

ADEPTUS MAJOR: Merciful Exempt Adept, I proclaim that Frater Adveniat Regnum (*vel nomen aliud*) has heard the voice of our loving Father, and that he looks in due time to pass through death to life.

ADEPTUS EXEMPTUS: Spirit of the Lord, attest it; spirit of the most High God.

ADEPTUS MAJOR: Soul of the Man, receive it; soul of the Man, attain; all ye who have been faithful unto death.

ADEPTUS EXEMPTUS: Auxiliary Frater Adeptus, as the gifts and graces of the spirit, at each stage of their descent, involve higher obligations, I ask now whether you will assume these with a real sense of their importance, and with a firm purpose to sustain them even to the end.

The necessary direction being again given by the Usher of the Grade, and still in an undertone, the postulant extends his arms in the opening sign of the grade of Tiphereth, and speaks, following his guide.

AUXILIARY FRATER ADEPTUS: Merciful Exempt Adept, I have been taught that the sons of the True Legitimacy do ever remember the yoke of their high calling.

ADEPTUS EXEMPTUS: So stand therefore, my brother, with your arms extended in the sacred cruciform sign, and say in your heart that which you utter with your lips ~

THE SACRAMENT OF A HOLY PLEDGE

The Celebrant-in-Chief gives a battery of one knock, and all rise.

I, Frater Adveniat Regnum (*vel nomen aliud*), Auxiliary Frater Adeptus in the glorious grade of Tiphereth, and brother of the Rosy Cross, do here, in this spiritual house of the Third Order, most solemnly confess and realize that the mysteries of the greater Initiation are protected by invincible seals from all knowledge of the profane, and that, albeit the outward signs may be manifested in the exterior world, the essential secrets are never openly formulated. I testify also that their communication is in the silence of the soul, even from the light which is beyond to the innermost depths of the understanding. In the faith hereof my arms are thus extended in the eternal sign of the cross. It is for this reason that, standing on the threshold of experience in a world as yet unknown, the only pledges which the Sovereign Headship of our Order can here and now exact, I here and now offer; and in place of a covenant to keep secret those things which exceed revelation, I promise that, in all good faith and zeal, I will maintain the mysteries of the sanctuary by a zealous preservation of the seals and veils thereof. In testimony hereto, I complete the sacred sign.

He crosses his arms upon his breast and ~ directed by the Usher of the Grade ~ bows his head reverently. The Celebrants and Members are seated. The Usher of the Grade returns to his own seat.

ADEPTUS EXEMPTUS: We know, beloved brother, that something ~ at its allotted time ~ must open the doors of eternity; and the mystical paths and gates of this august grade are in your respect set open already in our hearts by the pledge which you have now taken. Mighty Adeptus Major, what are the present dispositions of our faithful companion?

ADEPTUS MAJOR: He has heard the call of the union, the still small voice speaking in the heart of longing; and he knows in his inward being that the Center draws him back.

ADEPTUS EXEMPTUS: It is symbolized by the sacred Rose centered in the cross of our mystery at the meeting point of the arms. He who has been manifested on the cross must be enfolded and withdrawn therein. So only does he enter in his own being into the life of the Rose.

ADEPTUS MAJOR: He has stilled the life of the senses; he has sought detachment in the heart from the accidents of things without, that he may be established in the permanence of those things that are within.

ADEPTUS EXEMPTUS: I bid him remember the still state which is that of the spirit in God.

ADEPTUS MAJOR: Merciful Exempt Adept, I testify that he desires to ascent, at what cost soever ~ even from the holy mountain into Eternal life.

ADEPTUS EXEMPTUS: God save us, Fratres et Sorores. By the task that we have undertaken, it is imposed on us to aid our beloved brother in the need which has thus arisen. Let him kneel in his place between the pillars, while we, on our part, turn for light and assistance to the Source of strength and light.

This is done by the postulant. The Celebrant-in-Chief turns eastward, standing with extended arms. The other officers and brethren kneel, facing the east.

THE PRAYER OF THE CELEBRANT IN CHIEF

O Merciful and Divine Mistress of the life which is communicated within, thou hast called this man and our brother, who in the secret places of his heart has heard the word of Thy summons. We beseech Thee to grant him the gift of perseverance, that he may not fail in the trial of his fortitude but may keep his soul in the contemplation of concentered love, till the great light shines through the hush and the darkness. May Thy word again go forth, full of power and salvation. May he rise in his renewal by a resurrection in the spirit. May he know that within the veils of judgment there is the High Palace of Thy Clemency, even the Palace of the King, fixed at the center for ever. May he hail Thee in that day by Thy true name, receiving the light from the Crown. We pray Thee also to have mercy on us, even as upon him who we have chosen under Thy guidance, our beloved frater Adveniat Regnum (*vel nomen aliud*), that having assumed to ourselves the care of his decreed passage through the halls of Thy loving chastening, we may raise him gloriously at the end, to the honor of Thy Holy Name and his everlasting exaltation in Thee. Praise unto the spouse and the spirit, through the years and the ages, even unto the union which is in God. Amen.

The Celebrants and Brethren resume their seats. The postulant rises and remains standing between the pillars, a single pace behind them.

ADEPTUS MAJOR: I testify concerning the still rest which is that of the spirit of God.

ADEPTUS EXEMPTUS: I utter the watchwords of the risen life in Christ.
ADEPTUS MAJOR: I show that the whole process is one of the joy in dying for life's most true sake, that it is therefore a work of glory, and that this death is rapture.

ADEPTUS EXEMPTUS: The state of being hidden with Christ in God is the state of union with TSURE, the Prototype of our nature, the Supernal Part, which does not leave the Supernals, and this is the end of being.

ADEPTUS MAJOR: The Divine Union is the unfolding of our consciousness in God.

ADEPTUS EXEMPTUS: (*Knocks once*)

ADEPTUS MAJOR: (*Knocks once*)

Here ends the First Point.

THE SECOND POINT,
BEING THE SECOND PATHS OF GEBURAH

The postulant remains in his place and does not pass through the pillars at this point.

ADEPTUS EXEMPTUS: I bid you observe that the altar in this grade is cubical, like that on which you were pledged at the beginning of your initiated life. It is now ~ as it was then ~ the altar of your life, presented before you in a symbol. It was unfolded as a cross in Tiphereth, but in Geburah, which you are about to enter, the cross shall fold up its arms and again become the cube. You who have been manifested in the holy assembly, leading a life of regeneration, which is called the life of the cross, are about to be withdrawn for a period into the state of hiddenness. It is a state of inward being illustrated by the veiled lights upon the pillars between which you stand.

The Celebrant-in-Chief indicates the great symbols of the paths.

ADEPTUS EXEMPTUS: The expounded mystery of the two paths which open toward Geburah from below may be found in the great symbols of the paths, which are shown here on the altar. Between them lies a human skull, facing toward the door of the sanctuary. It is in a sense their synthesis or summary. Because of their meaning, and that which is intimated by the link or bond between them, I bid you remember the light which shines amidst darkness, leading to the mystic end and the Life of life. Remember also the gate of that death by which the living man passes into the realizations of the spirit.

The Second Celebrant has risen and turns inward toward the altar.

ADEPTUS MAJOR: All true paths are paths, my brother, of the unity; and those who have been received into the mysteries know that man returns by many ways whence he came. The channels of communication from Sephira to Sephira in the scheme of the Tree of Life are the allotted paths of ascent in the Order of the Rosy Cross. Those which communicate with Geburah on the way of ascent in the Tree are the paths of Kaph and Mem. They are termed in our secret tradition the Intelligence of Desire ~ or the Rewarding Intelligence of those who seek in their zeal after things Divine and the Stable Intelligence, which testifies to permanence of being.

Geburah itself is called the Radical Intelligence, by allusion to that state in which there is kinship with the Supreme Unity. The letter Mem is referred to the cosmical element of Water, and the great symbol of the path of Mem represents a Crowned Master, submerged beneath the Waters of Creation, as if reposing therein. The face is turned to the beholder, but the eyes are closed in sleep. The figure ~ as a whole ~ recalls in broad outline the symbol of a swastika cross, and thus suggests that the Crowned Master, though to all outward appearance he is dead and indeed buried, is the fountain of life in the universe. His Divine nature is indicated by the golden nimbus which encircles the head and by the rainbow which extends above the entire figure. It is in analogy with that other rainbow, in sight like unto an emerald, which was about the Throne of God in the vision of Patmos.

The Crowned Master signifies the Divine immanent in creation, and you who behold this great symbol for the first time should remember how our elder brethren discovered in the house of the Holy Spirit the body of their founder, our loving Father Christian Rosy-Cross. The inward sense of that finding, within the measure of the microcosm, was unfolded in the grade of Tiphereth. Here now is its macrocosmic meaning. The sanctuary of the house was draped in rainbow colors, and our Master reposed in the center, represented by the Celebrant-in-Chief. It was shown to you then that, being dead, he yet speaks ~ from that place of which he says in his legend; I have made this inner sanctuary of the most hidden God a sepulcher for myself. The God who is concealed in creation, hidden within the sanctuary of his own building, testifies also from within it to those who have awakened in the spirit. But the history of man, my brother, is that of the greater universe. In him the Divine spark is immersed within the waters of his own material existence. The Crowned Master is within us, and so also is the founder of the Rosy Cross. These things are true in the microcosm, as they are true in the world without, and the symbol with which we are dealing has the same Rosicrucian analogies in both cases.

I say unto you that, within and without, the Crowned Master and all that which is symbolized by Christian Rosy Cross in the sepulcher of his own making are not dead but sleeping, and they awaken in you. Observe in this symbol how the ocean of phenomenal life supports on its surface the mystical ark of Noah, which ~ in one of its aspects ~ signifies the vessel of correspondences, wherein the types of all things are collected from the wreckage of the old initiations for transmission through a new era.

As such, it belongs to the symbolism of instituted mysteries; but it has another and deeper sense. It is the ship of humanity, poised on the waters of the world. It is man, collective and individual, man in possession of his sense and also limited by these. There is that within him which is not put to sleep less utterly than is the great symbolical Master. There is that which is hidden in the body, as God in his own creation, that which is Divine within you, as the Divine abides in the universe. You know these things intellectually through the sacred rites of our Fellowship. As an old son of its mysteries, you should know them also ere now by the realization of living experience, and you will thus understand inwardly that there is yet another aspect under which we may regard the ark, for by many issues the great emblems open upon the infinite which they show forth, though it is after the manner of a reversed glass through which they are seen as if from very far away. From this point of view, the ark represents the house mystical of all the holy processes which the masters of experience have built about us who are following the quest of God. But it is above all the house of contemplation, understood in the sense of the masters and summarized in the Rosy Cross. An exit is found therefrom, or even from thought itself, into the world of direct experience. The grade of Geburah represents this flight of the soul, and I bid you therefore remember that in the ark of old there was a window, through which the mystical dove passed and repassed ~ now in frustrated flight, because wings may beat vainly at the golden gate ~ now bearing an olive branch of peace, as the promise of a new world and another life therein. But, in fine, there came a day when the dove returned no more, because the aspiration and outreaching of the soul do at length attain their term.

The Second Celebrant resumes his seat. The Celebrant-in-Chief rises and faces inward toward the altar.

ADEPTUS EXEMPTUS: Auxiliary Frater Adeptus, you have looked upon the path of Mem, by which the Divine Influences flow down from Geburah to Hod. You have dwelt at its threshold in contemplation. But there is also the path of Kaph, and it is by this that you will enter from Tiphereth the house of Justice in Geburah and the sanctuary of the Holy Sekinah. From Binah, which is the great Sabbath ~ the rest whereof we desire ~ there is an influx to the path of Kaph. It is part of the mystery of union and the ineffable mystery of the Presence. Now it is said that Geburah can be withstood only by those who have restrained their concupiscence, and the reason is that it is a Supernal Tribunal, wherein the love which overcomes death is prepared by death for the bridal. Geburah is a house of death, and the path by which it is entered is one of the paths of Shekinah. The mystery of the spirit is behind it, and there is no other means given unto man by which he shall pass into his rest, shall hear the Voice of the symbol, and after the cloud and the darkness, in a secret light of all, shall behold his way of resurrection into the life of union. The deep things of spiritual life are in correspondence with life manifested in the material world. Similar bonds of comparison subsist between physical and mystical death. Both are a veil, and the curtains in both cases are parted from within, to show that there is life behind. The great symbol of the path of Kaph is a symbol of mystical death and the price of immortality attained in conscious being. The pentagram which enshrines the human figure represents the state of Geburah and its holy sanctuary. Frater Adveniat Regnum (*vel nomen aliud*), I say unto you that the old Adam ⁓ which dies on the cross of Tiphereth at a certain hour of sunset ⁓ is buried for ever in Geburah, but the new Adam comes forth alive. Remember the dispassionate equilibrium which is poised between life and death. This is the state of the entranced figure before you, folded in the sleep of ecstasy, but drawing therein from the fountain of life in the universe. On the threshold of adeptship you were born again in the symbolism of the Rosy Cross. You have led in Tiphereth the mystical life of regeneration, and in Geburah you are taught how to die.

Here ends the Second Point.

THE THIRD POINT,
THE RITUAL OF THE HOLY CROSS

As the speech of the Celebrant-in-Chief draws to its close, the Usher of the Grade has left his place quietly, and concurrently with the last words he extinguishes all lights in the temple save those of the veiled candles on the pillars. He withdraws the curtain from the cross of Tiphereth, which is exposed for the first time. He comes round with the sun, and facing the postulant puts him back from between the pillars of the western end of the temple, where he faces the Celebrants, having his back to the cross. He is left leaning on his wand and the Usher of the Grade returns to his own place. The Celebrant-in-Chief has resumed his seat.

ADEPTUS MAJOR: The glorious sun of Tiphereth has set upon the life of man.

ADEPTUS EXEMPTUS: Spirit of our Master Christ, spirit of the Great Master, I have entered the path of ecstasy.

ADEPTUS MAJOR: I have known the sanctity of death in the halls of silence.

ADEPTUS EXEMPTUS: The Christ-Spirit is within me. I have risen with the Great Master, and behold I am alive for evermore.

ADEPTUS MAJOR INITIATION

ADEPTUS MAJOR: The path of death is also the path of Glory.

There is here a pause of some moments.

ADEPTUS EXEMPTUS: Behold, I have gone before you in the way, O brother of the Rosy cross. I bear witness to the resurrection of the adept, the body of redemption, the Christ-Life in the spirit and the law of mercy in Chesed. On the cross of holy obligation, which is the cross of life in Tiphereth, you have attained the crucifixion of the adept in conformity of will, the consecration of desire, dedication of mind, and the purification of your earthly part. The six years of Tiphereth are the working days of your creation, and thereafter comes a Sabbath.

There is here a pause of some moments.

ADEPTUS EXEMPTUS: Honorable frater Peregrinus Vallis, keeper of the precincts appertaining to the valley of silence, bind our beloved postulant to that cross which symbolizes his inward spiritual life and the time of his passion.

The postulant's wand of an Auxiliary Frater Adeptus is taken from him and laid at his feet. He is put upon the cross wearing his vestments and insignia. He recalls thus the old pictures of Christ in the reverence of priestly garments, as on a cross of glory. The Usher of the Grade returns with the sun to his place.

ADEPTUS MAJOR: Fratres et Sorores, abiding in the halls of Geburah, amidst the mysteries of sacred Darkness, behold him who is uplifted. Let us pray that he may draw after him all things which are capable within of eternal life.

ADEPTUS EXEMPTUS: O secret doctrine of the union. I testify that we come forth from the Center and that the Center draws us back.

ADEPTUS MAJOR: O life which is beyond nature, lift up and assume unto thyself the life which is in the midst of death belonging to our natural humanity.

ADEPTUS EXEMPTUS: To you, Frater Adveniat Regnum (*vel nomen aliud*) I unveil the mystical story of your inward progress through all grades of our Order. At a certain epoch of your manifest life there began to be formulated within you a desire for Divine Things, for the spiritual life as a path that leads thereto, for the depths of the riches of union, for living knowledge ~ beyond all knowledge and union attained in the ways of earth. It was a first intimation within you of an eternal desire in the Christ-Spirit, Who is the spouse and lover of souls, to enter into bonds of divine marriage with your conscious being, that it might attain itself in Him. The desire on your own part signified a loving stirring and kindling, awakened ~ by the unfolding of the Christ-Spirit ~ from a state of immanence to a state of manifestation within you. It opened, as if in summary, all modes and measures of the prospects which stretch through eternal being. You saw in a glass and darkly the beginning and end of union. The correspondence in ritual and symbolism was your experience in the First Portal grade of the Rosy Cross. The loving secrets of the path were unfolded subsequently by successive stages, corresponding to the later grades. The stable of your earthly personality was made ready in the rite of Zelator for the mystery to come, by purification of the bodily part. As a frater Theoreticus, your mind was prepared, consecrated and filled with the thought thereof. Afterwards, in the grade of Practicus, the heart was restored in purity and consumed with hunger and thirst for the desired end. The will, in fine, was consecrated by the Philosophical grade and the purpose turned thereto.

The will and its purpose were held in a sacred suspension, awaiting the declaration therein of the Divine intention and will. With a sense of the mystery on the Threshold, you stood then as one who knows that his Redeemer lives, that the temple of his natural personality must be rebuilt in God, that the Christ-Spirit shall reign within it, even as a King in Israel. But this Spirit was working already within, and that toward which it was working was the making of a new creature and a rebirth in God. It comes above for this reason, that the second Portal of the Rosy Cross is a grade of Regeneration, a grade of the second birth. The beloved soul is transformed by the Lover of the Soul and remade in His likeness. For the fulfillment of this mystery you reentered Yesod, because it is a mystery of sex spiritualized, wherein is the fount of grace, regeneration and life to come. In the grade of Tiphereth you were set to grow in the likeness of the Soul's Lover, and for this reason all its symbols and ceremonies, with all its epochs, are depicted as a figurative mystery of the Christ-Life enacted in your own life and your proper personality. The same imagery obtains throughout the grades of the Third Order, and they are all intimations of union between Christ mystical and the soul. The experience of the second birth corresponds to the soul's vision of the Lover and Betrothed therein. That life which follows the birth is a preparation of bridal garments. Thereafter comes a marriage, and this ~

my brother in the spirit ~ is the day of your bridal, the end to a life of separation and the death of all that hinders the joy of ineffable union. O soul, chosen out of thousands, pass on through death to life, knowing that this death is a secret of the union, and that the life to come is a glorious life of resurrection. No more through mysteries of symbol, rites and the pageants of these, pass thou henceforth through mysteries of real experience, and find therein that whatsoever is enacted here in this holy temple sets forth ~ in living words and moving pictures ~ the successive states and stages of the soul which goes to God.

There is a pause of complete silence. The Usher of the Grade renews the incense and it fumes through the temple.

ADEPTUS EXEMPTUS: It is I, O beloved brother, who ordained in days long ago that you should take up your cross and carry it. I, being an Unknown Master, and a symbol of the Christ-state, have come out of the far distance to be present at that mystical death which closes the life of Tiphereth. Fratres et Sorores, that which was begun upon the cross, on the cross also is finished.

There is another pause. The Usher of the Grade strikes the ninth hour upon the gong. He then moves with the sun to a point beside the cross of Tiphereth.

ADEPTUS EXEMPTUS: The spirit of the world dies and gives place to the Spirit of Christ. Herein is the folly of the cross, which is a scandal to the wise of earth. Our beloved brother dies in the mystical sense on the cross of Tiphereth, when the purpose of the crucified life has been fulfilled within him, when he has become himself the cross, and has immolated thereon whatsoever in his natural personality has no place or state in eternity. There is a moment when his perishable state cries out in the last throes of its ordeal: why has Thou forsaken me? There is a moment when the immortal part commends its being into the hands of God, Who is its source. There is a time when the higher and lower unite in saying: it is finished.

The Usher of the Grade has bent the head of the postulant to the right side, gently and firmly. He sees that this position is maintained. The Celebrant-in-Chief has spoken slowly and in a somewhat subdued voice. The Second Celebrant rises and flings up his arms, crying in a loud tone:

ADEPTUS MAJOR: Consummatum est.

There is a hushed murmur throughout the temple, the Fratres et Sorores repeating: It is finished; Consummatum est; Into Thy hands. *In this manner there is produced a certain confusion of sounds, albeit in an undertone. Under special circumstances, the words of the Second Celebrant may be also followed immediately by the springing of a muffled rattle. When there is again silence, the Celebrant-in-Chief points to the postulant on the cross.*

ADEPTUS EXEMPTUS: Blessed is the death which is suffered in respect of impurity and attachment to things that are transitory. Grant unto the self-knowing part, O Ineffable Master of all, the realization of the Divine within it, of the eternal end which is in Thee.
There is a complete silence for a short space.

ADEPTUS MAJOR: Angel of liberation, Shekinah, Mother in transcendence, grant that in his death he may behold Thy Holy Face, that he may know the life which is Thou.

ADEPTUS EXEMPTUS: Honorable Frater Peregrinus Vallis, let the postulant be taken from the cross.

When this has been done, the Usher of the Grade stands at the right of the postulant, both facing toward the east.

ADEPTUS EXEMPTUS: Fratres et Sorores, our brother has put away that which hindered, and the path is free before him. The death on the cross is literal, in the sense that the old life has ended; but the death is also mystical, because it is not a dissolution of the physical part. It is all a work of the will in the personality itself, by the re-ordination of desire and thought, with the consequent suspension of attraction toward the lower order of things, and thereafter by attachment to those things that are above. In virtue of all the holy hypotheses and all the witness of experience, there is a co-operation from the Divine Side in the work of grace, and it is known that this is fuller as the channels open within us, in the process of separation. There may come even that stage when the work is done for us and in us. Frater Adveniat Regnum (*vel nomen aliud*), you who have been manifested on the cross of Tiphereth and have become the cross therein are now to be withdrawn into the sacred silence of the Rose, that you may in turn become the Rose. You are in the care of him who is an Abider in the Valley of Judgment. Thither, where you are now called he has passed before you. As you follow his faithful leading, I direct you to set aside all external images and to realize that in so far as you are moving, it is in the thought-body alone. Your progress is a progress through the shadows.

Here ends the Third Point.

THE FOURTH POINT, THE GATE OF THE SANCTUARY

The postulant is drawn rather than moves on his own part, and is placed between the pillars. The Usher of the Grade returns to his seat.

ADEPTUS EXEMPTUS: Being divested of that which seems, we desire ~ God willing ~ to set aside all veils and go forth unclothed, as we came.

ADEPTUS MAJOR: We came forth naked into manifestation. We go out naked at our call, having put away the things that were before. We enter into a new sphere of being, and therein we are clothed upon.

There is a pause of a few moments, and the Usher of the Grade still maintains the incense, so that its fumes fill the temple, rolling about the pillars. The veiled candles are clouded yet more deeply.

ADEPTUS EXEMPTUS: Beloved brother, it is through many types that we pass ultimately behind the veils. I have something to say to you concerning Philosophical Mercury, the symbol of which you bear upon your left side, as an Auxiliary Frater Adeptus. The Keepers of the secret tradition tell us in their parables that it is coagulated by its own Sulphur, which is the conjunction of their Sun and Moon, or the marriage of Adam and Eve. Now this is to be understood mystically, for they say also that it is a union of heaven and earth. The explanation of such hidden language is to be found in the Tree of Life, as this is understood by the Order of the Rosy Cross. The natural principles of our humanity, symbolized in their correspondences with Fire, Water, Air and Earth, are collected in Malkuth, which is the world of Action, and are centered therein upon things manifested. The thoughts, desires, and will of man are contained within earth and his senses. In other words, the native mercury, sulphur and salt have not been made subject to the operations of Divine Wisdom. They begin to be purified and prepared in the World of Formation, containing three Sephiroth, allocated respectively to mind, desire, and will, and corresponding to three spiritualized planets, the Moon, Mercury, and Venus. These Sephiroth constitute the second reflected triad in the Tree of Life. The World of Creation, or Third Order of the Rosy Cross, is the first reflected triad, and it answers to the same principles of our nature, when they have been changed by the work of Wisdom. That which corresponded in Yesod to the reflected light of the Moon has become Philosophical Mercury in the grade of Tiphereth, or the Mind permeated and transmuted by the sun of Righteousness.

You will understand therefore that in the higher grades of the Third Order, analogous transmutations of desire and will are symbolized, so that in the language of the secret tradition they become Philosophical Sulphur and Salt. The transmutation of Desire fixes Mind, and hence Mercury is said to be coagulated by Sulphur, while transmuted Will and its Purpose direct all the inward principles of love and understanding to that Divine World which is first in the Tree of Life. The triad becomes a unity, which is the state of the Mystical Stone, at once tinctured and tingeing. But in the World of Divinity, the Three Principles are symbolized as Kether, the divine Mind, Chokmah, the Eternal Wisdom, the goodwill and good pleasure of Gods purpose, and Binah, the Eternal Love. They subsist in an ineffable unity. So are the worlds completed, interlinked at every point, and man attains God by a union of principles which correspond and are one at the root. As regards Mercury, it is affirmed that we know it now as it exists imprisoned in a body, but a day will come when it shall be liberated from present limitations and manifested as a pure, fixed, intelligible, constant fire. It is a fluidic and volatile substance, to fix which is the work of Wisdom. I say unto you that our Mercury is mind, and that in fixity, rest and simplicity it can attain a Divine Mode. Thought is reduced therein to the point at which it vanishes for a period, and the Mind of God testifies to mind in the silence.

There is here the pause of a moment.

ADEPTUS MAJOR INITIATION

ADEPTUS MAJOR: The natural reason of man is earthly above all things, but the ascent of the Tree of Life carries us far from earth, far from the ways and forms of material thought. The imprisoned and liberated Mercury are contrasted states of mind; one of them errant in the world of sense and confined therein, the other emancipated; one volatile, the other fixed by wisdom. Unto this shall be given in the stillness that word which has been sought in all initiations, which is reversed and transliterated, is substituted after every manner, and is recovered only by the soul in a state of union at the Center. This is the Word of Life. The Absolute exceeds thought, but in a certain suspension it enters to fill the heart, and so is God realized within us.

The Celebrants rise. The Usher of the Grade rises and passed quietly to the door of the sanctuary, from which he draws back the veil, exposing the symbol of the setting sun, which is thus displayed suddenly to the postulant. He then returns to his place.

ADEPTUS EXEMPTUS: Fratres et Sorores, Adepti Majores, behold, I have found in the symbolism of my high office and testify from its seat of experience that the kingdom of God is within.

The Celebrants approach the postulant and face him as he stands between the pillars.

ADEPTUS MAJOR: Looking toward that Center which is beyond all thought and form, which communicates to the purified soul amidst a stillness of ineffable love, we draw you forth in sanctity, O seeker of Eternal life.

They have brought him from between the pillars and have faced with him to the east, the Celebrant-in-Chief being at his right on the southern side and the Second Celebrant on his left. They move very slowly through the northern part of the temple.

ADEPTUS EXEMPTUS: In the grade of Tiphereth you entered the sanctuary of life by the gate of Venus. You approach now the gate of the setting sun, by which you will enter the sanctuary of mystical death.

ADEPTUS MAJOR: The Christ mystical Who is manifested in Tiphereth as Divine Life enters the hiddenness of Divine Death in the sacred halls of Geburah. Let us traverse the Path of mystical death.

ADEPTUS EXEMPTUS: The passage of this Path is a journey through great darkness. Thought is stilled in fixation. Desire is sharpened to a needle's point.

ADEPTUS MAJOR: The journey to the Center lies through the gate of the tomb ~ as understood in the sense of our Order; that gate is the death of the kiss.

ADEPTUS EXEMPTUS: Honorable Frater Peregrinus Vallis, I call upon you to open the gate, and may God lead our brother into the risen life beyond.

ADEPTUS MAJOR: Amen, brother. May God be now with him and His peace with thy spirit.

The door of the sanctuary is set wide open. The Usher returns to his place. The Celebrants and postulant reach the threshold. They pause thereat and there is silence for a very brief space, during which the postulant sees the funeral litter, the catafalque and the candles of the dead.

ADEPTUS EXEMPTUS: The correspondence to your present situation, my brother, in Christian symbolism, is the bearing of the dead Christ to that rock-hewn sepulchre wherein no one had lain previously.

ADEPTUS MAJOR: Having put away the earthly substance of the mind, may that which is imperishable within you be joined to that which does not pass in the universe.

The Celebrant-in-Chief faces westward, with high extended arms.

ADEPTUS EXEMPTUS: Fratres et Sorores, pray for the great peace of the perfect stillness, and for the sudden light therein,

He turns again eastward. They enter the sanctuary. The postulant is led to the northern side of the litter and is there left. The Celebrant-in-Chief takes up his position at the due east, facing west. The Second Celebrant passes to the south, where he faces the postulant.

ADEPTUS MAJOR: Let us enter into the mystery of death.

ADEPTUS EXEMPTUS: It is the body of our infirmity which dies upon the cross of Tiphereth, that in the sacred tomb of the adepts the soul may know God at its own center.

ADEPTUS MAJOR: The analogy of this inward event is the descent of the Lord Christ into the prison of the fathers.

ADEPTUS EXEMPTUS: Such a descent takes place between mystical death and resurrection. It is the state in which the seeker for Eternal Life goes to the uttermost end of his being, as on a journey into the underworld, the abyss within self-knowledge.

ADEPTUS MAJOR: When the last veil is parted, there is union of being in God.

ADEPTUS EXEMPTUS: Ashes to ashes, and dust to dust, in the death of the natural body. Spirit to soul in God, life to life, communication of ineffable being.

ADEPTUS MAJOR: Hereof is the death of the mystic, and hereof the death which is in Christ, our leader into the life of glory.

ADEPTUS EXEMPTUS: I testify that such death is the marriage of the adept, and that here is his bridal night.

The Second Celebrant leans across the litter and with both hands assists the postulant to assume a recumbent posture thereon. His arms are crossed upon his breast and a red pall is laid over him, but leaving the head uncovered. The Celebrant-in-Chief closes the eyes of the postulant, saying:

ADEPTUS EXEMPTUS: It is I who put to rest in Geburah. It is I who give back to the Father.

There is a moment's silence, and when this is beginning to be felt the Celebrant-in-Chief lifts up his arms and says:

ADEPTUS EXEMPTUS: There are many witnesses, and above them are the High and Holy Wardens. Their unfailing care shall watch over you in the grace of the solemn vigil. By the will and testament of the mysteries, I bequeath you to the sacred shadows. May you be brought in a final passage from the things which perish into those that remain for ever.

The Celebrants proceed with the sun to the western end of the sanctuary, where they pause, facing the litter.

ADEPTUS EXEMPTUS: By the power to me committed, I pray and beseech the Frater of Grace and the Auxiliaries of the Divine Will to pour down upon you, our brother, the living Power of the Word and the Love in Light thereof.

They turn westward and the Second Celebrant says, with outstretched arms:

ADEPTUS MAJOR: Blessed in the sight of the Lord is the death of His holy ones.

The Usher of the Grade has drawn the curtain over the holy cross of Tiphereth. He has reversed the seats of the Celebrants, so that they are now turned to the east. The Celebrants leave the sanctuary and take up their places on either side of the altar. The door of the sanctuary remains open to its fullest extent. The Usher of the Grade goes before it and says:

FRATER PEREGRINUS VALLIS: Hic jacet frater Adveniat Regnum (*vel nomen aliud*).

He returns to his place.

Here ends the Fourth Point.

THE FIFTH POINT,
THE OFFICE OF THE HOLY WATCH

There is a period of complete silence. The Usher of the Grade continues to maintain the fire in the pot of incense, and the fumes of it fill the temple. The door behind the sanctuary opens suddenly and silently. The Priestess of the Rite comes forth, wearing the violet vestures and veil of Binah. The veil covers her from head to foot, and is embroidered with the symbols of Shekinah. She bears in her hand the sacred Rose of Geburah. She stands at the head of the catafalque and is seen through it, leaning over the bier. The Usher of the Grade rises in his place and ~ without moving therefrom ~ says slowly and clearly:

FRATER PEREGRINUS VALLIS: Blessed be the glory of the Lord in the place of His Shekinah.

He resumes his seat. There is the pause of a few moments, and thereafter:

THE PRIESTESS: I have opened a door in the darkness, and the Light of the Supernals is in my heart. I am the Shekinah in transcendence, the Great Mother in Binah, appearing as virgin-wisdom and testifying to Eternal Life in the kingdom. I am the token of the Divine Presence issuing from the mercy-seat and reflected from the overshadowing Cherubim. I am the guiding spirit of all the holy assemblies; I am the bride in the Christ-State; and I am Divine Understanding, disposing all things sweetly to the great true ends of all. As the Shekinah in the temples below, I have been the guide of all your paths. With you I have been in exile, O brother, and with you I enter into liberation. I bring the grace of mystical death to those who practice the law of holiness. I am the well of prudence for the elect. I lift up my holy symbol of life in the indrawn state, the red rose of Geburah, which is manifested also in Hod, wherein is the beginning of continence for the part of desire in man. In the grace of mystical death, the elect shall behold my glory. On the threshold of the inward journey, pass in my peace, O brother, receiving the kiss of the Shekinah.

The Priestess presses the rose on the mouth of the postulant. The pressure continues for a few moments only, and yet so long that there shall be no doubt of the experience and its realization by the postulant. He sees the arm of the Priestess and her figure bending over him, but he does not behold her face, by reason of the veil which covers it.

THE PRIESTESS: Enter into mystical death. Pass into its deep degrees. Thou hast received the visit of Matrona. Go forth to the palace of the kings, which is a palace at thine own center.

The Priestess remains at the head of the bier. In the ceremony which follows, the Usher of the Grade strikes the hours and half hours on the gong. As regards these times and those of the grade generally, the symbolical convention is that when the postulant enters the temple in the First Point it is the hour of sunset – fixed at six o'clock. The figurative death upon the cross occurs at the ninth hour. That which follows, being the passage through the path of Kaph and to the moment of the first watchword, is a period of thirty minutes. The stroke of the gong in connection with this utterance represents half-past nine. The hours and half-hours sounded subsequently are up to and including three o'clock in the morning, which may be taken to represent the hour of perfect darkness. The watchwords of the vigil are recited by the Priestess from her place within the sanctuary, and their utterance comes immediately after each striking. The actual time occupied by the ceremony should be about thirty minutes.

THE FIRST WATCHWORD: This vault is the tent of the Shekinah. This bier is the bed of Solomon. The place is peace.

THE SECOND WATCHWORD: Forget the body of thy mortality and the crucified desires of flesh. Sacrifice the Bull of Earth.

THE THIRD WATCHWORD: Still also the mind within thee, all the makers of images. Sacrifice the Man of thought.

THE FOURTH WATCHWORD: Winds upon the waters of the soul. Say unto them: Peace, be still; peace upon the turbid waters; still the soul in death; sacrifice the Winged Eagle.

THE FIFTH WATCHWORD: The will is strong within thee; the will is keen; into the hands of God; into his holy charge. Offer up the Great Lion. These things, my friend, are dead. They have died in him.

THE SIXTH WATCHWORD: His image only is within thee – last thought, last symbol, last desire of all. I say unto thee; quench this also. Love unto love, my brother, from thee and me apart. And God uplifting thy consciousness shall fill that which is emptied.

THE SEVENTH WATCHWORD: Thou enterest on the great journey. Be of a steadfast heart. Thou passest, seeking the Presence. Darkness of death is around thee. Enter into the great darkness.

THE EIGHTH WATCHWORD: The darkness deepens in thee. The void is there. Self is alone with self.

THE NINTH WATCHWORD: All has passed from thee. Thou alone remainest. Self upon self, reflect no more an image. Spirit of the man unclothed, spirit of the man within, thou wast, thou art, and art to come. Unto everlasting, Spirit. Know thyself in God.

THE TENTH WATCHWORD: The sleep of this mystical death is shadow of an eternal Sabbath.

THE ELEVENTH WATCHWORD: Spirit in the height and deep, realize the God within.

THE TWELFTH WATCHWORD: Spirit of the All and One, Spirit of the eternal God, know this man in Thee.

The voice of the Priestess ceases at this point. She rises, and moving very softly with the sun, passes from the sanctuary into the temple. The Usher of the Grade is standing already by the door, and he goes before the Priestess, carrying the wand of peace. He escorts her to a seat which he has placed previously between the pillars. She sits there, looking eastward, but the veil still covers her. The rose of Geburah is now seen upon her breast. A space follows during which there is complete silence in the temple and holy sanctuary. The Usher of the Grade continues to burn incense, and the place is clouded.

Here ends the Fifth Point.

THE SIXTH POINT,
THE INWARD RESURRECTION

The period of silence has ended. The Celebrants remain in their places.

ADEPTUS EXEMPTUS: It is defined by the wise masters that Mercury kills and makes alive.

ADEPTUS MAJOR: Under the operation of its own Sulphur there is destroyed one mode of its being, but thereafter it arises to the life of another form. Hereof are death and resurrection in the mysteries of the Rosy Cross.

ADEPTUS EXEMPTUS: It is a work of the spiritual sun in Tiphereth, and when it is in fine completed, the postulant enters the state of Geburah through the door of the sun. That sun represents the perfect union of the three philosophical principles and of the second reflected triad in the Tree of Life. This is why the grade of Tiphereth is a summary of the Third Order. But, in the succession of grades, the mind is transmuted in Tiphereth, the desire part in Geburah, and the will in Chesed, the three principles working thereto in each as one principle only; and this is the Christ-Spirit.

ADEPTUS MAJOR: In virtue of that working, the life of regeneration enters into mystical death by a union at the Center, as a marriage with the Life of life, and in the glorious mysteries of resurrection from death, it enters into the life of union, which is wedded life in Christ.

ADEPTUS EXEMPTUS: Fratres et Sorores, Adepti Majores, our beloved brother has gone out through that door which opens on the inward world. He has made unto himself a sepulcher. All symbols of the external world have dissolved. Its essence remains in the heart. He has passed into the cloud of darkness; unto him be the light beyond. May the Christ-Spirit in the darkness be unto his soul a light. May there be a meeting of the spirit and the bride. So in his inward being shall be find that God is within, that the soul has ever its Christ in the hidden center, and that man, or woman, in the flesh, the woman and the man are we. The Great Work is for the soul to find the Spouse, to know and to be known with Him.

ADEPTUS MAJOR: In witness also to the other side of symbolism, I pray that having been crucified with Christ, having died and been entombed with him, having gone down into the underworld, the postulant may rise up with Christ and so come into the kingdom.

The Celebrants leave their seats and proceed to the door of the sanctuary. The Celebrant-in-Chief turns westward with uplifted arms.

ADEPTUS EXEMPTUS: Fratres et Sorores, it is I who bring back to life, that the work of holy manifestation may be carried to is completion.

The Celebrants enter the sanctuary and take up their places east and north of the bier. There is silence for some moments, and thereafter:

ADEPTUS EXEMPTUS: The watches of this sleep are holy. The watches of sleep are long.

ADEPTUS MAJOR: It is time now to awaken.

ADEPTUS EXEMPTUS: He has followed the Great Quest. He has finished the journey therein. He has reached the term of search in the hiddenness of his own center. He knows that it is the center of all.

ADEPTUS MAJOR: He has passed behind that veil which earthly hands sought in vain to draw. The light which is above reason dissolves its folds.

ADEPTUS EXEMPTUS: In the shadow of death he has found the path of Life. He shall not see death for ever.

ADEPTUS MAJOR: He has lifted up his eyes to the star that shines at morning, knowing that his Redeemer lives.

ADEPTUS EXEMPTUS: I say unto you that there is light in this sepulcher and that the bier is a bed of peace. The soul of the man herein has found the Spirit which is Christ, the immanent and hidden God.

ADEPTUS MAJOR: There has been silence in the inward heaven for the space of a half an hour.

ADEPTUS EXEMPTUS: The word of the Lord recalls him. The power of the Lord gives back.

The Celebrant-in-Chief lifts up his arms.

ADEPTUS EXEMPTUS: He that was dead shall rise.

Again he lowers his arms and extends both hands over the bier.

ADEPTUS EXEMPTUS: Thou who hast beheld the Light, which is all light, in the darkness, I call thee back. Soul out of space and time, I draw thee to time and space. After the rest in God there is an awakening in him.

He passes to the southern side of the bier.

ADEPTUS EXEMPTUS: I say unto thee: Arise and come forth.

The Celebrant-in-Chief raises the postulant and brings him into an erect posture beside the bier. He then places his hands on the postulant's shoulders.

ADEPTUS EXEMPTUS: I raise thee by the kiss of peace. May the consciousness of thy true Self abide within thee, henceforth and forever.

The Adeptus Major comes round with the sun to the south, and the postulant is led to the door of the sanctuary, where he stands between the Celebrants. In the temple without, the Usher of the Grade raises the veiled lights.

ADEPTUS EXEMPTUS: Blessed is he who has entered into the place of darkness and out of the shadow of death comes forth alive.

ADEPTUS MAJOR: It is written that the Eternal Fount of Love is found in Geburah, though this is also the place of judgment.

The Celebrants lead the postulant from the sanctuary and through the southern part of the temple. They reach the western side of the altar and stand, facing towards the pillars.

He beholds in this manner the Most Holy Priestess of the Rites who has risen and stands veiled from head to foot between the pillars. With arms outstretched, her outlines form a pentagram, and she wears a great pentagram as a lamina on her breast. The red rose of Geburah is in the center thereof.

ADEPTUS EXEMPTUS: You have passed, O Frater Adveniat Regnum (*vel nomen aliud*), from the sanctuary of mystical death, having been raised in that light which has dawned in your own being, and in its hidden center. By the symbolism, however, you are still in the hidden world, amidst the aftermath of your experience within. It is a light of memory and a rapture of contemplation thereon. It corresponds to darkness without, because the world does not share therein. It corresponds also to the half light which fills this sacred temple, where those who have dwelt in the center are brethren of a new spirit, and this spirit ~ outside all forms of words ~ bears witness to its presence in the world, and draws those who are prepared. Moreover, in the holy assembly of those who know with you the watchwords and the counsels of experience can pass freely. You can testify concerning yourself, and your co-heirs will testify to you. Hereof is the life in Geburah and hereof the raising therein. It is a retreat of three mystical days, during which there is speech in the rose, and the mind prepares its symbols, so that in the life of resurrection it may have power from the inward heaven to express on earth in efficacious sacraments the Word of the Soul to man.

The Usher of the Grade has reversed previously the seats of the Celebrants. The Second Celebrant returns to his seat on the northern side of the altar.

The Celebrant-in-Chief places the postulant with his back to the north and faces him.

ADEPTUS EXEMPTUS: By the power in me vested and in virtue of my high office, as not indeed I but the Christ-Spirit speaking within me, I give you speech in the rose. You who have been bound in Tiphereth are unloosed in Geburah. Henceforward let the servant usurp no longer the place of Matrona.

Still holding his wand, he raises it in both hands over the head of the postulant.

ADEPTUS EXEMPTUS: He preached unto the spirits in prison. Testify to the light of the Spirit in the Hidden Center. The glory shall be revealed in us, the manifestation of the sons of God.

The Celebrant-in-Chief leads the postulant to the pillars, where the veiled figure of the Priestess continues to form the pentagram in broad outlines. He indicates its several points in the lamina on her breast.

ADEPTUS EXEMPTUS: Bear witness in the rose, my brother, and say after me:

I dedicate my feet to the paths of Light. (*The Celebrant-in-Chief points to the left basal angle of the Pentagram.*) I dedicate my mind to the great quest. (*He points to the right basal angle.*) I dedicate my heart to the Divine rapture. (*He points to the left upper angle.*) I dedicate my will to the Supernal Mother of souls. (*He points to the right upper angle.*) I dedicate my entire self to the union of true being in the Christ who is God within me (*He points to the angle at the apex.*), awaiting the perfect resurrection, which is the union of three in One.

The Priestess resumes her seat. The Second Celebrant comes round by the south and takes charge of the postulant. The Celebrant-in-Chief returns to his own seat. The postulant is placed again with his back to the north, and the Second Celebrant faces him. They occupy points which are parallel to the two pillars.

ADEPTUS MAJOR: The sign of the 6=5 grade is given by raising the hands to the face, with the palms turned inward and the little fingers joined at the tips. It refers to the indrawn state of Geburah, encompassed by the Tree of Life. The grip or token is given by the left hand clasping the right thus, or alternatively by the right hand clasping the left. In either case it forms the pentagram, which is the lineal figure of the grade. The symbol is Hiddekel, which is the third river of Eden. There are two grand words or sacred names, referable respectively to the left and right hand pillars of the Tree of Life. The first is Taboonah, or understanding, a title of Binah and of Matrona, the Great Mother. You should know that the desire of the Great Mother must fill the heart of the postulant in his passage through the ineffable degrees, for our attainment is ~ in and through Her ~ in the great sea of Binah. Therein is the mystery of the bride, who is united with the spouse in Chokmah. The second sacred name is Yah, being Yod, He, signifying the union of Jehovah and Elohim, or God and his Shekinah in Kether. From this name is derived the mystical number of the grade, which is 15, the synthesis of which is 6, alluding to the years of your regenerate life in Tiphereth, while the correspondence is 33 or 3 + 3 = 6, being those of the Christ-Life in Palestine. The mystical title, which I give you hereby and herein, is Peregrinus Vallis, a traveler in the valley of death. In Geburah there is above all things a grade of union, but a grade also of separation, in fine completed. Its symbolism is therefore not only one of espousals but of severity and judgment. Before the union can take place, everything that belongs to separation must go absolutely – without dispensation, without remission, without mercy. The position of master and servant falls under this sentence. It is service henceforth in unity; and the soul shall say no longer: behold the handmaid of the Lord; but rather: My beloved is mine. The judgment is in order that Shekinah may manifest in the temple of the soul, between the Cherubim on the mercy seat. The bond of union is She, and the spirit is the Light within Her. Look to it therefore, my brother. May your Cherubim fold their wings over the throne of the Presence. May you dwell henceforth in the condition of eye to eye.

The Second Celebrant places the postulant before the Priestess and returns to his seat. The veil of the Priestess has been raised. She bends forward and fastens the rose of Geburah on the breast of the postulant.

THE PRIESTESS: Keep in your heart the precious knowledge of the spirit and the memory of where you have been. So shall you fulfill your mission, which is to raise the worlds that are below the Throne to the height of those which are above. Brother, abide in peace. Restore your world to the union, to that supernal state wherein there is no distinction between Shekinah and the Holy One.

A chalice containing red wine has been placed on the western side of the altar by the Usher of the Grade. The Celebrant-in-Chief raises it and, accompanied by the Second Celebrant, proceeds to the pillars. He hands the chalice to the Priestess. The postulant is directed to kneel. The Celebrants stand on either side of the postulant. The unofficial members, led by the Usher of the Grade, form a semi-circle behind them. All these kneel down. The Priestess lifts up the chalice, holding it in both hands.

THE PRIESTESS: Blessed be the dew which waters the garden of apples. Blessed be the wine which maintains the soul rather than the body of man. It is the wine of liberation, which raises the world below to the height of that which is above. Let us drink of the wine reserved for the elect from the beginning of time.

The Priestess makes the sign of the pentagram over the chalice, and drinks. She administers the chalice to the postulant, who drinks and bows his head. The Priestess hands the chalice to the Celebrant-in-Chief, from whom it passes to the Second Celebrant, and Adepti Majores in succession of grade, and lastly to the Usher of the Grade, by whom it is replaced upon the altar. All return to their seats. The Usher of the Grade leads the postulant to his own seat, and removes the vestments and insignia of an Auxiliary Frater Adeptus. He is clothed in the white habit, with the girdle of Geburah and the Rose-Cross belonging to that of Sephira. This is done in silence, and the postulant takes the place of the Usher.

Here ends the Sixth Point.

THE SOLEMN OFFICE OF CLOSING THE HOUSE
AND SANCTUARY OF ADEPTS IN THE GRADE OF GEBURAH

The Celebrants are seated facing west by the altar, and the Priestess is seated between the pillars, facing east.

ADEPTUS EXEMPTUS: Fratres et Sorores, Adepti Majores, I testify that the mystery which we have finished is in communion with all the mysteries, that things which are above being analogous to things that are below, the ineffable grades of advancement beyond this present grade are identical as to the root therewith, and so also are those which are below, because one experiment is concerned throughout therein. Mighty Adeptus Major, do you ratify on your own part?

ADEPTUS MAJOR: I am least among the faithful witnesses, but I have seen the end of the quest. I also have come from afar. The experience of the worlds within and without is laid up in my heart.

ADEPTUS EXEMPTUS: What do you testify concerning the world without?

ADEPTUS MAJOR: I speak in the sense of the mysteries and proclaim that it was even as the pilgrimage of natural life, from birth to death. But the birth was according to the spirit; there was life under the spiritual sun; and the soul of the man was commended at the close of all to the care of the Spirit of God.

ADEPTUS EXEMPTUS: After what manner did you enter the world within?

ADEPTUS MAJOR: Through the gate of the setting sun. But I speak in the sense of mysteries and proclaim that the life of the mystic is a loving preoccupation with one Divine Image shining in the heart. The hour comes when he is drawn into the deeps of that image by a mystical death, and so passes through it, leaving the world of images, to abide in Divine Darkness.

ADEPTUS EXEMPTUS: What is this place of darkness?

ADEPTUS MAJOR: It is the world within, stilled in the waters of contemplation, and these are waters of love.

ADEPTUS EXEMPTUS: Who testifies therein?

ADEPTUS MAJOR: Soul unto soul in the darkness, love unto very love, desire in the heights above to desire in the deeps within. Then it is silence of silence. The soul, for a brief space, becomes that which it contemplates, for the center opens within, and light shines in the unity.

ADEPTUS EXEMPTUS: Might Adeptus Major, I beseech you in your charity to show forth some part or shadow of that most sacred state; and I testify that all the holy assemblies shall hearken while you announce the tidings.

ADEPTUS MAJOR: Merciful Exempt Adept, I am he who has risen in the twilight, and my speech is an echo in the heart. But at that center I knew the Inmost and Divine Self about which the universe resolves. Behold, I am that which I sought, and the end of my desire is with me. I have found the light of the Presence and mine is the love of my heart.

All present rise up. The Priestess extends her arms, standing between the pillars.

THE PRIESTESS: The waters of life are love. Whosoever wills, let him drink of the waters of life freely. I testify that the Rose of Sharon is also that of Shekinah, for the spirit and the bride are One, and this is the life of the Rose.

ADEPTUS EXEMPTUS: Mighty Adeptus Major, in the grace of this sacred mystery, I depute you to close the house of the spirit in the grade of Geburah.

ADEPTUS MAJOR: O House of Divine Death. House of Eternal Love. By that which overcomes death, I close the House of the Spirit in this grade of Union. (*Knocks three times, pauses, knocks twice, pauses, knocks once.*)

ADEPTUS EXEMPTUS: (*Knocks three times, pauses, knocks twice, pauses, knocks once.*)

HERE ENDS THE SOLEMN OFFICE OF CLOSING THE HOUSE AND SANCTUARY OF ADEPTS IN THE GRADE OF GEBURAH.

The Third Order of the Rosy Cross

World of Creation

Part IV

The Ceremony of Admission
to the
Grade of Adeptus Exemptus

7 = 4

Being the Most Holy Grade of Chesed
and the Paths Pertaining Thereto

Id Est
Mysterium Resurrectionis

Privately Printed

1917

The Fellowship of the Rosy Cross

—

Grade of Adeptus Exemptus
7=4

—

BEING THE MOST HOLY GRADE OF CHESED
AND THE PATHS APPERTAINING THERETO

—

PROLEGOMENA

*The grade of Exempt Adept falls naturally into four divisions, of which
three are connected with those paths in the Tree of Life which communicate with Chesed from below. The fourth division is the ritual of the grade
itself, and this is in two sections. The ordinary mode of advancement from
Sephira to Sephira in the Fellowship of the Rosy Cross is recalled by this
arrangement, but ~ the natural analogy notwithstanding ~ there is one
important distinction. While there is, as usual, a single path of entrance
into Chesed, the other paths are those of return. The grade itself is therefore
communicated between the passage of the first and the transition to the
second and third paths. They are paths of return because he who attains
the grade of Exempt Adept is an ordained priest and teacher, who comes
down in the lower Sephiroth of the Third Order for the celebration of the
mysteries therein, and is also reflected into the Second and First Orders,
where he is represented by the Master of the Temple. The postulant enters
Chesed from the side of Geburah and leaves it for a life of ministration in
the holy assembly from the side of mercy. According to Zoharic Kabalism,
the pillar of severity, resumed in Geburah, is that of going in, while the
pillar of mercy, resumed in Chesed, is that of coming out. The paths of*

communication with Chesed are those of Teth, Yod, and Lamed, being the lines of junction respectively with Geburah, Tiphereth, and Netzach.

The preparation of the postulant for the grade of Adeptus Exemptus is made during the three symbolic days of his life in the indrawn state of consciousness, represented by the rose and denominated Life in the Rose. He has passed, at least in symbolism, through the ineffable experience of Divine Union, which is that of mystical marriage, and the three days are an aftermath of this ecstasy. The Word has entered into his heart, and he bears testimony thereto within the precincts of the holy assembly, with whom he dwells in the halls of Geburah. This is the speech in the rose. It is not a light of teaching, but that of a state attained, being manifest dedication to the path of Light; to the great quest and its term; to the Divine Rapture of the union; to the supernal Mother of souls, as the principle of union and of love; and to the Christ-Spirit, who is God and the spouse within. After this manner does the Adeptus Major raise in his own person the worlds that are below to the height of those which are above, and so prepares for his resurrection.

Herein is the preparation of hidden life, and when the postulant has received his call to advancement, the prescribed act of preparation is a single day of silence, to be passed in prayer, aspiration and thanksgiving. The adept shall concentrate in mind and heart on his ceremonial progress through the grades of the Fellowship up to the present epoch; on the inward meaning of the grades, according to the interpretation communicated in the grade of Adeptus Major; on spiritual love as the key to the grand mysteries; and on the power and the grace which are essential to one who having been drawn to things that are eternal, should receive a commission to lead others in the path. The silence of the postulant must be preserved until his mouth is opened in the course of the ceremony itself.

THE CELEBRANTS OF THE MOST HOLY MYSTERY

1. The Celebrant in Chief, *id est*, Adeptus Exemptus, Lord of the House of resurrection.

2. The Most Holy Priestess of the Rite, *id est*, the Lady of Shekinah.

3. The Usher of the Grade, who is also Keeper of the Threshold and Spokesman of the Adepti Exempti.

4. The Mighty Adeptus Major, 6=5, bring the postulant at the Gate of

Easter, who, as in the grade of Adeptus Major, is also in a certain sense an officer of the grade, having a rank corresponding to that of the Second Celebrant in the ceremonies of Tiphereth and Geburah.

5. The Celebrant within the Sanctuary, who is either the Imperator of the Rite or his delegate, lawfully appointed. He represents the grace, power and authority which are beyond the Third Order and from which its warrants are derived.

The clothing of the Celebrant in Chief, or Merciful Exempt Adept, is the same as in Tiphereth.

The Most Holy Priestess wears the white habit of the Third Order, with the veil and girdle of Binah.

The Usher of the Grade wears the white habit and the girdle of Chesed, with the Rose-Cross belonging to this Sephira. He carries a wand surmounted by a dove of peace, similar to that of an Ostiarius in the worlds below Tiphereth.

The Celebrant within the sanctuary wears a white habit and robe. He is girt about the waist with a golden girdle. His collar is of white silk, from which depends a gold lamen, having the wheel of the spirit within the circle, and on the circle itself is the inscription: Mysterium Ineffabile. His biretta is white and on its front is emblazoned the word Unitas, in letters of gold. He bears the wand of Imperator.

The postulant wears the vestments and insignia of Mighty Adeptus Major in the grade of Tiphereth.

The clothing of unofficial members is that of the Usher of the Grade.

The Solemn Ceremony of Opening the House and Sanctuary of Adepts in the Grade of Chesed

The arrangement of the house follows the unwritten precedents. The door of the sanctuary is closed, and a curtain of the color of Chesed is drawn in front of it. At the extreme western end of the temple hangs the red curtain of Geburah, bearing the symbol of the setting sun. Beneath it is the funeral litter, having its head toward the north. At a certain distance in front are the two pillars of the Fellowship. There are no candles of the dead, and there is no catafalque. The candles on the pillars are lighted. The altar is placed in the middle way of the temple and is in the form of a double cube, draped in Chesed violet. The symbols of personality belonging to the grade of Tiphereth are placed thereon, but the cup is empty at this stage, and the lamp is not lighted. The sacred pictorial symbol of resurrection is fixed upon the western side of the altar, looking toward the pillars.

The Celebrant in Chief is seated alone in the east, having the door of the sanctuary behind him. The seat of the Priestess is between the pillars, facing east. That of the Usher of the Grade is at a convenient point in proximity to the temple door. Beside him is a lighted brazier, from which smoke of incense rises. The temple is in full light. The Fratres et Sorores of the 7=4 degree are assembled and clothed. It should be observed that the western end of the temple in the first and second points represents that side of Geburah which opens on the path of Teth. The orientation in these parts of the ritual is therefore arbitrary.

The Merciful Exempt Adept opens the sacred ceremony with a battery of one knock and proceeds as follows:

Adeptus Exemptus: The grace of Chesed is peace. Fratres et Sorores, peace of God be with you, the peace of His high places; and between us be the counsels of peace.

There is here a pause of a moment.

Adeptus Exemptus: Merciful Exempt Adepts, sons and daughters of the sacred doctrine, dwellers in the house of resurrection, in the union of our common heritage, which is a sacrament of the union that is above, I invite you to join your intention with mine in the solemn act of opening this holy house in the Grade of Chesed. (*Knocks once*).

All rise.

ADEPTUS EXEMPTUS: By Chesed the world was made. By Chesed it is remade in Christ. O ye who have been faithful unto death, who have attained the mystery of union and the marriage of soul therein, I proclaim the day of resurrection.

THE PRIESTESS: It is the living union of the lover and beloved in mind and heart and will.

ADEPTUS EXEMPTUS: It is also the word attained and the mission which follows therefrom. It is the Christ purpose in the world and a priestly sacrifice. In the Holy Order of the Rosy Cross, resurrection is therefore a return. It is the soul's regression to external life, bearing with it a Divine experience, the Word realized in the soul.

THE PRIESTESS: Light in the eternal east; Light from the sun of glory. All hail, thou morning of Easter.

ADEPTUS EXEMPTUS: It is in union with the Center that the Word is sought and found. We sought it in the written law. We suffered the yoke thereof. We sanctified the flesh therein. We sought it in the holy mysteries ~ the inward sense of revelation. They gave us many words in the mysteries; in their utterance they were words of grace. By the light of the secret law we were called as sons of the doctrine. The galleries of mind were enlightened. All lights rose up therein. Still we were far from the term. The desire of the house of the Lord carried us on wings of fire ~ wings over the great waters. How long, O Lord, how long? The secret of the will in its surrender brought us to gates of regeneration. To the spirit of Thy will they opened. We knew Thy will within us. We beheld our path in Thee, as children of the Second Birth. A message came into our hearts that we must ourselves become that Word which we had sought through the ages. We found that the Word was within us. Thy Light descended within us, O Lord of Light, uplifting our lower Sephiroth. The path in Thee became a Way of the Cross, which is the way of the Word on earth. Hereof is the imitation of Christ. All that is immortal within us was lifted into the glory of Calvary. All that was perishable within us died on the cross of sacrifice. Passus et sepultus est. O grace of death in the Lord, sacred retreat into the darkness of the world within. Light which shineth in the darkness, and God which fills it entirely. I testify on the part of the Masters, I testify on my own part, that He entered into the dark places. Descendit ad inferos. The Word is crucified within us; the Word is upfolded within us, in the deep inward state. We are also received into the Word, and after the realization therein it possesses our whole being in a glorious resurrection. Tertia die resurrexit. And this is the glory of adeptship.

THE PRIESTESS: May the Light of the Word encompass us. May the Word abide within, for so it is attained only. May its efficacious grace assist us, from greater fullness even unto greater fullness, to manifest the Word in life. The vestiges are about us everywhere; it is formulated in all our ways, but is realized in the heart alone.

The Celebrant in Chief and the Most High Priestess advance from their respective places and stand, facing one another, east and west of the altar.

ADEPTUS EXEMPTUS: The spirit and the bride say: Come.

THE PRIESTESS: Herein is the call of Chesed.

ADEPTUS EXEMPTUS: The spirit is the heavenly spouse, and the spouse is Christ.

THE PRIESTESS: The bride is the bride of Messias, She whom the secret tradition has termed Shekinah in records that shine for ever.

ADEPTUS EXEMPTUS: Hail unto the perfect bride. Behold, She is supernal understanding, the state of consciousness in union. She is the union of souls in Christ. She is the community of Israel in election. She is the communion of saints. She is the hidden church of the chosen ones.

THE PRIESTESS: The soul becomes a robe of glory for Christ in each and all who enter into the Christhood. The souls that are called lost are souls traveling through the aeons and the spaces without the Christ-Spirit, the spouse. Bring them, O Master of all, to the end of their exile, that these also may be one in Thee.

ADEPTUS EXEMPTUS: Hereof is the prerogative of mercy in the Exempt degree. Hereof is our election in the grade. For this, O Adepti Exempti, we return at need whence we came, carrying glad tidings. O Adepti Exempti, by the power to me committed, in me also vested, and in the name of the hierarchy which is above, I declare that this house of the Holy Spirit is open in the grade of Chesed, for the works of grace and providence that belong thereto.

THE PRIESTESS: Fratres et Sorores, it is open in all grades. The voices of those who are beneath unite in the cosmos of harmony, and the silence that is above concurs with all the rumors of the quest attained.

ADEPTUS EXEMPTUS: Unite also with us, ye Adepti Exempti, looking for redemption in experience.

THE PRIESTESS: This is the day of the Lord, which comes to restore all things.

They give the sign of the grade, which is the clasping of both hands ~ the union of the Lover and Beloved. It is given with arms extended across the altar.

ADEPTUS EXEMPTUS: The name of the bride of Heaven on the day of supernal union is the name of glory.

THE PRIESTESS: Enter under the wings of Shekinah.

ADEPTUS EXEMPTUS: When God said: it is not good for man to be alone ~ he created on earth the symbols of that union which is above.

THE PRIESTESS: The wings of Shekinah are extended over Chesed and Geburah.

ADEPTUS EXEMPTUS: Worlds of the glory of life ~ worlds without end for ever.

THE PRIESTESS: And one world of union.

ADEPTUS EXEMPTUS: (*Knocks four times*)

ADEPTUS EXEMPTUS INITIATION

THE PRIESTESS: (*Knocks three times*)

The Celebrant in Chief and the Priestess return to their places.

Here ends the solemn ceremony of opening the House of the Adepts in the grade of Chesed.

THE FIRST POINT

The Celebrants and members are seated, with the exception of the Usher of the Grade, who proceeds to extinguish the lights of the temple, save those of the candles on the pillars. There is a brief pause, of complete silence. The fumes of incense from the brazier shroud the light of the candles. The Usher of the Grade is seated.

ADEPTUS EXEMPTUS: The light of the world to come is the Light of the Holy One. The darkness of the earthly world is the hiddenness of God. The gift of vision is the uplifting of a cloud from the sanctuary of our inner consciousness. It shall lead through the light and the darkness into the glory of the Presence. The way is clear before us, and the path is straight. We go into our own country, and God's peace is on our life ~ we in Him and He in us. So, after all the warfare, we repose upon our arms.

THE PRIESTESS: Peace profound, my brethren. Immanuel, God is with us.

ADEPTUS EXEMPTUS: Fratres et Sorores, the secret tradition which reposes in the sanctuaries of adeptship, as in places of inward life, bears witness that a high experience has been known always in the world and that this is an experience of self-knowledge explored in its heights and deeps on the quest of God. They who attained it desired to lead others in the same most holy path, and their guidance was after many manners, but chiefly by the awakening of a still small voice in the hearts of those who were prepared. I testify that the hidden school is working at this day more strenuously than ever. The doctrine of the hidden school abides within the creeds, even as a foundation stone, a pearl beyond price. It is the life and grace of all symbols. It is a realization of the great mystery concerning that

Divine Nature which for us is asleep in the universe until it quickens in the hearts of those ~ chosen out of thousands ~ who can utter the awakening words to the Divine which dwells within them.

THE PRIESTESS: The voice of the turtle heard in the land is the Word of the Holy One. The greeting of Jacob and Rachel is the world above kissing the world below. May the kiss of Tetragrammation be as waters of life upon us. O brethren of the Rosy Cross. May the kiss of the four spirits who carry its sacred letters visit us in the ineffable mercy which flows from their union. Declare unto us the secret doctrine, O Master of the Temple; what are the awakening words?

ADEPTUS EXEMPTUS: They are contained in no formulary of outward speech and are uttered only by the voice of the secret soul. I testify to that which I have heard; for I know ~ even I ~ that my Redeemer lives, and that standing before Him, or ever I doubted and quested, He placed my hand within the mystic cube, saying; because I shall be buried in thee, behold, I am with thee all days. It is for this reason that He is nearer than hands and feet.

The Usher of the Grade, in his capacity as Keeper of the Threshold and Spokesman of the Adepti Exempti, rises in his place at the threshold.

FRATER CIVIS REGNI SUPERNI: Of those who abide in our holy house of adeptship, some have received the Word by the light of communication in a symbol, but other some have attained it by the grace of an inward experience. These are the first and highest circle of our Fellowship. There are those also who have been called at a later time and have answered thereto within the measure of their gifts. Of these some are still in the lower grades, and their hour is not yet; but other some stand on the threshold of adeptship. Again, some are in the grade of regenerated life and have not cried to be dissolved; but other some have passed through mystical death. Among these I commend to your indulgence the Mighty Adeptus Major, Frater Adveniat Regnum (*vel nomen aliud*). The providence of the present hour ordains that we, who have been brought already from death to life, should give him happy issue from the rock-hewn sepulcher, through the power to us committed in the Grace of Christ.

ADEPTUS EXEMPTUS: For no other purpose have we raised the temple of God in the inmost heart or externalized its shadow here. Do you testify that our elect brother will come quickly, seeing that his reward is with us?

FRATER CIVIS REGNI SUPERNI: The Word of the Lord is heard in the hidden deeps, and he that was dead shall rise.

The Usher of the Grade advances to the altar, from which he takes the extinguished lamp. He gives the saluting sign of the grade and leaves the temple in silence. He proceeds to the vestibule, where the postulant is kneeling on a prie-dieu in full light, having a scroll in his hands containing versicles on the mystery of resurrection and the life of union therein. He is greeted by the Usher of the Grade saying:

FRATER CIVIS REGNI SUPERNI: The Word was dead in us. We have followed the purified life, in order that I might be reborn in us. We have died mystically, that again it might be alive in us. In its restoration we rise again.

The postulant ~ who has been cautioned previously to preserve the rule of silence ~ is appareled already in the white habit of the Third Order. The Usher of the Grade now prepares him further by clothing him in the full regalia and vestments of a Mighty Adeptus Major. While this is being done:

FRATER CIVIS REGNI SUPERNI: The grade of Exempt Adept is the grade of the Voice which falls from the great height and renews the heart in stillness. Hereof is the day of the Lord, which comes to restore all things. I bid you remember that one of the titles of Chesed is Foedus Carnis, which is the covenant of resurrection in the complete man ~ three in the union with Christ, but also three in one. So closes the mystical work of the soul's creation in God, under the light of the Rosy Cross.

The preparation being finished, the Usher goes before the postulant carrying the extinguished lamp. They pass from the vestibule to the door of the temple, where the Usher gives the battery of the grade (four knocks, a pause, then three knocks). The door is opened for their admission. While this has taken place in the precincts, there has been silence for a brief period in the temple within, and what follows is so timed that the Usher of the Grade enters, leading the postulant, during the course of the colloquy. The seat of the Priestess has been removed, and she stands between the pillars.

ADEPTUS EXEMPTUS: Those who study the Law shall be given a radiant vesture.

THE PRIESTESS: The seventh day is a Sabbath, and this is the rest in Geburah.

ADEPTUS EXEMPTUS: Those who are in Geburah desire the perfect body of resurrection.

THE PRIESTESS: The slave recovers his freedom after the year of jubilee.

ADEPTUS EXEMPTUS: Geburah is a place of desire for the salvation of the world.

At or about this point the Usher of the Grade has placed the postulant immediately in front of the funeral litter, with his face toward the east. The Priestess has turned between the pillars to the west. The Celebrant in Chief has risen. As the Usher of the Grade stands beside the postulant, on his right hand:

FRATER CIVIS REGNI SUPERNI: There was darkness on the River Gihon.

The Priestess moves to the head of the funeral litter and is seated thereat. The Usher of the Grade places the lamp on the altar. He proceeds to the foot of the funeral litter and is seated also. The Celebrant in Chief lifts up his arms, holding his wand of office.

ADEPTUS EXEMPTUS: I have laid down myself in nakedness, in the place of great darkness. I have cast out all the images. Thou has come to me in the hiddenness, in the secret places of love. I have attained the nuptials of the spirit. Thou hast come to me in the light of Thy knowledge. I have seen the desire of mine eyes. I have arisen and returned to testify. I have come in the fire of Thy love. I come to cast fire upon the earth. I am consumed with the zeal of fire, because of the glory of Thy love, in the sanctuary of Thy holy house. Thou hast given unto me Thy word of service.

The Celebrant in Chief resumes his seat.

THE PRIESTESS: Mercy and judgment remain in their places, and between them lies the path of union.

Frater Civis Regni Superni: It is God who says: Arise, and come forth ~ to those that are dead in Geburah.

The Usher of the Grade rises and goes to the altar, where he lights the lamp. He passes behind the postulant, and raises it over his head.

Frater Civis Regni Superni: The dawn of the morning of Easter.

He sets the lamp on the altar, and returns to his seat at the litter.

Adeptus Exemptus: Salutation and peace and joy and holiness of heart be with you, now and henceforward, O son of the mystical resurrection. We know your titles and warrants, in all the paths and grades which lead up the mountain of God, the holy mountain of initiation, unto the great height.

There is here a pause of a moment.

Adeptus Exemptus: Fratres et Sorores, our beloved postulant stands mystically within the rock-hewn sepulcher. It is also the mystic cube. From the moment that the tomb is entered, all that takes place in the grade of Adeptus Major is really an experience therein. He has passed through a spiritual resurrection and in the deep state of consciousness has known the Divine within him, in the union of mind and heart. But the plenary resurrection takes place when the Divine Nature permeates all parts of personality and is with him in all his ways. This is manifestation from the tomb. Till then he is in an underworld of consciousness, in the place of inward experience. In our symbolism, it is in that world of thought which goes before the uttered word. It is the night of mystical espousals and not the life of spiritual marriage. According to our secret tradition, the Word existed from eternity in the form of thought, but it was manifested only in creation, when thought was transformed into the Word. The Word was articulated in creation, which is thus like an opening of the mouth. It is in expression that the Word is made flesh. The speech in the rose conferred in the previous grade is a mystery of thought suspended in inward stillness. In the hiddenness of your self-knowing part, in the sleep of mystical death, wherein the soul holds communion with the Divine and the Divine manifests to the soul, there is a realization which is like speech in Heaven. The speech in the rose is the soul's communing with itself in the aftermath of an ineffable experience. At a later stage in the symbolism, it is also the secret intercourse with all who have entered into union. You are called now to pass from this state of the stillness, from love hidden in the heart to love at work in the world, from the mystery of thought in silence to the mystery of uttered thought. Your repose in the sanctuary of Geburah was like that of the Divine Word before it manifested in creation. In the grade of Adeptus Exemptus you shall yourself become the Word, according to the sense of our symbolism, and this is resurrection from the dead, as it is also the life of espousals between the Christ Spirit and the soul.

Frater Adveniat Regnum (*vel nomen aliud*), before the altar in this house of the Lord, there must be a pledge between us and you, and God shall watch upon the covenant for ever. The time is long dead and gone when you were required to certify that such bonds would be assumed freely, for by many dedications you have been integrated in the Rosy Cross. I say unto you, lift up your hands (*it is so done accordingly*), and the testimony which I utter on my own part in the fullness of the manifested Word, you shall recite in the inmost heart and secret soul. The pledge of the grade of Chesed, on the threshold of the path of Teth, is taken in silence and is therefore like a spiritual communion, for the mouth of the postulant is not opened as yet in earthly life.

The Celebrant in Chief gives a battery of one knock and all rise. The Usher of the Grade places the postulant between the pillars.

THE THRICE-GREAT PLEDGE OF FIDELITY

I, Frater Adveniat Regnum (*vel nomen aliud*), who look for the resurrection of the adept, the body of Redemption, the Christ-Life in the soul, and the reign of clemency in Chesed, having undertaken heretofore to maintain the mysteries of the sanctuary by the due preservation of the seals and veils thereof, do ratify hereby and herein my former pledges, from the last even unto the first. Standing in this house of the spirit, built upon the summit of the Third Order, in the Presence of the Lord my God and on the steps of the throne of Christ, in the presence of the Adepti Exempti and of you, O priest of the temple, chief of the paths below and Prince of the Light above, I covenant to communicate that which I receive in the sense and way that I received it. I will impart the Word in symbols, which are the tongue of earthly speech. In the grace and power of the Word I will draw unto me the chosen hearts, from the deeps beyond Malkuth, through all the holy houses of the Rosy Cross, into the Portal of the Third order, and thence into the life of the cross. I will sustain them on the arms of the cross; I will put them to rest in Geburah; and at the end I will raise them gloriously, when their Easter dawns in the soul. The pledge of silence has become the pledge of speech ‑ in heaven, on earth, and in the rose.

There is silence from some moments, during which the postulant remains with uplifted arms. The Usher of the Grade moves round the pillars, passes to the altar, takes up the lamp in both hands and raises it toward the postulant to the full height of his own arms.

FRATER CIVIS REGNI SUPERNI: Be thou a light of revelation to those who are called and chosen, the glory of this house of adeptship.

The Usher of the Grade restores the lamp to the altar and returns to his previous place. The postulant lowers his arms.

ADEPTUS EXEMPTUS: Seeker for the last mysteries of the Third Order, I bid you lift up your head, remembering that above the first reflected triad there is the light of the Supernal Sephiroth. Remember also the morning of the soul, after the sacred darkness and the mystical sleep in God. It is the morning of Easter. Those whom that orient visits shall hold a treasure within them, by which they can glorify the world. We who are pledged like you have seen that light in our hearts. It is in virtue thereof that we have proceeded thus far in this office of mercy. Between the pillars in the house of the spirit, you stand now on the threshold of the path of Teth, which is called in the secret tradition a fountain of life, communicating with a place of the world wherein men do not die. This is the place of resurrection, and it is Chesed in the Tree of Life. The path by which it is entered is a path of love, maintained at white heat in the heart and in the aftermath of ecstasy. It signifies also the ascent from the mystical underworld, the translation from mystical death, from the marriage of the soul to the ineffable life of the union. The path of Teth is love in its perfect transmutation, and the union of subject and object has already begun. As such, it is reflected from Daath, which is super-perfect love in the indrawn state, apart from all distinction of subject and object, of thee and me, of lover even and beloved. There God is All in all.

The Priestess has risen in her place and, moving round the pillars, she faces the postulant.

THE PRIESTESS: Finally, the path of Teth is called in the secret tradition a path of all spiritual activities. The fullness thereof is from the benediction of the bride in transcendence on the throne of Binah and from the glory of all glory, which is that of the spouse in Chokmah. It leads into the activity of Chesed, which is the life of mission, for he who has attained the greatest of all human experiences must bear true witness through the world, that by his mediation, others who are called thereto may attain also in their turn. Frater Adveniat Regnum (*vel nomen aliud*), postulant for the life of resurrection, standing between the pillars of the temple, I bring you forth from the life of the rose.

She draws him through the pillars, and taking her place beside him, she leads him a short distance and pauses, midway between the pillars and the altar.

ADEPTUS EXEMPTUS: The lesson in chief of the path of Teth is indicated by the great symbol of the path. The crowned Titan, who was shown to you in the path of Mem, submerged beneath the waters of Creation and in the deeps within your own nature, has arisen as the Christ of glory, for in the world of Chesed, the Divine in the universe and in your own soul, my brother, is shown forth in the realization of the adept. The day of resurrection is the day of the high light, which has come into manifestation, and the world is restored therein. That which is concealed in the deeps shall be proclaimed from all the heights. It is the solstice of eternal summer. Again the rainbow encompasses the whole figure, but its nimbus has greater radiance than in the previous symbol. Shadowed in the light above are the wings of Aima Elohim, typifying the power of the supernal Sephiroth, set toward the channel of manifestation for the utterance of the word.

The Priestess leads the postulant directly to the altar. The lamp is placed in his hands.

ADEPTUS EXEMPTUS: The will comes out from the sleep of perfect conformity to do the work of Divine Will.

In response to a silent direction, the postulant raises the lamp to his lips and then replaces it.

ADEPTUS EXEMPTUS: He is clothed with purpose as a light, and plenary activity is restored to him.

The Priestess pours red wine into the cup. It is placed in the hands of the postulant.

ADEPTUS EXEMPTUS: Wine of the world to come. Wine from the Tree of Life. The ecstasy of Divine Love is the mystic wine of the Kingdom.

In response to a silent direction, the postulant raises the cup to his lips and drinks therefrom.

ADEPTUS EXEMPTUS: He shall be clothed with ineffable desire, that he may utter the Word with power in the holy assemblies. He shall carry the tidings of the house and the Mystic City over the whole mystical earth.

THE PRIESTESS: The secret law is wine. The law shall hallow thy desire. Thou shalt drink in holiness.

ADEPTUS EXEMPTUS: He is girt about with desire, and with a garment woven of many waters.

The postulant has laid down the cup upon the altar, and the Priestess now places the symbolic dagger in his hands.

ADEPTUS EXEMPTUS: The mind shall be clothed with new images. Behold, I make all things new.

In response to a silent direction, the postulant raises the dagger to his lips, and then replaces it on the altar.

ADEPTUS EXEMPTUS: Give unto him Thy mind, O Lord, the viaticum of Thy sovereign reason.

The Priestess now places the silver chain in the hands of the postulant.

ADEPTUS EXEMPTUS: Give unto us Thine own life, O Lord, in all the parts of being.

In response to a silent direction, the postulant places the chain about his neck.

THE PRIESTESS: Let us look for the glory of God in the manifestation thereof.

In response to a silent direction, the postulant removes the chain, raises it to his lips and then replaces it on the altar.

ADEPTUS EXEMPTUS: Divine Love enters into veils of flesh and becomes redeeming love on earth.

The Priestess leads the postulant round the altar and direct to the Celebrant in Chief, saying as they pass:

THE PRIESTESS: The spirit and the bride say: Come ~ to all that has elements of redemption in the manifest side of man.

The vestments of a Might Adeptus Major are removed from the postulant and are received by the Usher of the Grade, who comes up for this purpose. He returns with them whence he came, and lays them with the wand on the litter. The postulant is now standing in the white robe of adeptship, without insignia of any kind.

ADEPTUS EXEMPTUS: We desire to put off mortality and to be clothed again in God. He gives back to us all our vestures in the Light of His Glory.

The Celebrant in Chief invests the postulant with the girdle and Rosy Cross of Chesed.

ADEPTUS EXEMPTUS: One like unto the Son of Man, clothed with a garment down to the foot and girt about the paps with a girdle.

THE PRIESTESS: To the glory of heaven in its clearness and to the brightness of the everlasting light.

ADEPTUS EXEMPTUS: Blessed is he that watches and keeps his garments. He shall be a priest of God and of Christ.

The seal of the Priestess has been replaced between the pillars, and she returns thereto.

ADEPTUS EXEMPTUS: Frater Adveniat Regnum (*vel nomen aliud*), I give unto you the last mystery of the path of Teth. It is the return of the soul into the manifest world, illuminated by experimental certitude of the Divine Union. The maxim of this path is: the transmutation of the world of images.

The Celebrant in Chief lifts up his arms over the postulant and says, in the person of the Christ of Glory

ADEPTUS EXEMPTUS: I have sought my soul through the ages. I have sought my body of life. I have been born in Thee as the man of sorrows. In Thee I have been acquainted with infirmity. I have carried my cross in Thee. I have been crucified, dead and buried. I have gone down with Thee to the underworld. I have risen gloriously from death, because I have returned in Thee. All power is given to me in heaven and on earth, that I may ascend with Thee to the father.

The Celebrant in Chief resumes his seat. The postulant remains in his place.

Here ends the First Point.

THE SECOND POINT
THE RESURRECTION IN THE LIGHT

The Usher of the Grade turns up all lights, so that the temple is made brilliant throughout. This is done quickly, and then standing at the head of the funeral litter he points toward it and says:

FRATER CIVIS REGNI SUPERNI: Behold the place where they laid him.

THE PRIESTESS: Chesed is Easter morning, the hour of perfect clemency in its manifestation. Let us enter into the joy of the Lord, even the freedom of His service.

The red curtain of Geburah is drawn across the western end of the temple to conceal the funeral litter.

ADEPTUS EXEMPTUS: It is said that the postulant in the sacred halls of Geburah goes into his true self, as a priest into the holy place. He comes forth as one who is truly sealed with priesthood, and it remains only that what has been received within should be ratified and proclaimed without, in the sacred temple. The term of adeptship in this our sanctuary of the mysteries, declared in Christ, offers therefore to the elect in God a visible ordination and an exempt license for the fulfillment of those offices of mercy which inhere therein. The man of grace is in Chesed, and this also is a house of priesthood. Frater Adveniat Regnum (*vel nomen aliud*), I bid you therefore kneel down, being made and vowed as you are. Bow your head, fold your arms upon your breast, and say in your heart with me: Cleanse my heart and my lips, O Holy God, who hast cleansed those of Thy prophets, even as with burning coals. Cleanse also my reins and my hands, that I may communicate faithfully to others the symbols of the Divine Word in the same sense and manner that they are this day communicated to me. Amen.

The Celebrant in Chief rises and lays aside his wand of office.

The Usher of the Grade brings up the vial of consecrated oil on a salver covered with a white cloth. All rise.

ADEPTUS EXEMPTUS INITIATION

The Prayer of Ordination

Adeptus Exemptus: I pray Thee, O Merciful God, Lord of the life in Chesed, and the numerations above and below, that the great white light which I invoke upon the soul of this postulant, who has risen to the life in Thee, may descend also upon myself in the operation of Thy sacred mysteries, so that I may faithfully and validly, with clean and holy hands, exalt him by a priestly rite, a sacred rite of ordination, as a Merciful Exempt Adept, in the perfect resurrection of Chesed. And do Thou, I beseech Thee, O Lord, abide henceforth with him. Strengthen, sustain and lead him in the fullness of Thine efficacious grace, that he may pass in perfect purity from the inward region of Divine experience in Geburah, which is a foretaste of eternal union, to the place of Thy clemency in Chesed, which is the world of the uttered Word.

The Celebrants in Chief anoints the postulant on the head in the form of the Sephirotic cross.

Adeptus Exemptus: The priesthood is of the inward spirit in Geburah, but of the body also in Chesed. Per Spiritum Sanctum revivisimus. Be thou anointed with oil, my brother, in the Name of the Lord.

The Celebrant in Chief has removed the oil from his hands, using the napkin on the salver. The vial is replaced thereon; the Usher of the Grade carries the vessel of ordination back to its place, and takes his seat by the door. Other members are seated.

The Celebrant in Chief lifts up his arms.

Adeptus Exemptus: Fratres et Sorores, by the power to me committed from the hierarchy which is above, I raise unto you a priest in Chesed, your peer and co-heir for ever.

The Celebrant in Chief raises the postulant.

Adeptus Exemptus: Give unto us, O Lord, that priesthood which comes not by the laying on of hands. Impose on us Thine own spirit. Establish Thy spirit within us.

THE PRIESTESS: We know, O Master of all, that those who have preceded us in the high mystery of Thy work fulfilled on earth have left something to be said in Thy Name. Impart Thy Word to us.

ADEPTUS EXEMPTUS: His voice as the sound of many waters, and out of his mouth went a sharp two-edged sword, which is the Life of the Spirit of God. Frater Adveniat Regnum (*vel nomen aliud*), it is said in the secret tradition that thought is the origin of all things and that the world subsists by the mystery of union between thought and the Word. Speech in the heaven of thought and speech in the rose and thine; in heaven, which is the Word found by realization within us, for so is the Christ attained; in the rose, which is the living testimony of the Divine Word abiding in the silence that is within. By the power to me committed, I give unto thee speech on earth.

The Celebrant in Chief places his hands on the shoulders of the postulant and breathes thrice upon his forehead.

ADEPTUS EXEMPTUS: (*at the first breathing*) For the testimony of the faithful witness; (*at the second breathing*) for the word delivered to man; (*at the third breathing*) for the life, which is love therein. In heaven, on earth, and in the rose, be thine the perfect speech; and in the mission of an Exempt Adept, which is the mission of mercy in Chesed, be thou the Word.

The Priestess rises and lifts up her arms.

THE PRIESTESS: It is written that the Word was made flesh and dwelt among us.

As directed by the Celebrant in Chief, the postulant folds his arms upon his breast and says:

ADEPTUS MAJOR: My Lord and my God.

ADEPTUS EXEMPTUS: Be therefore not faithless but believing.

The Celebrant in Chief and the Priestess resume their seats. The Usher of the Grade comes forward and leads the postulant to a seat on the eastern side of the altar, facing east. He then returns whence he came.

ADEPTUS EXEMPTUS: The resurrection from death in the grade of Adeptus Major is a resurrection inward to the realization of the Divine in consciousness. That of the Adeptus Exemptus is outward into the manifest world, and is for the liberation of those who have been prepared in the heart by one who has attained liberation. It follows the he who is to carry the sacraments of the Lost Word into the external order must have received its inward life into the deep places of his soul. That Word is the Life of life which restores the worlds, and it is the efficacy of those symbols by which it is shown forth. It is said that its utterance unites Chesed and Geburah, being communicated from the mercy side of the Tree to the side of holy severity. It is in this manner that speech in the rose is conferred on the adept in the grade of mystical death, which is the dissolution of self-realization in the rapture of union with Christ. In that union the Christ speaks to the soul, and the soul hearkens in its ecstasy. But in the aftermath, the soul is in communion of internal speech with the Christ Spirit. It is said also that Chesed is the world of the Holy One, which is the world of resurrection in God; and this, my brother, is the life of Christ in the soul. The resurrection of the adept is attained in the glory of Christ's union, by realization of the Christ within.

The first necessity of the postulant is therefore to know that his Redeemer lives, he in Christ and Christ in him, in virtue of which he shall accomplish the redeeming work in the world. The whole grade is a manifestation of the mystery of Christ within, and from within outwardly, through the vessel of the individual soul. It is in this sense that I have said unto thee; be Thou the Word. The Divine maxim of Chesed is: I am the Light of the World, and he that follows me shall not walk in darkness. The Divine name is Al, understood as a great attribute of eternal grace and benignity which is set above the supernal Tribunal. The password of the grade is AHAV, signifying love, and thence is derived the mystical Number, which is 8, being that of Christ the Spirit. There is also another password, ECHADUTH, signifying unity. In one aspect it is held mystically to show forth the union between Tiphereth and Malkuth, regarded as the Son and the bride. It is otherwise the congregation of Israel, when the male is joined to the female ~ that is to say, when there is mystical union between the Lover and the Beloved. It is the union between Christ and the elect in Chesed. The grade word is SHILOH, understood as the peacemaker, because Chesed is the grade of peace, attained in Christ. You return, therefore, to the world bearing in your mouth the two-edged sword of the spirit, which is the Word of God; but in your hands are the counsels of peace; and may that be about you on all sides which encompassed Solomon through all the glory of his reign.

The mystical Title of the grade is Civis Regni Superni, for those who are in the state of resurrection are citizens of the Kingdom of Heaven. It is in this sense that one of the denominations of Chesed is the world to come. It is also the fourth path, which is called the Intelligence of Reception, because it receives the influences of the supernal Sephiroth, that it may manifest them below. That which is below is sustained by the descent of the graces from Chesed, and those who, in the symbolism of our Fellowship, are seated on the thrones thereof, go forth from Chesed, carrying glad tidings of the Word realized in life.

The Celebrant in Chief rises, and in response to a silent intimation the postulant draws forward till he is immediately opposite the Celebrant.

ADEPTUS EXEMPTUS: The sign of the 7=4 grade is given with the arms forward and inclined upward from the elbows, the palms turned outward, and the thumbs joined at the tips. The whole face is visible above the hands and the eyes of the adept are upraised. It refers to the manifest state of Chesed, exhibiting the mystery of the Tree. The grip or token is a duplication of that communicated in the grade of Geburah, being given one to another with both hands (*the Celebrant in Chief and the postulant exchange the grip*). It symbolizes the union of the Lover and Beloved, and it bids us praise God because He is All in all. The symbol of the grade is Gihon, being the Second River of Eden. The maxim is: the sacrament of speech. In fine, Frater Adveniat Regnum (*vel nomen aliud*), the salutation of this grade is Pax Dei Tecum.

The Celebrant in Chief resumes his seat, while the Usher of the Grade comes up and leads the postulant to the western end of the temple.

Here ends the Second Point.

THE THIRD POINT
THE OFFICE OF THE SANCTUARY

The red curtain of Geburah, which has been drawn across the western end of the temple, so that the funeral litter is hidden, is itself hidden by a drapery of Chesed violet. The Celebrant in Chief rises and his seat is removed. He takes up his place at the door of the sanctuary, on the southern side. The Priestess rises and proceeds also to the door, standing on the northern side. The Usher of the Grade stands on the right of the postulant at the far western end, both facing east. The Usher of the Grade gives a battery of one knock.

FRATER VICIS REGNI SUPERNI: Enter into the treasures of the Lord. Enter into the good things in the land of the living.

He leads the postulant to the eastern end of the temple, where they kneel down, facing the sanctuary, at a certain distance from the threshold. Their arms are folded on their breasts. The Usher of the Grade directs the postulant to say on his own part:

ADEPTUS EXEMPTUS NOVUS: I have looked for the resurrection of the adept, the body of redemption, the mystical life of union and the Word declared in Chesed.

ADEPTUS EXEMPTUS: There is another and more glorious sun than that which dawns in Tiphereth, which shines and sets therein.

The Celebrant in Chief gives a battery of one knock.

He opens the door of the sanctuary to its full extent.

The High Priest of the sanctuary is discovered within, at the eastern end, in full vestments and regalia. On the circular altar before him are white roses, about the figure of a lamb bearing a white pennon. Behind this there is a chalice containing white wine and covered by a paten on which is unleavened bread, corresponding to the manna in Chesed, A white cloth is laid over these vessels. It is removed by the High Priest. He raises the paten.

THE HIGH PRIEST: The heavenly bread is the beginning of understanding in Israel. Give unto us the Bread of Heaven.

He sets down the paten and thereafter raises the chalice.

THE HIGH PRIEST: Those who have attained union with the spirit of Christ shall drink new wine in the Kingdom of the Father.

He sets down the chalice and proceeds to the consecration of the Elements according to the terms of the Pars Magna Secreta in the ritual of the winter solstice.

He replaces the paten on the chalice at the end of the secret working and covers both with the white cloth. He comes round to the western side of the altar and stands with uplifted arms in front of the postulant.

THE HIGH PRIEST: The vesture of thy death has perished. It died upon the cross of Tiphereth. The vesture of thy glory is upon thee. It is the body of resurrection in Chesed. The life of sin is over, from henceforth and for ever. The price in Christ is paid. Thine is the life in Him, and the second death has no power.

He takes white roses from the western side of the altar and fastens them on the breast of the postulant.

THE HIGH PRIEST: May the union which obtains above in the world of the supernals be fulfilled also below. God and His name are one. Be they one also in thee. The sacred names are roses. The symbol of clemency and mercy is the white and perfect rose. Be thou decorated in the risen body with stainless roses, at the highest point of the Order of the Rosy Cross, in the manifested degrees thereof.

He places his hands on the head of the postulant.

THE HIGH PRIEST: Be thou blessed by the mouth of Shekinah in all thy grades and degrees, in all the Sephiroth which have been sanctified and exalted in thee.

The Usher of the Grade prompts the postulant to say concurrently with himself: My heart is in the place of the Hidden Ones, the place of Christ in the transcendence, the place whence the Spirit comes down. I look for the Grace of the Spirit.

The High Priest lifts up his hands above the head of the postulant.

THE HIGH PRIEST: The great white Light is the Christ descending within us. May He therefore abide within thee henceforth and for ever. Be thou blessed with the mouth of the Holy One, blessed be He. May all the Masters of the doctrine and all the Holy Presences answer: Amen. May the Ineffable Lord of Sanctity and His Shekinah concur herein.

The High Priest passes round to the eastern side of the altar, where he uncovers the sacred Elements, saying:

THE HIGH PRIEST: The peace of Salem is Melchisedek.

He passes westward, bearing the sacramental vessels, and deposits them on the western side of the altar. He lifts up the paten and goes close to the postulant, without crossing the threshold.

THE HIGH PRIEST: The bread is the world below. That which is below is lifted to that which is above. That which is above descends to that which is below.

He places one of the Hosts in the mouth of the postulant.

THE HIGH PRIEST: The Lord visit His people in the breaking of bread.

He replaces the paten on the altar, and turns westward with the chalice.

THE HIGH PRIEST: The wine is the world above. Thou shalt bind the world below to the world above in the bonds of thy priesthood.

He places the chalice to the lips of the postulant.

THE HIGH PRIEST: Be the odor of thy sanctity as a field which the Lord has blessed, and as the wine of Lebanon.

He turns eastward, replacing the paten on the chalice and covering the vessels with the cloth of white linen. Again he turns westward, raising the sacred vessels.

THE HIGH PRIEST: Abraham was in the likeness of Chesed. Go forth therefore as Abraham, father of elect nations. But unto him came Melchisedek, carrying bread and wine. He was King of Salem, which is peace. Chesed is grace and Salem is above Chesed. Unto those who dwell therein is given the title of peace, and the priest thereof dwelleth in hiddenness therein.

The Usher of the Grade assists the postulant to rise.

THE HIGH PRIEST: The warrant of the Exempt Adept is conveyed to him, as for himself and others, in the form of bread and wine. May the grace of the Lord attest it; I give unto thee wine and bread.

The High Priest places the sacred vessels in the hands of the postulant.

THE HIGH PRIEST: The cession of the warrant carries a guarantee in symbolism that the Divine Power remains with the Adeptus Exemptus for the expression of the Word in life, so that the symbols shall be in veridic analogy with inward truth, and shall therefore be sacraments ~ that is to say, efficacious channels of grace. It is in this sense that God stands round His people as the hills stand round Jerusalem. Go forth as the Word alive. Go forth with the symbols of the Word. The Word is the power of resurrection, and its realization is thine own rising. Go forth in the power of the Word. The adept on his return is carried by wings of healing. We learn in this manner that the deep mystical states which are inactive apparently on the external side are not for such reason without office in the world. We take nothing into the stillness save that which is inalienable from ourselves, but we bring back in due season the messages of saving grace, or restoring peace, and, after the sleep of the faithful departed, a great Light of awakening.

The Usher of the Grade leads the postulant slowly to the eastern side of the altar, in the middle place of the temple. It is the altar of his own personality, transmuted in sacrifice.

While this is being done, the door of the sanctuary closes from within. The

Celebrant in Chief resumes his place in the east, and the Priestess ~ passing westward ~ takes up her original position between the pillars.

The Adeptus Exemptus Novus sets down the sacred vessels upon the altar. A white scroll is handed to him by the Usher of the Grade, and he reads therefrom.

ADEPTUS EXEMPTUS NOVUS: There is famine on earth when celestial mercy is separated from celestial severity. It is famine of celestial things. But Chesed is above and below, so that mercy is on every side. So also are the Bread of Life and the Wine of the Spirit.

The Adeptus Exemptus Novus uncovers the sacred Elements. He lifts up the paten, still reading from the scroll, and its rubrics.

ADEPTUS EXEMPTUS NOVUS: I have taken unto me the Law of Mercy. I will give my life for the world.

The Adepti Exempti come forward. The paten is passed round and they partake of the Hosts.

The paten is replaced on the altar. The Adeptus Exemptus Novus lifts up the chalice.

ADEPTUS EXEMPTUS NOVUS: So far as in me lies, I will leave my spirit in the world by the works therein.

The chalice is passed round, and the brethren drink thereof.

The Adeptus Novus reveils the elements.

The Usher of the Grade lifts up his arms.

FRATER CIVIS REGNI SUPERNI: He was known of them in the breaking of bread.

The Usher of the Grade leads the new Adeptus Exemptus to the western side of the altar, looking toward the east.

Here ends the Third Point.

THE FOURTH POINT
THE PATHS OF RETURN

The Adeptus Exemptus Novus remains, in recollection, by the altar. The Usher of the Grade returns to his place and stands thereat. The Celebrants and other members are seated. The Usher of the Grade speaks in the person of the postulant.

FRATER CIVIS REGNI SUPERNI: The Lord who dwells within me is a fountain of glory and Light. Behold, I have received the Word and the Life of its understanding in the heart. I have asked and obtained power to bear witness in the holy assemblies and to draw the elect therein. The measure of mercy is also the measure of knowledge, and those who know God are channels of Divine Compassion flowing upon the world below. I have seen how the world has changed, for I bring my light with me. It is the radiant time of morning, and especially the morning which is within. It is the glory of the world of symbols, when the symbols speak in the heart, when they utter a joyful shout. It is the marriage of type and anti-type.

The Usher of the Grade resumes his seat.

ADEPTUS EXEMPTUS: It is said in the secret tradition that the pillar of severity, summarized in Geburah, is the way of going in, while the pillar of mercy, resumed in Chesed, is the way of coming out. The science of the paths which communicate with Chesed belongs to the root matter of resurrection itself, which involves return in its meaning. To attain resurrection, the postulant must traverse the path of Teth, but thereafter he comes forth out of Chesed, holding the warrants from above, and proceeds downward, returning on his road to manifest the Word. He takes the part of the Master in Geburah and Tiphereth. He opens the door of Tiphereth which looks toward Yesod. He is reflected into Netzach as the Master of the Temple in the Second Order and in him also comes back, even into Malkuth.

The Celebrant in Chief leaves his seat, joins the Adeptus Exemptus Novus at the altar, and faces to the west with him.

The great symbols of the paths of Yod and Lamed are suspended before the curtain at the western end of the temple.

ADEPTUS EXEMPTUS: The paths of return are traveled in thought only. The Adeptus Exemptus Novus stands at the gates and looks. The gates and paths of return are represented by the great symbols of the paths. (*The place of these is indicated by the Celebrant in Chief.*) The path of Yod is called in our secret tradition the Intelligence of Will. It is the preparer, on the return journey of all created being, so that they shall manifest the glory of the beginning. Yod is the sign of the covenant, in virtue of which Divine Graces are communicated below from above, or from God to man. It contains the measures of mercy reflected from the supernal triad. The great symbol of the path represents the keeper of the secret tradition and the mysteries of the Rosy Cross, who descends from Chesed to Tiphereth, clothed in white raiment, bearing a wand surmounted with the triple cross of the Tree of Life and having in his left hand the Light of the Word. From one point of view the figure signifies the return of him who has attained in the mountain of the Lord. He bears the glad tidings that the Word is found, because of resurrection from the dead, and is shown forth in the flesh of man; but it is uttered in symbols only and clouded in forms of speech. For this reason the light shines through a lantern. The figure recalls therefore the Adeptus Exemptus, but it has the vestments of a higher grade, being those which you saw for the first time when the sanctuary of the house of the spirit was opened in the Third Point of the mystery of Chesed. In its perfect understanding the figure represents therefore the power and authority of the Fourth Order, dwelling in the light of the world within, the World of Ascension, and holding the secrets of the King. It enters Chesed under the veils of bread and wine, for the communication of Divine Substance to the soul, and thence it sends forth its messengers ~ bearers of the secret tradition which formulates Divine Experience in Geburah and Tiphereth. But the path of Lamed, extending from Chesed to Netzach is not traveled in our system, which is concerned with the descent of the graces through the channels of the secret church.

The great symbol of the path of Lamed represents the official church, in the person of a sovereign pontiff adorned with all his insignia. It is placed at this point because the Order of the Rosy Cross comes in the sign of peace and not of the sword. It is at peace with all the churches. They are leaders of humanity at large by the manifest ways of life, and they open doors to the Center. In our secret tradition, the path of Lamed is called the Intelligence of Faith, and this is personified in the most appropriate manner by the pontifical figure of the symbol, which is also an image of magnificence. The path of Teth is another path of return, but the experience of its mysteries is with you. In summary therefore, my brother, your mission henceforward is to raise up the fallen Sephiroth, including Malkuth, and those who dwell therein, looking for worlds of redemption in the light of the Rosy Cross. But the saviors of men must realize in all their modes the truths which they are called to communicate. In the light of this realization the Word of Life is formulated. May Christ be with thee for ever hereby and herein. The paths of return are paths of the Christ-Life made manifest. The maxim of the path of Teth is: I am the Resurrection and the Life. That of the path of Yod is: Behold, I come quickly, and my reward is with me.

The Celebrant in Chief turns the Adeptus Exemptus Novus to the east and goes back to his place. While he stands thereat:

ADEPTUS EXEMPTUS: The search for the Word has culminated. The mouth of the postulant has opened in the three worlds. It is now the reign of the restored world, and Malkuth is the kingdom of God. O Frater Adveniat Regnum (*vel nomen aliud*), He in you and you in Him. I testify that the crown of all is not remote for the Kingdom. Herein is the mystery of Chesed, and above is the world of Atziluth, where all things are within. It is the place of eternal union, and it reflects into Daath, which is the Portal of the Living God.

The Celebrant in Chief resumes his seat, and the Adeptus Exemptus Novus takes his place in the temple.

Here ends the Fourth Point.

THE SOLEMN CEREMONY OF CLOSING THE HOSE OF THE ADEPTS IN THE GRADE OF CHESED

ADEPTUS EXEMPTUS: Fratres et Sorores, I testify that Chesed and Geburah remain in their places, not ascending higher. What is therefore the hope of Chesed?

THE PRIESTESS: It is imparted after a veiled manner on the authority of the Masters, who have given us the Word Daath, being a mystery of Knowledge, as a gate and way of the Supernals.

ADEPTUS EXEMPTUS INITIATION

ADEPTUS EXEMPTUS: I pray you to declare in your wisdom so much of this ineffable mystery as appertains to the grade of Chesed, for the benefit and consolation of the elect.

THE PRIESTESS: I testify that there is a lineal way which leads upward from Tiphereth, and it is called the path of Cheth. But in the Supernal Sephiroth all things are infinite, all things holy, and all are also within. The passage is therefore no longer from subject to object, as in grades of manifest life, or even the hidden life which is led in the holy assembly. The way of ascent is in Daath, as if through a great door, which eye hath not seen, save only in symbol.

ADEPTUS EXEMPTUS: It is written that Daath is the mediator between the upper and lower Sephiroth. It conciliates on the right and the left. It is the equilibrium in the height, and a place of ineffable union where God is known of the heart.

THE PRIESTESS: Daath is the Ark of the Eternal Covenant. The hope of the height is the hope of ascension therein. It is indeed the World of Ascension, wherein is a living stillness. It is the place of the Word in its fullness, an undifferentiated deep of being, withdrawn in the Supernals forever. But as it withdraws inwardly, so also it sets forth toward utterance and from the Word in Daath flow down those symbols which are thought and speech at the highest.

The Celebrant in Chief gives a battery of one knock and all present rise up.

ADEPTUS EXEMPTUS: Ecce, Regnum Dei Intus. And this, O Adepti Exempti, is that which is declared in Chesed, in virtue of which we return at need whence we came, carrying the glad tidings. We that were bound in Tiphereth and unloosed in Geburah do stand here to show forth that which has been given us at the summit of the Third Order. But we know that there is another silence, and in its stillness there is rest. The closing in this grade is therefore a solemn discharge or permit, whereby we are sent to preach the gospel of mystical life unto every prepared creature.

The Most Holy Priestess, standing between the pillars, extends her arms.

THE PRIESTESS: I am she who beholds the Vision. I am the Vision and the Eye which sees. I am the union of subject and object at the great height. I am the Dweller in the Supernals. The soul has wings, and the white ship has sails. I am the soul with wings. I have taken unto myself the wings of the dove. I have entered into the great rest. With those who are in separation, I dwell through many exiles, and with them I enter into union. I am that which attains and leads. Behold, I am with all the brethren, and I dwell in unity. I am myself and no other through all. I am in the High Palace of the King, but the stained and tattered garments of the prodigal are also mine. When the Fellowship of the Rosy Cross dissolves in the Light of the Supernals, I stand between the pillars of the temple. JAKIN and BOAZ are my witnesses through all generations. From the summit of the Third Order, I who come from Daath, look back upon the Portal of the Union.

She clasps her hands in front of her.

THE PRIESTESS: I point the path thereto.

The Celebrant in Chief and the Most High Priestess advance from their respective places and stand facing one another, east and west of the altar.

ADEPTUS EXEMPTUS: Chesed and Geburah remain in their places.

THE PRIESTESS: It is Tiphereth which ascends to the height.

ADEPTUS EXEMPTUS: The height stoops down to Tiphereth.

They give the sign of the grade, with arms extended across the altar.
THE PRIESTESS: And so all things are made one.

ADEPTUS EXEMPTUS: In the union of the Lover and Beloved, world without end.

They unloose their hands and return to their places. As they stand there-at:

ADEPTUS EXEMPTUS: Fratres et Sorores, I close our holy temple in the grade of Chesed. (*Knocks four times*).

THE PRIESTESS: (*Knocks three times*).

HERE ENDS THE SOLEMN CEREMONY OF CLOSING THE HOUSE OF ADEPTS IN THE GRADE OF CHESED AND HERE ENDS THE THIRD ORDER OF THE ROSY CROSS.

The Fourth Order of the Rosy Cross

World of Supernals

Part III

The Ritual of Return in Light

Privately Printed

1924

Ordo Sanctissimus Rosæ et Aureæ Crucis

—

The Ritual of Return in Light

—

The first Portal Grade of the Rosy Cross has been celebrated for the reception of a novice in the mother house of the Holy Spirit, and the Imperator of the Rite has fulfilled his part therein. He has made the sacramental oblations at the altar of Neophytes, has communicated in the four elements to himself and has administered to the Master of the Temple. He has returned to the east and stands in front of his throne, facing west. The communication continues from officer to officer and then among Adepti Exempti. Thereafter one of the Adept brethren, being an Epopt of the Rite, but wearing only the girdle of Tiphereth over the black habit of the temple in the Worlds of Action and Formation, goes before the Imperator bearing the Banner of the East and leads him by south from the temple, all other Epopts following. The Banner is delivered to the Ostiarius in the hither side of the Portal, and he restores it to its place in the east.

In their absence the sacramental communication continues, with the Master of the Temple in charge. The Auxiliary Frater Zelator returns to his station without receiving. The Neophyte also has not been led to the altar. An instruction follows, as it may be, the questioning of the grade, the interlocutors being the Master and Auxiliary Frater Zelator. Alternatively according to circumstances and arrangement made previously, there may be organ music and chants proper to the time. Meanwhile the blessed company proceeds to a vestry of the house and there assumes the clothing and insignia of the Epopt grades, the Imperator being vested as High Priest. They enter the secret temple, where the candles on the altar have been lighted about the sacramental Elements and all is arranged as at the solemn office of closing the hidden church according to the ceremony of contemplation on the further side of the last Portal grade.

The High Priest stands at the lowest altar step and there turns west. The banner in chief of the Rosy Cross and the hermit lamp are delivered into his keeping. He lifts up the hermit lamp. The banners of all Sephiroth and all paths are congregated about him. The silver bell sounds long and sweetly. The banners are exalted. The High Priest makes the:

Most Solemn Invocation of the Holy Spirit of God

HIGH PRIEST: Spirit of understanding, spirit of eternal counsel, keep us in Thy bonds of service. We have assumed our work as Thine; make it Thy holy work. Those who have dedicated themselves do Thou accept and dedicate. On us who descend below in the ministry of this sacramental rite do Thou come down and bless. Thine are our ways and Thine our worlds and paths. Sanctify our signs, illuminate, inform our symbols. Take unto Thyself those whom we bring to Thee. From day to day exalt our ministry below and make it Thine above. In the name of Thine eternal Mission, in love that is Thine and Thou, give us Thy work for ever. Plead with the hearts who we shall call in rites transformed by Thee. Thy voice is in our hearts sounding from far away. Bring us to that state in Thee when only Thy voice henceforth shall speak within us. Melt us in the crucible of love and shape us according to Thine own image and the law of Thy likeness. O All in all, reveal Thine All in us, that we may abide for ever in the All of Thee.

The voice of the High Priest ceases. The banners are lowered. The notes of a stringed instrument sound exceeding softly and die into the stillness. Another voice intones the golden anthem of the order: SILENCE IN THE MOUTH OF THE ALMIGHTY ONE. *Alternatively, it is uttered by the High Priest. The blessed company is hushed in deep contemplation. And thereafter:*

HIGH PRIEST: It is here and now; the heart and hands are filled. Mission is life in us, and life is filled with mission. Come down, Creative Spirit; we who invoke are called, call and are called in Thee. Call us, and choose and take us; hallow in Thy high election. Inform us with Thine holy fire; endue this rite of Thine. We have no part therein, except in Thee. Shape it to Thine ends for man. Let the sense of our possession pass; it is not ours but Thine. Make it a river of Life, and make of us Thy vessels, serving its waters freely. O quiet waters over all the ways; waters of inspiration, waters of secret knowledge, waters of immortal life. Tree beside the waters, Tree of supernal knowledge, Tree of Life; gifts of the Spirit, manners of fruit thereof. Teach us by these and all to heal Thy stricken nations.

The High Priest ascends the altar steps and again turns west.

HIGH PRIEST: Sub Nomine, Fratres et Sorores. Through paths and Sephiroth, and thus from world to world, the soul goes up, even unto Daath, the threshold of Being in union. It does not cross the threshold, save only in intimations of vision, as a waking space between white pillars of sleep. Beyond the images of mind and heart, beyond all thought and word, this state of Being lies. The soul comes back therefrom because of mission to the world. The Order therefore in the height of Daath presents the doctrine of return. The practice follows after. In yet another sacramental pageant, and that is this, the sacred rite shows forth the soul's return, carrying the gifts and graces. All worlds are bound together, and God is the chain of union. Unity of nature, unity of life, unity of heart in life; the work of transmutation waits us in the world below. It proceeds through all Sephiroth, even to Malkuth, wherein the light of the crown, which is said to be emanating light, and creation, manifests within us the correct path beyond. It is by Daath through Tiphereth and Malkuth that man, bound in heart and soul, can be returned to the Light from which he was created. The key of such theosophy on its individual side is that he who was Neophyte in Malkuth is raised as an Epopt in Daath. It is for this reason that Daath descends to Malkuth from the threshold of ineffable mystery, carrying all the symbols that appertain thereto, and these are the signs of Melechizedek.

Fraters et Sorores, the path of ascent in the Tree is the path of trial, and this is the way of attainment. The path of descent in the Tree is the path of the glory coming down and the return of those who have attained, carrying their branches of palm. The lower Sephiroth are drawn upward into all exaltation, and they are brought down transmuted. This is signified by the great banners of the supernal grades descending from numeration to numeration, uplifted by their proper officers. The rite bears witness thus unto the restored world, and the world is restored in the Holy One. The banners of the Rosy Cross are displayed in Malkuth as signs of restoration, and Kether is declared therein. The novice is married to the quest, and in the name of the Divine quest the Order receives the novice.

The banner of the Rosy Cross is erected at the east side of the altar. The High Priest takes the monstrance from its shrine in the pillared cupola and turning elevates it in sight of the blessed company. The banners are exalted and then again lowered. The High Priestess, covered with the veil of the sanctuary but wearing all her insignia beneath its folds, moves from her place in the holy assembly and kneels down on the lowest step of the altar, with clasped hands.

THE PRIESTESS: The rendering of the Holy Grail: it passes through the worlds of the Tree. Visit me in waking life; visit me in dreams of sleep, in visions beyond the dreaming, in the white light of the stillness that shines behind the vision, the rest within the stillness.

That which follows belongs to the world of Atziluth.

HIGH PRIEST: The mysteries of Divine communication are declared on the threshold of the supernals. There is no life but Life and God is God therein.

THE PRIESTESS: There is one Life alone, and That is Thou.

HIGH PRIEST: Apart from all the vestures, within and behind the worlds, it is Thou and no other. Receive our being in Thee.

THE PRIESTESS: After the life of separation, give us the life of union.

HIGH PRIEST: Thou who hast made us man because of the ways without dost open also the way of the worlds within.

THE PRIESTESS: In another land of the living we have seen the greater good.

HIGH PRIEST: As at Thy bidding, far and away, so high and low, we have explored the self ~ a thousand kingdoms ~ and have rejoiced therein.

THE PRIESTESS: Thanks be to God for the kingships, the crowns thereof and rings of high profession.

HIGH PRIEST: Thanks be to God for one pool still and deep through which we looked and say as in an open eye.

THE PRIESTESS: Within that shining all the worlds went past. O "something not ourselves," O All in all, become the self within. Thou and Thou only was; Thou art within, not we but Thou for ever.

HIGH PRIEST: We knew thereby, beyond the need of self, another thirst and hunger, the want and ministry of other love, the promise also of another food, of marriages made in holy Heaven of God, not in the earth of flesh. We sat at tables never dressed by man, and in the troth of God we plighted vows.

THE PRIESTESS: The eye is not satisfied with seeing, but the soul is filled with God.

She is prostrated for a few moments on the steps of the altar, and then the Priestess rises. She receives the monstrance at the hands of the High Priest and it is again elevated in the sight of the holy assembly, amidst the exalted banners.

THE PRIESTESS: We have sung our daily masses in the twelvemonth of this earthly life. Now after all the moons and Sabbaths, high days and holy, give us the mass of union. Proclaim it; Missa Est, but Ite is not heard. The Sanctus sounds on earth, a Veni chants, and instituting words ineffable are uttered on the altar of the soul.

This is said from the level of the temple floor, and the High Priest testifies from his place above.

HIGH PRIEST: Its Tantum Dic Verbo the soul responds, once and once only in the rapture of dying self. Then it is an eternal Eucharist, and in the soul of Man is God, Eternal Life.

THE PRIESTESS: After our daily bread, our wine of longing, break all our bread and spill our cups of wine. Take back the self Thou gavest, and after love in separation marry us into Thine own being.

HIGH PRIEST: Hereunto therefore is the mystery of host and cup, declared in the world of the supernals, on the sacred threshold: in knowledge, and that is love.

THE PRIESTESS: It is manifested under veils in this reflected life of earthly things; it is withdrawn in every soul that finds the Holy Grail. Then are the veils removed.

HIGH PRIEST: The soul beholds the spiritual things. Yet a little while, and that which sees becomes That which is seen. The soul goes back therein, the soul attains, which takes this Gospel to its heart of life.

THE PRIESTESS: So is the Grail withdrawn, from that which is without to that which is within, Amen. God speed it.

HIGH PRIEST: The end of all becoming is the transubstantiation of the soul in God.

The part of Atziluth ends at this point and that which follows belongs to the world of Binah. The High Priest takes the chalice from its place on the altar and elevates it in sight of the blessed company, amidst the exalted banners. The monstrance is elevated again at the same moment.

THE PRIESTESS: O signs uplifted in the risen world, signs of Divine substance: in the great grace behind them may our souls be fed.

HIGH PRIEST: Fathers and mothers before us gave the body of flesh. The soul elect in God that follows on the call builds up thereby the holy body of redemption.

THE PRIESTESS: O Risen Life in God and Living Bread, which doth that Life sustain.

HIGH PRIEST: The wine is Thou.

THE PRIESTESS: Signs of the wedded life in God, maintained by mission through the worlds of being; sense plenary of the Presence in the Great Work that is His.

HIGH PRIEST: Vision of the gates beyond, which open at the term of service for those who are called to go in – if ever, while the cosmos lasts. Beyond the golden gates that vision which is He, the life of eye to eye.

THE PRIESTESS: Give us the blessed vision until we end in Thee.

HIGH PRIEST: Thou the desire of being; it is Thou and no other.

THE PRIESTESS: From the worlds within the Signs are united. The flesh of the worlds within, bring forth the vision that is He.

HIGH PRIEST: Bring us forth from body to body. He to Man, and Man to He, for the transubstantiation has begun.

THE PRIESTESS: God give this service life for hearts we draw within. So shall we build them in: so grows our hidden church.

HIGH PRIEST: Presanctified; when we go forth on wider work of mission, in worlds that stretch beyond, our sacred rite in God shall have built about us also a body of redemption, meet for the ways to come; Thy ways of life, signs united by He.

THE PRIESTESS: Second birth of the soul; life, which follows thereon; sleep of the soul in love; sleep of consecrated souls; great awakenings to come; ways of the underworld and another sun that lights them; glory of risen life. O the great states of being and ministry of grace therein, as food of souls. In the name of all reality we raise the sacraments of union.

It is so done accordingly and that which follows belongs to the world of Yetzirah. The High Priest descends the altar steps and stands on the right of the Priestess.

HIGH PRIEST: As that which is bred in the bone comes out in the flesh, so that which is known in the soul shall dawn at length in the mind.

THE PRIESTESS: But that which is known in the soul is its root, O Lord, in Thee: a sap, a marrow, a life within the life; thereby are we formed in God.

HIGH PRIEST: The mind and heart are formed, the will is His. Our inward nature turns into another channel. This is the path by which we come out of separation, from darkness into light; but the path is travelled within.

THE PRIESTESS: O alchemy of God, transmuting all our modes.

HIGH PRIEST: The desire after Thee is soul, and the soul is love. It is the great secret of self and that within it which makes for full redemption.

THE PRIESTESS: There is a part of pure virginity within us, predestined to Divine nuptials, and amidst all our divagations incapable of a lower union. O form our parts of being, that this may manifest within.

HIGH PRIEST: The sacrament of the Eucharist is the sacrament of that reception, the significance of which is that the Spirit dwells within. And this is the Christ Spirit. The secret tradition hereof is a great memorial concerning a great experience. The macrocosm is the body of Christ, the microcosmic soul of man is in the image and likeness hereof; there is union between Christ in the macrocosm and Christ in the soul of Man.

THE PRIESTESS: O Hidden Master of the Rosy Cross, unknown without, revealed to love within.

The part of Yetzirah ends at this point and that which follows belongs to the world of Assiah. The sacramental Elements are elevated as before and the grouped banners exalted.

THE PRIESTESS: Make Thou our daily bread the food of souls.

HIGH PRIEST: Our signs and symbols of the soul attained are taken up to hallow and brought down to bless.

THE PRIESTESS: O truth and goodness, bring the True and Good.

Here ends the high office of the secret temple. The High Priest ascends the altar steps, sets down the chalice and remains in contemplation thereby, facing east. He is followed by the High Priestess, who turns west, midwise on the step beneath, the monstrance still in her hands. A Soror Electa comes forward and drapes the sacred vessel in red samite, set about with stones and gold.

The door of the secret temple is put open and the first procession is formed, id est: (1) An Elect Soror, having a basket of wild flowers, or others in winter season: this may be sweet herbs; (2) An Epopt bearing the great banner of the Rosy Cross; (3) The High Priestess holding the veiled monstrance; (4) The Junior Haeres, with hermit lamp uplifted; (5) The Celebrants of the Third Order wearing their full vestments and regalia of office. It descends to the lower temple and the battery of the Neophyte grade is given on the door without. The Ostiarius opens. The battery of the Master sounds from the east within and all present are upstanding. The procession is met by the Thurificans and Aquarius, who turn and proceed in front, censing and sprinkling. The flowers and herbs are strewn. The strains of sacramental music fill the holy place. The great mystery of all sacredness passes through the lower temple. The versicles proper to the time are recited or intoned amidst the reverential progress. The temple is circumambulated once only and slowly.

THE SACRED VERSICLES

• Soror Electa (*strewing flowers or herbs*) – Flowers in the garden of this world; the flowers of the garden follow a gospel-pattern. Their breath is like the offering of incense; their eyes are lamps in the sanctuary.

• The Banner Bearer – Shadows of life are we; be Thou the life within us.

• Adeptus Exemptus – Glory of all the glory; enlighten, shine within.

• Adeptus Major – We are the tabernacles of Thy presence; set upon us Thy jewels of grace.

• Adeptus Minor – The sun is Thy vesture; shine upon our human veils.

• The High Priestess – Take off our veils in fine; then is it Thou and no other.

The procession has reached by south the extreme west of the temple and now returns as it came. The Thurificans and Aquarius resume their proper stations. Having entered the secret temple, the High Priestess ascends the altar steps and replaces the monstrance within the pillared cupola. She retires with the Celebrants of the Third Order to the vestry; they remove their pontifical vestments and insignia. They are now in their white albs and golden girdles. This is done quickly.

The second procession is formed within the door of the secret temple, id est; (1) A Standard Bearer, carrying the banner of Daath; (2) The High Priest, in the full insignia of the secret sanctuary and carrying a golden crook; (3) A Standard Bearer, who displays the banner of Chokmah; (4) the Bearer of the banner of Binah; and he is followed by (5) one uplifting with great reverence the exalted Standard of Kether; (6) The Epopts of the blessed company, including her who has officiated as High Priestess and the Celebrants of the Third Order.

The procession descends to the lower temple and the battery of the Neophyte grade is given on the door without. The Ostiarius opens. The battery of the Master sounds from the east within, and the brethren who have resumed their seats are again upstanding. The procession is met by one who bears the Banner of the East, and by the Thurificans and Aquarius who turn and proceed in front, censing and sprinkling. The strains of sacred music fill the holy place. The manifestation of Daath begins in this manner and Kether is declared in Malkuth. The temple is circumambulated once only and slowly. The High Priest recites the versicles proper to the time amidst the reverential progress.

The Sacred Versicles

• Gates of the world of Spirit; gates that open, as hidden years unfold within the heart of youth.

• The meanings of life are heard in the heart of love, through the rush of the time-sea, the sea of images, the roar of its great voices.

• That sea has also its secret speech in season, and of Thee it tells alone; it is then like a soft wind in the organ when no one touches the keys.

• Dreams of the heart bodied forth in images, dreams of Thee; a world of dreams behind and a dream in front.

They have reached the western end of the temple and proceed direct to the altar at its eastern side, the Thurificans and Aquarius resuming their proper stations. The High Priest faces west, the Banner Bearers grouped about him according to the Sephirotic points. Other Epopts return to their places.

HIGH PRIEST: The life of the kingdom is not without its crown. I testify to the crown and the kingdom; the witness of God is ever in the house of God, the Presence is in the Holy Place. Praise of the inmost heart, praise in the heart of love; let silent praise go up to the Maker of All, in the day of small things for the hand of God therein and a place of the meeting of lives, in the world of life for the sacred quest of death, which opens on immortal realms.

A pause of recollection follows.

HIGH PRIEST: O still Eternal Reality; the vibrant stillness fills the heart with longing.

The Auxiliary Frater Zelator brings up the novice of the day to a kneeling stool on the western side of the altar.

HIGH PRIEST: Hallows in the Holy of Holies; hallows in the Holy Place: God's veils are also there. The hallows in the court of the temple abide in the grace of the Holy One. The inward virtue sanctifies the outward form. To thee, my brother, in holiness. (*He communicates the bread and salt to the Neophyte.*) Be thy body as the court of the temple, thy heart as the Holy Place, thy soul as the Holy of Holies. To thee, my brother in the Life of the life to come, and this is He, world without end. Amen. Thine be the body of redemption, the salt of the second birth. (*He communicates the wine to the Neophyte.*) The cup of thy desire; be thou desire in God. The desire of the house in its beauty shall be beauty in thy house of life. (*He presents the roses and binds one upon the breast of the postulant.*) Light in the mind, enlighten; come down, O Holy Light. (*He places the lamp in his hands and bids him lift it up.*) Purpose and will transform. (*The Neophyte replaces the lamp. The High Priest raises the postulant with both hands.*) Thou art dedicated now and henceforward to the glory of God in the Highest.

The Auxiliary Frater Zelator leads back the postulant. The High Priest proceeds to his throne in the east by way of the pillar of severity. He is followed by the Banner Bearers and the Epopts of the rite, who are grouped about the throne. The charge in brief of the Neophyte grade is then given.

HIGH PRIEST: Fratres et Sorores, there is no room for anything in this temple but God. Let the postulants received herein and all brethren of the Order, in their spiritual progress through the great succession of grades, from the first even to the last, remember this, and that only in so far as they are seeking the Divine Union and approaching that end by love do they belong to our holy Sodality. The motto to be written in our minds until it is realized in our hearts is One in One, looking towards that time when there shall be no distinction between the soul and the Holy One.

A brief pause follows and thereafter:

HIGH PRIEST: Honorable master of the Temple, I call upon you now to ordain the closing of this holy house in the grade of Neophyte, remembering that it is open always in the Spirit, and from henceforth and for ever, to us and those who are with us, is a Place of the Presence.

The Master of the Temple proceeds to the eastern side of the altar and communicates to the Auxiliary Frater Zelator. The temple is closed according to the ritual of the Neophyte grade.

HERE ENDS THE RITUAL OF RETURN IN LIGHT, WHICH IS A BOOK OF THE HOLY ASSEMBLY AND BLESSED COMPANY.

www.ingramcontent.com/pod-product-compliance
Lightning Source LLC
Chambersburg PA
CBHW030422100426
42812CB00028B/3065/J